Ancient Law, Ancient Society

Ancient Law, Ancient Society

Dennis P. Kehoe
and Thomas A. J. McGinn, Editors

University of Michigan Press
Ann Arbor

Published in the United States of America by the
University of Michigan Press
Manufactured in the United States of America
♾ Printed on acid-free paper

2020 2019 2018 2017 4 3 2 1

A CIP catalog record for this book is available from the British Library.

Library of Congress Cataloging-in-Publication Data

Names: Kehoe, Dennis P., editor. | McGinn, Thomas A. J., editor.
Title: Ancient law, ancient society / Dennis P. Kehoe and Thomas A. J. McGinn, Editors.
Description: Ann Arbor : University of Michigan Press, 2017. | Includes bibliographical references and index.
Identifiers: LCCN 2017011930| ISBN 9780472130436 (hardcover : alk. paper) |
ISBN 9780472123025 (e-book) Subjects: LCSH: Law, Greek—History. | Roman law—History.
Classification: LCC KL4121 .A45 2017 | DDC 340.5/38—dc23
LC record available at https://lccn.loc.gov/2017011930

Foreword

Susan D. Martin

One measure of Bruce Frier's legacy will ultimately be seen in the contributions that his students have made in their respective fields. Bruce's scholarly interests encompass an astonishingly broad range, both chronological and disciplinary, extending from Roman law, classical studies, and social and economic history to modern jurisprudence and legal pedagogy. The diversity of the titles in this volume reflects his impact on students spanning many disciplines and eras. Bruce's effectiveness as a teacher and mentor of future scholars owes much to several characteristic traits that many of his students will have observed: a voracious enthusiasm in his intellectual pursuits, an unwillingness to accept obvious answers, a delight in complicating the questions, and, above all, the breadth and constantly evolving nature of his interests.

Just a glance at his published work demonstrates this breadth. In the earlier years of his career, as Bruce was working on *Landlords and Tenants in Imperial Rome* (Princeton, 1979), there was a sense of exhilaration that comes from true innovation in scholarship. Bruce was working out how to integrate a broader view of Roman legal studies, which had been dominated by doctrinally focused continental scholarly and pedagogical tradition with methods drawn from the discipline of ancient history and classical studies in general. The question was how to respect the doctrinal, legal nature of the sources while mining them as the rich resource they are for Roman social and economic history. From the perspective of the student, this meant understanding and respecting the work of the Roman jurists in the creation of analytical jurisprudence, a type of thought that was not typically part of the training of classical studies and that required a different sort of mindset, one having more in common with "thinking like a lawyer" than with the world of the classicist. Only through this new way of formulating scholarly issues would it be possible to appreciate fully the contribution of the jurists to their world and legal history. This brought with it a host of problems as well: to what extent did this body of intellectual work influence practice in the Roman world? Bruce insisted on understanding the legal contribution of the jurists as well as the challenge in melding it to an analysis of the Roman world. Many of the questions he asked then cannot be resolved, but the questions themselves are important. Bruce also demonstrated an eagerness to explore new theories and approaches across disciplines and to adapt these tools fruitfully to his own work. The fact that many of his students who are now university faculty teach Roman law using his tools and methods—although adapted to our own particular interests and styles—is another lasting impact.

To his students of my generation, at least, the ringing and often-heard phrase "Much to commend, much to deplore" signaled the return of another draft or chapter of the dissertation. Combined in this phrase were Bruce's unflagging enthusiasm for the work as well as his rigorous critique and a wealth of creative suggestions. While not sparing the "much to deplore," he also, usually, found at least something to commend. The result of his assiduous attention and commanding example is what you will find exemplified in the chapters of this volume: an impressive command of sources ancient and modern, innovative use of theories and cross-disciplinary approaches, willingness to explore new territory, and a trajectory of accomplishment that is already yielding pathbreaking work. There is much to commend, I think.

Acknowledgments

This volume originated as a series of papers presented at the University of Michigan on October 26, 2013, to honor Professor Bruce Frier's distinguished service at the university and to mark his retirement from the Department of Classical Studies. The title of the conference was "Ancient Law, Ancient Society: A Conference in Honor of Bruce Frier." The contributions at the conference were all by Professor Frier's former PhD students, whose careers have been launched over many years, from 1981 to 2014. We are very grateful to Ruth Scodel, then chair of the Department of Classical Studies, for her initiative and inspiration in organizing the conference and for all her work and hospitality in hosting us. We also thank Sandra Andrade Chumney, events and communication coordinator in the department, for all her hard work in making a wonderful day, for the honorand and the speakers. In addition, we thank Ellen Bauerle for supporting the publication of this volume at the University of Michigan Press and Mary Hashman for her efforts in helping the publication to proceed smoothly. We also thank Jill Butler Wilson for her care and skill in copyediting our volume. Lastly, we editors owe a debt of gratitude to Bruce Frier for his intellectual inspiration in the field of Roman law and, more important, for his constant support and friendship throughout our careers.

Dennis P. Kehoe
Thomas A. J. McGinn

Contents

Introduction

Ancient Law and Ancient Society

Dennis P. Kehoe
Thomas A. J. McGinn

The purpose of this volume of essays is to explore a number of ways in which the study of law is crucially valuable for understanding ancient societies, particularly in the Greek and Roman world. It is inspired by the work in Roman law of Professor Bruce Frier, who has shown, through his scholarship in many areas of this broad field, the close connection between Roman law and Roman society. His scholarship, which draws on the rich literature from contemporary debates on the relationship between law and society, understands the law both as a product of the society in which it has developed and also as one of the most important forces shaping that society. The essays collected here are all, in some measure, inspired by the approach that Bruce has taken in his own pioneering work on Roman law, but they do not represent any single methodology. Instead, they demonstrate how ancient historians and legal scholars can come to a deeper understanding of ancient law and society when they apply imaginative and innovative perspectives that allow them to ask new questions. This volume addresses the economic aspects of law and legal institutions, the efficiency of law in deterring harmful behavior, the relationship between local provincial law and Roman law in the Roman Empire, concepts of justice in provincial Roman society, the degree to which Roman legal rules are embedded in social values, the role that political forces played in shaping legislation in the Roman Empire, and the usefulness of law and legal institutions for various levels within Roman society. The idea for this volume originated at a daylong conference honoring Bruce Frier on the occasion of his retirement from the Department of Classical Studies at the University of Michigan. The conference, organized by the editors at the request of Bruce's colleague and department chair, Ruth

Scodel, was held on October 26, 2013, and featured papers by a number of Bruce's PhD students over the years, working both in the fields of Roman history and law and in Greek history and law. Since the conference, we have added several papers to round out the volume.

As mentioned above, most of the essays in this volume seek to use contemporary debates drawn from the fields of law and the social sciences to come to a better understanding of the role of law in ancient societies. Such an approach has characterized the scholarly work of many of this volume's contributors. We editors recognize that this approach to understanding law has generated considerable controversy. For example, in the view that he develops in his provocative book *The Poverty of Clio* (2011), Francesco Boldizzoni argues forcefully that economic institutions in premodern societies are exclusively the product of historical factors and that any effort to apply contemporary economic theory to analyzing a premodern society is bound to fail, since the assumptions about modern economic activity—for example, that individuals are motivated by a desire to maximize their profits—are themselves the product of social values particular to our age, ones that were not shared by past societies. To apply Boldizzoni's perspective to the issues covered in this volume, any effort to analyze or understand Greek and Roman law in terms of economic concerns is misguided: the law, like economic relationships, was the product of historical factors that shaped society, and it cannot be understood in terms of modern economic concepts like efficiency or creating incentives. In his contribution to the *Cambridge Economic History of the Greco-Roman World* (2007), however, Bruce Frier suggests ways in which methodologies drawn from the new institutional economics (NIE) can help us to understand better both the consequences for Roman society of the law's definitions of property rights and the possibilities that the law created for resolving disputes.[1] Since the publication of the *Cambridge Economic History*, a number of scholars, including several of the contributors to the present volume, have used theoretical approaches drawn from NIE and other areas of the social sciences to enhance their analysis of ancient legal, economic, and social institutions. We believe that the essays in the present volume confirm that law and society can be approached usefully from a number of theoretical perspectives. These essays are both a tribute to the influence of Bruce Frier's scholarship and teaching and a demonstration of the importance of the study of law and legal institutions to the broader field of classical studies.

1. B. W. Frier and D. P. Kehoe, "Law and Economic Institutions," in W. Scheidel, I. Morris, and R. Saller, eds., *The Cambridge Economic History of the Greco-Roman World* (Cambridge, 2007), 113–43.

Three of the essays in this volume deal with the law in classical Greece, particularly Athens. The essays are well crafted to test an important theme arising from Bruce Frier's own work, whether we should view ancient institutions and practices primarily as products of unique cultures and value systems or whether such institutions and practices are amenable to analysis using social science methods developed to study contemporary societies and institutions. In "Collective Sanctions in Classical Athens," Adriaan Lanni examines the role that collective sanctions played in the enforcement of Athenian law. Collective sanctions provide an interesting test case for the best way to understand an ancient institution. On the one hand, collective sanctions, such as the punishment imposed (but then rescinded) on the entire population of Mytilene after its unsuccessful revolt from Athens in 427 during the Peloponnesian War, can be viewed simply as a crude and brutal product of Athenian democracy. At the same time, some collective sanctions, such as those imposed on entire families for various offenses, such as on the Alcmeonids for their role in the Cylonian conspiracy, were connected with ritual pollution, which attached to all members of a group related to the original individual perpetrator of an offense. On the other hand, collective sanctions could have an instrumental function to deter wrongdoing. One such sanction that Lanni studies, the dishonor, or *atimia*, imposed on state debtors and their heirs, provided a way to deter financial misconduct by officeholders, as well as a means to enforce the payment of debts, since heirs of state debtors would be freed of their disadvantageous status when they discharged the debt. As Lanni points out, some of the collective sanctions in Athens were actually innovations of the democracy and thus cannot be viewed as crude holdovers from the past. They seem to have been particularly useful, in the absence of a public prosecutor, to deter crimes committed against the community rather than against individuals, for whom private prosecutors would emerge to seek justice. This function of collective sanctions seems to have been especially well designed for boards of magistrates responsible for finances, since their collective liability would provide members an incentive to monitor one another's activities.

In "An Economic Perspective on Marriage Alliances in Ancient Greece," Michael Leese analyzes an institution basic to every society—namely, marriages among the elite—in terms of economic incentives. Certainly, such marriages can be analyzed in terms of prosopography, to trace over time how the alliances among various elite families from Athens and other parts of the Greek world help to explain political change. Leese seeks to understand elite marriage differently, however, in that he examines how families used marriage alliances to accumulate financial resources. For many families, dowries represented the single most important occasion for acquiring capital. Families might seek husbands for their daughters precisely at the time in which a dowry would be especially welcome for a family's political ambitions. Leese's analysis suggests a complicated relationship between economic interests and social practices in the Greek world. Certainly, even in analyzing ancient economic structures in terms of NIE, one has to account for the role that historical factors, such as social institutions and beliefs, play in affecting decision making in economic matters. Thus, from one perspective, elite marriage practices in the Greek world represent a case in which economic activity can be regarded as "embedded" within social institutions. Leese's analysis takes this notion one step further by showing how major economic decisions were often carried out through customary social practices. In his interpretation, social institutions were embedded in economic activity.

In "Assumption of Risk in Athenian Law," David D. Phillips seeks to understand the Athenian law on homicide in terms of modern legal analysis. The problem that Phillips addresses concerns the legal justification in Athenian law for exonerating a killer from liability for murder in certain situations, such as killing an adulterer. Phillips suggests that a concept borrowed from modern tort law, assumption of risk, helps to explain how Athenians conceptualized the situation of the victim in the types of killing he considers. In addition, Phillips' approach, as he notes, invites comparison with Roman law: in the juristic discussion for liability for damage to property under the *lex Aquilia*, a similar concept of assuming risk plays an important role in determining liability.

Turning more emphatically to the Roman world, Cynthia J. Bannon's "Rivers, Rights, and 'Romanization'" examines the development of the Roman law surrounding the use of public waterways for irrigation. Access to water was a crucial issue in much of the Mediterranean world, since modest rainfall levels and frequent droughts reduced yields and increased the risks surrounding agriculture. In the Roman period, substantial investment in irrigation in many places in the empire, including Spain, North Africa, and Egypt, made possible the more intensive use of land—with increased investment in viticulture, among other types of agriculture—and thus increased the production of food and materially supported the empire's urban culture. But reliance on irrigation often involves disputes over water rights, and Bannon's scholarly work has examined how agricultural communities in the Roman world overcame the "tragedy of the commons" and developed systems of sharing water that allocated water in an equitable manner while preserving the resource for the future. Bannon examines this issue by considering how provincial solutions to this problem affected Roman legal doctrine. Two important inscriptions, the *lex rivi*

Hiberiensis from Spain and the Lamasba decree from North Africa, record how local communities developed systems to share water from public sources, while the definition of rights to water in a rescript of Marcus Aurelius and Lucius Verus (Pap. Iust. *D.* 8.3.17) shows the influence of provincial practice on Roman law. To demonstrate the importance of understanding the Roman solution to sharing common-pool resources, Bannon's analysis draws on the rich literature on this topic in the field of economics, particularly that of Nobel laureate Elinor Ostrom.

In "Justice in Aelian's *Miscellaneous History*," Lauren Caldwell seeks to come to a better understanding of how Romans conceived of justice in the age of the Severans, by examining the moralizing anecdotes in the Greek author Aelian's *On Animals* and *Miscellaneous History*. How people in the Roman Empire understood justice at this time is especially important because the Severan Age saw the centralization of the administration of the law: the jurists Ulpian, Papinian, and Paul wrote extensively on Roman law but also served in the most important posts involved in the administration of the law throughout the empire, that of the *a libellis* and the praetorian prefecture. Aelian often uses the Persian king from a legendary past as the person who determines what is just, even in areas of the law that were debated in the Severan Age, such as the power of life and death that a father exercised over his children. Caldwell's essay suggests the importance of seeing the work of the jurists against a broader background of intellectual trends in the Roman Empire.

In "Agency, Roman Law, and Roman Social Values," Dennis P. Kehoe investigates and ultimately defends the usefulness of drawing on methodologies from the fields of law and economics and from new institutional economics to understand the complex relationship between law and the Roman economy, by focusing on agency, a basic component of economic activity in any society. The contract of mandate (*mandatum*) and the related quasi contract of "unauthorized administration" (*negotia gesta*) are suitable for an investigation of this type because they were important to Roman economic life throughout the period of the empire but were also rooted in Roman aristocratic social values. The major point of Kehoe's essay is to show that, in their treatment of mandate and unauthorized administration, the Roman jurists and emperors consistently interpreted the rights and obligations of the parties in terms of their conception of Roman upper-class values of duty and reciprocity, the values that are generally agreed to have inspired the development of mandate. At the same time, however, a careful analysis of their treatment of mandate and unauthorized administration indicates that the jurists and emperors confronted agency relationships that went beyond the purely upper-class arrangements that inspired the development of mandate. In this circumstance, consideration of the economic incentives of the parties in an agency relationship, as well as the economic implications of legal rules and authoritative legal institutions, helps us to attain a better understanding of mandate as a social institution of the Roman Empire.

One of the major questions scholars who seek to understand the social role of Roman law must confront concerns the extent to which a broad class of people, as opposed to a small group of elite property owners, had access to the protection of law and legal institutions in the Roman Empire. In "*Cui Bono*? The True Beneficiaries of Roman Private Law," Thomas A. J. McGinn examines the widely held assumption that Roman law and legal systems exclusively or chiefly served the interests of the rich and powerful, suggesting that it would not have been possible for the Romans to operate a legal system successfully for so long if it were simply characterized by a blatant and exclusive assertion of elite advantage. Certainly, the legal authorities intervened occasionally, if not regularly, on behalf of less privileged, though not unimportant, segments of society, against the interests, narrowly conceived, of the wealthier and better connected, with the goal of advancing the ideals of utility and justice. This thesis, which has been developed by two other students of Bruce Frier (also contributors to this volume), is placed in the context of an important study by Edoardo Volterra that relies on the evidence of the *Digest* and *Codex* to advance the idea that the system of private law served the needs not of the very well-off and powerful but of those at a more modest social and economic level. The truth is likely more complicated: the law generally developed to serve the interests of the elite, but this observation by no means tells the whole story. McGinn offers a more nuanced understanding of the law, arguing that the political and legal authorities did seek to accommodate the needs of a relatively wider sector of society than one might otherwise assume, even if one purpose in doing so was ultimately to benefit the elite as a class.

In "*Libertas* and 'Mixed Marriages' in Late Antiquity: Law, Labor, and Politics in Justinianic Reform Legislation," Charles Pazdernik demonstrates the value of understanding the precise circumstances behind the promulgation of legal rules, in this case, imperial constitutions that were incorporated into the *Corpus Iuris Civilis*. Pazdernik focuses on a constitution preserved in five fragments in the *Codex* of Justinian that this same emperor issued in 533, when the publication of the *Institutes* and the *Digest* were anticipated. The constitution concerned reforms to the *Senatus Consultum Claudianum* of 52 CE, specifically as regards women of free status who married registered bound tenants, *adscripticii*. Justinian, who generally sought to protect people's free status, was forced to respond to the concerns of property owners who, under his own recent reforms, stood to lose the services of the offspring of such unions. Pazdernik sets this constitution in a political context in which the emperor was developing *libertas* into an important imperial theme as his troops under Belisarius were fighting to regain Africa and soon would invade Italy.

Finally, this volume's afterword is an assessment of Bruce Frier's contribution to the study of ancient law. Clifford Ando examines the influences of Professor Frier's work and approaches on the essays by the contributors to the volume.

CHAPTER 1

Collective Sanctions in Classical Athens

Adriaan Lanni

The topic of collective sanctions (i.e., collective punishment of a group, such as a family or tribe, as opposed to individual liability) offers an opportunity to consider a debate relevant to Professor Bruce Frier's work:[1] should we view ancient institutions and practices primarily as products of a unique culture and value system (what we might call a "traditional anthropological approach"), or are they amenable to analysis using social science methods developed to study contemporary societies and institutions (what we might call a "sociological approach")?[2] Collective sanctions have been interpreted through both these lenses: for some, they reflect a distinctively "primitive" conception of collective guilt and responsibility; for others, collective sanctions are an instrumental method of promoting deterrence. Of course, these two approaches are not mutually exclusive. Collective sanctions can have cultural roots while furthering functionalist ends.[3] Conversely, institutions that serve functional purposes always exist within a specific cultural context, incorporating a society's unique beliefs and values.[4] Nevertheless, it is, I think, a meaningful question to ask whether a given collective sanction was contemporaneously understood pri-

1. I am honored to be included in this collection celebrating Bruce Frier's career as a scholar and as a teacher. Bruce's works using modern legal theory and new institutional economics to shed light on ancient Rome—in particular, Frier and Kehoe, "Law and Economic Institutions" (2007); Frier, *Rise of the Roman Jurists* (1985); and Frier, *Landlords and Tenants* (1980)—have been important models for my writing on ancient Athens.

2. For discussion, see Lanni, "From Anthropology to Sociology" (forthcoming).

3. For example, Dodds, *The Greeks and the Irrational* (1951) 33, argues that the concept of inherited guilt served to sustain the belief in divine punishment because it explained how wrongdoers who appeared to escape punishment in their lifetime would eventually be punished through their descendants. Cultural beliefs and practices that also serve functionalist ends may be more likely to endure.

4. For example, the functional explanation offered here for collective sanctions incorporates distinctively ancient notions both of the inheritability of bad character and of the importance of maintaining one's hereditary line.

marily as punishment of collective guilt or as a device that punished the innocent along with the guilty in an effort to promote deterrence.

The answer is complicated, but I think the Athenians understood collective sanctions primarily in instrumental terms. While the long pedigree of collective sanctions in Greek literature and culture made these punishments less morally repugnant to the Athenians than they are to moderns, the relatively rare uses of collective sanctions in classical Athens do not support a cultural account. At the same time, modern functional accounts only explain a small subset of Athenian collective punishments. Most functional accounts describe ancient collective liability as a form of indirect, delegated deterrence that encourages group members to monitor, prevent, and punish individual wrongdoers within the group. I argue that while this model applies to one form of collective punishment in Athens—group punishment of boards of magistrates—most cases of Athenian collective sanctions were aimed at direct, rather than indirect, deterrence. The first two sections of this essay summarize the major modern interpretations of collective sanctions and the use of collective sanctions in classical Athens. The third section offers some reasons to doubt that the cultural explanation is complete. Finally, the fourth section argues that the standard functional account of ancient collective sanctions does not explain the most common uses of collective punishment in Athens, and suggests an alternative functional account.

Modern Interpretations

The classical Athenians' use of collective sanctions (sometimes called "group punishments," "third-party sanctions," or "communal liability") has not received systematic treatment since Glotz's magisterial 1904 book,[5] but much has been written about collective sanctions in the ancient world more generally, particularly in biblical and Near Eastern law.[6] Scholars take one of two approaches to collective sanctions in ancient law. The first, which we might

5. Glotz, *La solidarité de la famille* (1904). More recent works focused on Greek or Athenian religion or penal theory often include a brief discussion of collective liability: Dodds, *The Greeks and the Irrational* (1951) 33–34; Parker, *Miasma* (1983) 198–206; Saunders, *Plato's Penal Code* (1991) 118–20. For discussion of specific types of collective liability in Greece, see Connor, "The Razing of the House" (1985); Johnstone, *A History of Trust* (2011) 127–47 (on collective liability of boards of officials); Rubinstein, "Individual and Collective Liabilities" (2012) (same).

6. On ancient liability generally, see Levmore, "Rethinking Group Responsibility" (1995); Lindgren, "Why the Ancients May Not Have Needed a System of Criminal Law" (1996); Parisi and Dari-Mattiacci, "The Rise and Fall of Communal Liability" (2004); Miceli and Segerson, "Punishing the Innocent along with the Guilty" (2007); Daube, "Two Notes on Communal Responsibility" (1944).

call the "cultural approach," views collective punishment as a reflection of religious and/or social beliefs in collective guilt or of a view of the family or clan, rather than the individual, as the relevant unit of moral and legal responsibility. Dodds' *Greeks and the Irrational* provides an example: "That these men . . . accepted the idea of inherited guilt and deferred punishment is due to their belief in family solidarity which Archaic Greece shared with other early societies and with many primitive cultures today. Unfair it might be, but to them it appeared as a law of nature, which must be accepted: for the family was a moral unit, the son's life the prolongation of this father's, and he inherited his father's moral debts exactly as he inherited his commercial ones."[7]

Those employing a cultural interpretation of collective sanctions often take an evolutionary approach, describing how collective sanctions are gradually replaced by individual responsibility regimes as the solidarity of the family weakens and the power of the state grows.[8] Glotz provides such an evolutionary account, tracing the decline in the use of collective sanctions in Athens over time. According to Glotz's narrative, collective liability was first banned in private law as the state curbed the practice of familial blood feud and claimed a monopoly of legitimate violence.[9] Collective sanctions for crimes against the city survived longer but were nearly completely eradicated by the fourth century.[10] For Glotz, the democracy played a critical role in developing the notion that the individual citizen, rather than the family or clan, was the relevant legal and moral unit for civic rights and duties and thereby for legal responsibility.[11]

Connor offers a somewhat different cultural and evolutionary account in his article on house razing in ancient Greece. He suggests that the use of house razing and hereditary *atimia* (loss of citizenship rights) as a punishment for tyranny, treason, and bribery may reflect a belief that these crimes were offenses against the gods, resulting in pollution.[12] Connor notes that "for many Greeks in antiquity acts that subverted the existing social and political order were not purely political or secular matters" but "offenses against the gods."[13] As such, they implicated Greek cultural beliefs in pollution, in which heinous crimes cause an infection or *miasma* that can extend to the criminal's family

7. Dodds, *The Greeks and the Irrational* (1951) 33–34.

8. The most well-known example is Maine, *Ancient Law* (1861) 121–22.

9. Glotz, *La solidarité de la famille* (1904) 466–69, 604–6.

10. Glotz, *La solidarité de la famille* (1904) 606. Glotz acknowledged the continuation of hereditary disenfranchisement for state debtors in the fourth century. He emphasized the absence of evidence for collective sanctions in antityranny laws after the late fifth century, but the discovery of Eukrates' law of 337/6 BCE, first published in 1952, undermined this argument.

11. Glotz, *La solidarité de la famille* (1904) 606.

12. Connor, "The Razing of the House" (1985) 86–88, 92.

13. Connor, "The Razing of the House" (1985) 92.

and future descendants.[14] Connor argues that the belief in pollution was supported by the social structure in archaic and early classical Greece.[15] The *oikos* (household) was the fundamental unit of social life; the close bonds and lack of privacy within each household meant that, as a practical matter, "responsibility was never individual."[16] According to Connor, beliefs in pollution waned as the bonds of the family weakened, making it possible to disaggregate the guilt of individual members.[17]

In contrast to the cultural approach that focuses on notions of collective blame and responsibility, legal scholars have explained the use of collective sanctions in ancient (and modern) societies in forward-looking, functional terms. Scholars such as Richard Posner, Saul Levmore, and Daryl Levinson have argued that collective sanctions are better understood as instrumental mechanisms that punish the innocent along with the guilty in order to boost the deterrence, detection, and/or punishment of crimes.[18] Levinson, for example, views collective sanctions as a "delegated deterrence regime": "group members may be punished not because they are deemed collectively responsible for wrongdoing but simply because they are in an advantageous position to identify, monitor, and control responsible individuals, and can be motivated by the threat of sanctions to do so."[19] Posner and Lindgren each discuss an additional functional explanation for ancient collective punishment: in systems that emphasize redressing wrongs by employing private compensation (e.g., the use of "wergild") rather than state-enforced punishment, group liability was necessary to insure that victims were sufficiently compensated, since individual wrongdoers might not have the resources to pay.[20]

Several scholars have argued that collective punishment is most attractive when the identity of the wrongdoer is unknown or uncertain, because the group sanction will induce group members to identify, prevent, and/or punish individual wrongdoers within the group.[21] For example, Miceli and Segerson argue

14. Connor, "The Razing of the House" (1985) 90–92.

15. Connor, "The Razing of the House" (1985) 93–94.

16. Connor, "The Razing of the House" (1985) 94.

17. Connor, "The Razing of the House" (1985) 94–99.

18. E.g., Posner, *Economics of Justice* (1981) 119–230; Posner, "A Theory of Primitive Society" (1980) 43–53; Levmore, "Rethinking Group Responsibility" (1995); Levinson, "Collective Sanctions" (2003).

19. Levinson, "Collective Sanctions" (2003) 348.

20. Posner, *The Economics of Justice* (1981) 193–94; Posner, "A Theory of Primitive Society" (1980) 43–44, 46. Lindgren, "Why the Ancients May Not Have Needed a System of Criminal Law" (1996) 32, 51–53.

21. Levmore, "Rethinking Group Responsibility" (1995) 88–89; Miceli and Segerson, "Punishing the Innocent along with the Guilty" (2007) 82. Parisi and Dari-Mattiacci, "The Rise and Fall of Communal Liability" (2004) 491, argue that individual incentives to reduce crime were diluted

that collective sanctions may offer a viable alternative to individual responsibility when detection of the wrongdoer is difficult or impossible or when punishing the innocent is not seen as costly (as in the case of military or international contexts, an issue to which I will return).[22] They find that their results broadly reflect the actual use of group punishment in biblical and ancient Babylonian law.[23] Levmore similarly argues that group liability is "firmly linked to uncertainty" in both the modern and the ancient world.[24] Focusing on biblical texts, he argues that collective sanctions may not have been as widespread in the ancient world as generally thought.[25] He suggests that the relatively rare instances of group responsibility that we do see in the ancient world involve either (1) international or military situations in which group punishment is acceptable because the burdens of punishing the innocent are not borne by members of the community[26] or (2) cases where there is "uncertainty regarding the identity of the narrowly-defined wrongdoer."[27] Interestingly, however, these rationales apply to only a small portion of the Athenians' use of collective sanctions. The Athenians had their instrumental reasons for imposing collective punishments, but they generally do not fit the model of delegated deterrence regimes that legal scholars use to describe communal liability in other ancient societies.

The Use of Collective Sanctions in Classical Athens

Unlike law in other ancient societies, classical Athenian law rarely used collective sanctions. Collective punishment was used in three main categories of public offenses:[28] (1) failure to pay debts owed to the state; (2) serious crimes against the state, such as bribery and attempting to overthrow the democracy;

with an increase in group size and group wealth, leading to a decline in collective punishments over time.

22. Miceli and Segerson, "Punishing the Innocent along with the Guilty" (2007) 81–82, 104. More specifically, their model indicated that when retribution is the goal and when the enforcer cannot invest in detection, group punishment is preferred to individual punishment, but when deterrence is the main goal and when the enforcer cannot invest in detection, individual and group punishment are equally attractive. By contrast, where the enforcer can invest in detection of the wrongdoer, individual punishment is preferred.

23. Miceli and Segerson, "Punishing the Innocent along with the Guilty" (2007) 84–85.

24. Levmore, "Rethinking Group Responsibility" (1995) 88–89.

25. Levmore, "Rethinking Group Responsibility" (1995) 119–21.

26. Levmore, "Rethinking Group Responsibility" (1995) 87.

27. Levmore, "Rethinking Group Responsibility" (1995) 88.

28. Athenian law does not include a distinction similar to the modern distinction between crime and tort. The Athenians distinguished between public suits (*graphai*) that implicated the public interest and could be brought by "anyone who is willing" (*ho boulomenos*), as opposed to private suits (*dikai*) brought by the victim or, in the case of homicide, the victim's family.

and (3) failure of boards of magistrates to carry out their duties. Before examining each of these uses of collective sanctions in detail, I should bracket a fourth potential category: collective sanctions against members of foreign cities.

Examples of collective punishments in the international context abound.[29] I will not include these kinds of collective sanctions against foreigners in my analysis below, because international collective sanctions were likely quite different in character from the Athenians' use of collective sanctions in the domestic context.[30] It is far from clear that the Athenians approached interactions with foreign states and their citizens as matters subject to the same restraints of justice and moral desert that applied in domestic courts.[31] Thus international collective sanctions clearly had functional motivations, but because notions of blame and responsibility were less central to decisions concerning treatment of foreigners, these examples do not shed much light on the central question of this essay: whether the Athenians thought of collective sanctions as punishment of a guilty collective or punishment of innocents to serve a utilitarian purpose. Even within a functional framework, Levmore has pointed out that collective sanctions may operate differently (and be more morally acceptable and functionally attractive) in the international context than in the domestic context, because the costs of punishing innocents in the international context are not borne by members of the community.[32] For these reasons, I will set

29. During the imperial period, if a citizen of a subject city killed an Athenian, it appears that the city was required to pay a fine of five talents (*SEG* 23.7–13, 99.1–3; Ar. *Peace* 164–72). It has been suggested that this provision applied only to cases in which an Athenian was killed in foreign territory by a killer whose identity was unknown, but it is impossible to confirm this for certain from our sources. For discussion, see MacDowell, *Athenian Homicide Law* (1963) 127–28. Athenian punishment for cities that attempted to revolt from or refuse Athenian rule was the killing and/or enslaving of a large proportion of or even the entire foreign population: see Thuc. 3.50.1 (Mytilene), 5.32 (Scione), 5.116 (Melos). In war, of course, enemy states could be destroyed, and their citizens, including noncombatants, could be intentionally killed or enslaved: see Lanni, "Laws of War" (2008) 479–82. One example of collective sanctions against foreigners that does not seem directly related to a military or imperial context was *androlepsia*: the relatives of an Athenian murdered in a foreign city had the right to seize any three citizens of that city as hostages until the suspected killer was extradited to Athens for trial (Dem. 23.82–83; Polyd. 8.50–51; *Lex. Seg.* 213.30–214.2). One late and not entirely reliable gloss even suggests that if the foreign city failed to deliver the killer to Athens, the three hostages would be tried and punished for homicide in the killer's stead (*Lex. Seg.* 213.30–214.2). For discussion of the many unanswerable questions about the details of *androlepsia*, see MacDowell, *Athenian Homicide Law* (1963) 27–31; de Ste. Croix, "Notes" (1961) 268 and n. 7.

30. On the differences between collective sanctions in international or war-related circumstances as opposed to domestic contexts, see Levmore, "Rethinking Group Responsibility" (1995) 85–87.

31. A victorious city, for example, had complete discretion over how to treat the citizens of its vanquished enemy, without regard to questions of justice or blame. See Xen. *Cyr.* 7.53; Ar. *Pol.* 1.6.6–7.

32. Levmore, "Rethinking Group Responsibility" (1995) 87.

aside the category of collective sanctions against members of foreign states and focus this analysis on the domestic use of collective sanctions in Athens.

Failure to Pay Debts Owed to the State

One category of collective sanction that remained in force throughout the classical period was the imposition of *atimia* (loss of citizenship rights) on the descendants of state debtors.[33] A citizen could incur a debt to the state in a number of ways: for example, because of a fine imposed against him in a court judgment or because he (or someone for whom he was serving as a surety) defaulted on a contract with the state, such as a tax-farming contract, mining lease, or lease of public property.[34] If a citizen failed to pay a fine or to keep up with the payment schedule in a public contract, officials recorded him as a public debtor, and he (but not his heirs) was regarded as disenfranchised, meaning that he was not permitted to hold office, speak in the Assembly or the courts, serve as a juror, or enter the temples or agora.[35] If he attempted to enter one of the forbidden areas or to exercise civic rights, any citizen who wished to prosecute him could do so.[36]

If the debtor failed to pay by the ninth of the ten Council meetings held each year (the ninth prytany), in most cases the debt was doubled,[37] his name was publicly inscribed as a state debtor, and his property was subject to confiscation. The confiscation procedure, *apographe*, like many aspects of Athenian law, relied on private initiative: any citizen could bring a confiscation action listing specific items of property that were owned by the debtor and that could be confiscated. If the volunteer prosecutor was successful in court, the confiscated items were sold at auction, and the proceeds were used to partially or

33. Lys. 20.34; Is. 10.17; Dem. 22.33–34; 24.201; 43.58; 58.1–3, 16–19. For discussion, see Hansen, *Apagoge* (1976) 71–72; Hunter, "Policing Public Debtors" (2000); MacDowell, *The Law in Classical Athens* (1978) 164–67; Todd, *Shape of Athenian Law* (1993) 143–45. In Athens, imposition of *atimia* did not require intervention by the state or its representative.

34. E.g., Dem. 24.134–35; 25; 58.1–3, 30–33. For discussion, see Hunter, "Policing Public Debtors" (2000) 22–25.

35. *Ath. Pol.* 47.3–48.1; And. 1.73; Dem. 58.48–49; Hunter, "Policing Public Debtors" (2000) 26; MacDowell, *The Law in Classical Athens* (1978) 165. It seems that at least in the case of debtors who had defaulted on state contracts (as opposed to those who incurred debts from a judgment), the Council had the option of imprisoning the debtor until the debt was paid: see Hunter, "Policing Public Debtors" (2000) 26–27.

36. We do not know for certain how penalties for exercising various civic rights were determined, but the death penalty was a possibility in at least some situations. See MacDowell, *The Law in Classical Athens* (1978) 75.

37. In the case of money owed to a religious sanctuary, the debt was multiplied by ten. See And. 1.73; Dem. 24.82, 59.7; MacDowell, *The Law in Classical Athens* (1978) 166.

completely retire the debt. Successful prosecutors likely received one-third of the state's recovery,[38] while prosecutors who failed to secure at least one-fifth of the jurors' votes were subject to a hefty fine.[39]

A state debtor could regain his citizenship rights at any time simply by paying the outstanding debt.[40] While the original state debtor was alive, his heirs suffered no punishment. But if the debtor died without paying, his *atimia* was passed on to his heirs, and they became disenfranchised. Just like the original debtor, those who inherited *atimia* could regain their rights at any time by paying off the debt.[41]

Serious Crimes against the State

The second category of offenses subject to collective sanction includes a number of serious crimes against the state, all of which were punished by hereditary *atimia* for the offender and his descendants. In some cases, *atimia* meant loss of citizenship rights; in other cases, it meant outlaw status, under which the offender could be killed with impunity. Unlike in the case of state debtors, for crimes in this category, *atimia* attached immediately to the offender's living descendants.

From the sixth century down to 336 BCE, we have several examples of hereditary *atimia* (mostly cases of outlawry) for crimes related to establishing a tyranny or attempting to overthrow the democracy. The *Constitution of the Athenians* mentions a sixth-century law that provided that anyone who establishes a tyranny would be outlawed, along with his descendants.[42] Plutarch re-

38. Dem. 32.2 suggests that the successful prosecutor in an *apographe* received a lavish three-quarters of the recovery, but several scholars have suggested that the text should be emended so that the actual reward was one-third of the proceeds.

39. MacDowell, *The Law in Classical Athens* (1978) 166.

40. Dem. 58.21, 49–52. Citizenship was also restored in cases where the sale of confiscated property through the *apographe* procedure completely retired the debt. See Hunter, "Policing Public Debtors" (2000) 28–29.

41. Lys. 20.34; Is. 1.17; Dem. 22.33–34; 24.201; 43.58; 58.1–2, 17, 59. For discussion, see Hunter, "Policing Public Debtors" (2000) 29; Hansen, *Apagoge* (1976) 71–72. The inscription preserving accounts of Athenian harbor officials includes several examples of debts retired by descendants of the original debtor. See Hansen, *Apagoge* (1976) 71 n. 6.

42. *Ath. Pol.* 16.10. Another possible collective punishment involves Themistocles: one source (*FGrHist* 338 F 1) states that he and his descendants were condemned to perpetual exile for his treason, but we know that his son returned to Athens, so the sanction against his descendants was either revoked or ignored. For discussion, see Phillips, *The Law of Ancient Athens* (2013) 472–74 (#367). An example of private collective punishment is the killing of Lycidas and his family for treason in 479 BCE (Hdt. 9.4–5; Lyc. 1.122). Lycidas' family appears to have been killed by Athenian women in a form of spontaneous popular justice. Somewhat earlier than our period, Draco's homicide law also provided that anyone who attempted to subvert the law was to be outlawed with his descendants (Dem. 23.62).

ports the impeachment of Archeptolemos and Antiphon in 411 BCE for their involvement in the short-lived oligarchy of the Four Hundred. Their sentences included house razing, confiscation of property, and disenfranchisement for them, their descendants, and anyone who tried to adopt their descendants.[43] Demophantos' decree on subversion of the democracy, passed in 410 BCE, did not provide for hereditary *atimia* but, instead, imposed outlawry on the offender and confiscation of property and charged all Athenians to swear an oath to kill anyone who subverts the democracy.[44] I will return to this unusual law later. Finally, hereditary *atimia* is again used in the 337/6 BCE Law of Eukrates on subverting the democracy. The law provides that anyone who cooperates in the subversion of the democracy may be killed with impunity, and it states that if any member of the Areopagus assumes official duties after the democracy has been overthrown, both he and his descendants are to be outlawed.[45]

Bribery (*dora*) and embezzlement of public funds (*klopē*) also carried collective penalties. Offering or accepting a bribe or embezzling public funds were punishable by a fine of ten times the amount of the money involved, plus immediate disenfranchisement for the offender and the offender's descendants until the fine was paid.[46] The enforcement of laws against corruption by public officials was not entirely dependent on lawsuits initiated by volunteer prosecutors: following their term in office, magistrates also underwent a mandatory accounting (*euthyna*), during which officials audited their financial accounts and invited the public to present any accusations of bribery or embezzlement to a jury.[47]

Boards of Magistrates

The nature of the third category of collective sanction—collective punishment for boards of magistrates—is somewhat less certain. Athenian magistrates generally served on boards (commonly with ten members) on which each member wielded equal power and on which decisions were made primarily by consen-

43. Plu. *Lives of Attic Orators* 833d–834b. It is unclear whether *atimon* here means "outlawed" or merely "disenfranchised." The reference to adoption was presumably intended to prevent the offenders' children from avoiding punishment by arranging to be adopted into another family.

44. And. 1.96–98.

45. *SEG* 12.87.

46. And. 1.74; Dem. 21.113. While we cannot date this law with any certainty, the reference to "the people" suggests that it postdates Cleisthenes' reforms of 508/67 BCE. See Phillips, *The Law of Ancient Athens* (2013) 468 (#361).

47. For a summary of these procedures, see MacDowell *The Law in Classical Athens* (1978) 170–72.

sus.[48] Several Athenian inscriptions from the late fifth century through the late second century BCE seem to suggest collective liability: these inscriptions typically instruct a particular board to carry out a specific duty (e.g., to collect a type of fine), for the failure of which "they" (the members of the board, in the plural) will either be liable to a penalty or will owe a specified amount "each."[49] The implication seems to be that no attempt will be made to determine which individual members of the board were at fault; rather, the board as a whole is held responsible. Rubinstein has shown that these types of regulations were widespread throughout Greece in the late classical and Hellenistic periods.[50]

Our interpretation of these inscriptions is complicated by evidence, from Athenian court speeches, of a few instances in which board members were given individual hearings in response to accusations of board misconduct.[51] Based on these examples, some scholars have concluded that despite the wording of some of the individual regulations, members of boards in Athens were always given an individual hearing during the *euthyna* (mandatory accounting) procedure.[52] Others contend that collective liability *was* used where the regulations appear to call for it.[53] In the course of discussing the late classical and Hellenistic evidence, Rubinstein points out that the right to an individual hearing is not necessarily incompatible with a notion of collective liability. As Rubinstein notes, most of the regulations implying collective liability involve acts of omission: the board is required to complete a specific task and is punished for failure to do so.[54] Whether tested in one trial or several, the regulation still called for collective liability. The *hellenotamiai*, for example, may have been tried individually, but all of them were convicted.[55] Moreover, where the regulation offered little opportunity for an individual defense, we may imagine that individual hearings might be quite cursory or even that punishment might be summarily imposed on the board and often not challenged by members, de-

48. For discussion of the process of deliberation and decision making on boards, see Johnstone, *A History of Trust* (2011) 111–26.

49. E.g., *GHI* 65.36–39; Dem. 24.22. For discussion and lists of examples, see Johnstone, *History of Trust* (2011) 130–33; Piérart, "Les *euthynoi* athéniens" (1971). It is important to note that there are also regulations that provide for punishment of the individual magistrate at fault.

50. Rubinstein, "Individual and Collective Liabilities" (2012).

51. Dem. 22.39: when the Council was accused of failing to build the prescribed number of triremes, every member had a right to an individual hearing at his *euthyna*; Ant. 5.69–70: when the *hellenotamiai* (the board that oversaw the finances of the Delian League) were charged with financial mismanagement, each member was convicted in a separate trial.

52. E.g. Hansen, *The Athenian Democracy* (1999) 223; Kahrstedt, *Untersuchungen zur Magistratur* (1936) 160–65.

53. Johnstone, *A History of Trust* (2011) 135.

54. Rubinstein, "Individual and Collective Liabilities" (2012) 341–42.

55. Dem. 22.38–39.

spite the formal right to an individual hearing.[56] In sum, although the evidence is far from certain, it seems likely that collective sanctions were sometimes used against boards that failed to carry out their prescribed duties.

The best-known example of collective sanctions from ancient Greece—the trial of the Arginusae generals[57]—also involved punishment of board members. But the Arginusae trial was an anomalous event and quite different from the deliberate use of collective sanctions provided for in laws and decrees that I have been examining thus far. The Arginusae affair is generally cited as evidence for an Athenian commitment that defendants have a right to a trial and to an individual assessment of guilt.[58] The eight generals in charge of the naval victory at Arginusae in 406 BCE were criticized for failing to rescue the shipwrecked sailors after the battle. In a highly irregular procedure, the six generals who returned to Athens (the two others fled the city) were tried together in the Assembly, and all eight generals were condemned to death in a single vote. An objection that trying the generals collectively would be unconstitutional was raised at the Assembly meeting but was withdrawn in the face of threats from the angry mob, and the Athenians regretted the decision almost immediately.

The Arginusae trial was an exceptional and unconstitutional imposition of a collective punishment that does not contribute much to our understanding of the use of communal liability in Athens. The Athenians' embarrassment over the Arginusae affair reflects the undisputed notion that individual responsibility was the norm in most of Athenian law; I have here been exploring the relatively rare exceptions to this rule. Although the Arginusae trial involved generals who served on a board, this case had little in common with the situations contemplated in the regulations calling for collective punishment of boards. First, the Assembly condemned not the entire board of ten generals, as we might expect in a standard collective liability regime, but only those who had been present at the battle and left the scene without rescuing the sailors. Moreover, we have seen that the collective liability regulations tend to apply to a board's failure to perform a very specific, prescribed duty—in other words, situations amenable to self-monitoring. The charges against the Arginusae generals, by contrast, amounted to incompetence or poor judgment. To be sure, the Athenians were not skittish about punishing generals for incompetence or even bad luck in losing a battle,[59] but these kinds of accusations were always

56. Rubinstein, "Individual and Collective Liabilities" (2012) 339 (describing non-Athenian evidence).

57. Xen. *Hell.* 1.7.9–35.

58. Lanni, "Judicial Review" (2010) 246.

59. As pointed out by Hansen, *The Athenian Democracy* (1999) 217, such accusations always had to be formally framed in terms of corruption or treason.

brought against individual generals through the *eisangelia* procedure.[60] Thus the outrage that the Arginusae generals were denied the usual individual determination of guilt does not undermine the argument that we should take the surviving inscriptions at their word and conclude that the Athenians elected to use communal liability in limited situations where a board failed to carry out its specified duties.

It may be worth pointing out that the Athenians seem to have employed collective sanctions only rarely and that the handful of examples occur in situations quite dissimilar from each other. Inheriting *atimia* along with a state debt did not always attract moral condemnation and may only loosely fit into the category of "punishment."[61] Fining amateur magistrates for failure to perform their duties similarly feels more regulatory than penal. In other cases, by contrast, collective sanctions are reserved for the worst of the worst: extraordinary situations in which the offender threatened to overthrow the democracy.[62] The common thread in these disparate examples may be that they involved offenses against the state rather than an individual, resulting in systemic underenforcement due to Athens' reliance on private initiative. I will argue that in some circumstances, collective sanctions may have served to enhance the severity of the penalty in an effort to boost deterrence for offenses that were less likely to be prosecuted.

Limits of the Cultural Model of Collective Sanctions

I turn now to the limits of the cultural explanation of collective sanctions in classical Athens. There is undoubtedly something to the cultural model. Notions of inherited guilt and collective sanctions, particularly imposed by gods, are commonplace in Greek literature.[63] Herodotus, for example, famously attributes Croesus' defeat at the hands of the Persians to divine punishment for the crime of his ancestor Gyges, who illegally seized the Lydian throne: "Croesus paid in full for the crime of his fifth ancestor, who, as a bodyguard of

---

60. Under this procedure, individual public officials could be indicted before the Assembly or Council for major crimes against the state and tried in the Assembly or, more commonly, in a court.

61. Throughout, I follow Levinson (2003) 349 n. 13 in preferring the term *sanctions* rather than *punishments*, the latter of which may imply moral condemnation and guilt.

62. The Arginusae trial may be another example of the use of collective sanction in response to an extraordinary offense that aroused moral outrage.

63. For discussion, see, e.g., Parker, *Miasma* (1983) 198–206; Dodds, *The Greeks and the Irrational* (1951) 33–37; Sewell-Rutter, *Guilt by Descent* (2007) 1–48; Gagné, *Ancestral Fault* (2013) 159–446. For discussion of divine judgment and punishment in Greek literature, see Bers and Lanni, "Disqualified Olympians" (2015).

the Heracleidae, was induced by a woman's guile to slay his lord, and assumed his high position, to which he had no right."[64] The intertwined concepts of individual guilt, inherited guilt, and fate are notoriously hard to unravel in Greek tragedy, but there is no doubt that the curse of the house of Atreus plays a role in the tragic events depicted in Aescyhlus' *Oresteia*. The Athenians' familiarity with the notion of divine collective punishments must have made them somewhat more receptive to the idea in secular law. But there are some reasons to doubt that the uses of collective sanctions in classical Athens should be primarily understood in terms of beliefs in communal, particularly familial, blame and responsibility.

First, as has often been pointed out, we see, from very early on, evidence that at least some Greeks viewed collective sanctions as punishing the innocent along with the guilty, rather than holding the family or group jointly responsible.[65] When discussing divine punishment of wrongdoers, for example, Solon describes how "innocent [*anaitioi*] children" or later descendants "pay for their [i.e., wrongdoers'] deeds."[66] In one of his poems, Theognis pleads to Zeus that it is not right for children who have done no wrong to be punished for the transgressions of a parent.[67]

Second, we have evidence that the Greeks could think about collective sanctions in functional terms in at least some situations. Thucydides' Mytilene debate offers an example.[68] Although the Mytilene episode takes place in the international context, I am using it here merely to illustrate that the Athenians could think through, in a sophisticated way, how the choice between an individual or collective punishment regime might affect deterrence.[69] After the revolt of Mytilene is quashed, the Athenians debate whether to kill all the Mytilenean men or only those who were implicated in the revolt. A central issue in the debate is whether collective or individual punishment would serve as a better deterrent for future revolts. Cleon argues that collective punishment is necessary for deterrence, partly because it prevents those contemplating revolt from holding out hope that they can escape punishment with a good speech or

64. Hdt. 1.91 (trans. Marincola and Selincourt).

65. For discussion, see Parker, *Miasma* (1983) 198–206; Dodds, *The Greeks and the Irrational* (1951) 33–37; Sewell-Rutter, *Guilt by Descent* (2007) 15–48.

66. Solon 13.25–32.

67. Theog. 731–52. See also Hdt. 1.55; Isoc. 16.2–3; Dem. 18.15–16.

68. Thuc. 3.36–50. Another example may be Hdt. 1.55.

69. Of course, we must be mindful that the focus on instrumentalism in the Mytilene debate may reflect Thucydides' narrative design rather than a true account of the Athenian debate. Discussions of the deterrent role of punishment are common in Attic court speeches, though I am not aware of any passages that specifically examine the effect of a collective versus an individual responsibility regime on deterrence. See, e.g., Lys. 30.23; Dem. 22.68, 34.50, 54.43, 56.48, 59.112.

a bribe if the rebellion fails. Although Cleon argues that all the Mytileneans are guilty since they did not join the Athenian siege, he also suggests that wrongly punishing innocent individuals might be required to hold onto the empire: "If, however, whatever the rights or wrongs of [imperial rule] may be, you propose to hold power all the same, then your interest demands that these too [i.e. those not directly implicated in the revolt], rightly or wrongly, must be punished. The only alternative is to surrender your empire."[70] In opposing the proposal to punish the Mytileneans collectively, Diodotus rejects arguments regarding justice and guilt as irrelevant[71] and focuses instead on which proposal better furthers deterrence. He argues that imposing collective punishment will actually be counterproductive: once a revolt starts, all the people will join in and fight to the death since they know that surrender means certain death.[72] Regardless of the accuracy of Thucydides' reporting here, the Mytilene debate demonstrates that Athenians could contemplate imposing collective sanctions primarily for functional reasons.

Third, we have seen that cultural accounts of collective sanctions tend to explain the relative rarity of these punishments in the classical period by relying on an evolution away from communal liability and toward individual responsibility. But the use of collective sanctions against state debtors and boards of officials are clearly not holdovers from an earlier time. The laws providing for collective sanctions against state debtors and boards were introduced after the democracy had been established, and both these forms of communal liability continued for the lifespan of the democracy. In fact, the use of group liability against boards appears to have remained a popular practice in Athens and elsewhere well into the Hellenistic period.[73] The evolutionary account does not apply to charges of overthrowing the democracy either. It had long been argued that the use of hereditary *atimia* was abolished as a punishment for treason and tyranny in 403/2 BCE, but the discovery of Eukrates' law demonstrated that the Athenians passed a law as late as 337/6 BCE imposing hereditary *atimia* for overthrowing the democracy. In the fourth century, the Athenians seem to have more often favored nonhereditary punishments for treason, but there was no fundamental shift in mindset, from collective to individual blame, that made hereditary punishments unacceptable.

Finally, the treatment of state debtors is particularly difficult to understand

70. Thuc. 3.40 (trans. Warner).

71. 3.44. He explicitly contrasts the issues of justice considered by domestic law courts with the present situation that calls for the Assembly to consider only questions of expediency.

72. Thuc. 3.46–47.

73. Rubinstein, "Individual and Collective Liabilities" (2012).

in terms of collective blame. The Athenians had no trouble disaggregating the guilt of the different generations during the debtor's lifetime: the heirs of the debtor remained unpunished while the debtor was alive and did not lose their citizenship rights until the debtor died. In addition, being indebted to the state was not considered the type of serious crime that typically called for group punishment. It did not implicate pollution or religious concerns, nor did it threaten the survival of the state. In fact, the speaker in Demosthenes' *Against Aristogeiton* states that some state debtors, such as those who incurred the debt by acting as a surety for a friend who defaulted, are merely "unfortunate" rather than criminal, and he suggests that some citizens "turn a blind eye" to state debtors who continue to exercise citizenship rights.[74] Moreover, the cultural explanation for collective treatment of state debtors is undermined by features of the law that seem clearly intended to compel prompt payment of the debt, such as the doubling of the debt if it is not paid off by the ninth prytany.[75] The unusual financial incentives for private prosecutors bringing confiscation actions further support the view that facilitating enforcement was an important consideration in crafting the rules regarding public debtors. In sum, the collective penalty scheme for state debtors seems to reflect utilitarian concerns rather than retributive ones.

Functionalist Approaches

If collective sanctions were not merely a form of primitive retribution, what was their purpose? What were the utilitarian goals animating the use of collective sanctions in classical Athens? As mentioned earlier, most functional accounts of collective liability in ancient societies involve a notion of indirect, delegated deterrence: the idea is to punish the group to which the wrongdoer belongs, so that innocent members of the group will identify or punish the individual offender or, even better, monitor and prevent individual members from com-

74. Dem. 25.85–91. Hunter, "Policing State Debtors" (2000), demonstrates that the attitude and treatment of state debtors varied enormously depending on the source of the debt: defaulting trierarchs and others who incurred a debt while performing a public service were treated very leniently and often continued to exercise full citizenship rights despite being formally *atimoi*; judgment debtors who observed the rules of *atimia* were rarely imprisoned and generally only faced property confiscation if a private citizen (often an enemy) took it upon themselves to initiate an action; those who defaulted on tax or rent contracts were treated most severely, often facing immediate imprisonment pending payment, possibly (at least according to *Ath. Pol.* 48.1) directly enforced by the Council. See also Hansen, *Apagoge* (1976) 59 and n. 22.

75. Imprisonment could also be used in certain circumstances to encourage payment, though uncertainty surrounding when this practice was used remains. For discussion, see Hunter, "Policing State Debtors" (2000) 25–30.

mitting offenses. This explanation makes sense when the identity of the specific offender is unknown to the punishing authority, and I think it may work in Athens for collective fines of boards of magistrates. But the penalties for state debtors and for serious offenses like bribery and subverting the democracy were not delegated deterrence regimes.

Liability for an entire board or committee fits best with the standard modern accounts of ancient collective liability. As Johnstone and Rubinstein have argued, collective punishment of boards that failed to carry out their duties probably did function as a form of delegated deterrence: it relieved the state of trying to figure out which individual official was at fault, and it encouraged all board members to insure that other members of the board did their job properly.[76] Rubinstein has pointed out that these provisions often involve "victimless" crimes—for example, cases in which a magistrate charged with collecting a debt was bribed into reporting back that the fine could not be collected because the debtor had no assets or in which a magistrate was bribed to ignore a regulatory violation.[77] In the absence of a victim to complain, these types of malfeasance would be difficult to detect during the routine accounting procedure; a collective liability regime might encourage board members to monitor and prevent wrongdoing by their colleagues. Johnstone suggests that collective punishment of boards also conformed to the democratic ideology of citizen equality,[78] but it seems more likely that it reflects a functional solution to the reality of citizen inequality: in a board composed of citizens of varying abilities and chosen by lot, collective liability encourages the more competent members to compensate for their less competent colleagues and insure that the required tasks are accomplished.

But the other forms of collective sanctions in classical Athens did not work this way. Most ancient collective liability regimes punished extended families, tribes, or even whole villages, often in cases where the identity of the specific offender was unknown to the punishing authority. But in the remaining classical Athenian examples—state debtors and serious crimes against the state—the identity of the offender is known, and only the offender's children and descendants are punished. Unborn descendants are obviously in no position to identify or prevent the offender's wrongdoing, and given the power of fathers over sons in Athens, it seems highly unlikely that living sons could serve

76. Johnstone, *A History of Trust*, (2011) 139–41; Rubinstein, "Individual and Collective Liabilities," (2012) 342–53. It is even possible that innocent members collectively fined under these regulations might informally exact payment from the individual at fault.

77. Rubinstein, "Individual and Collective Liabilities" (2012) 349–50.

78. Johnstone, *A History of Trust* (2011) 147.

this function either.[79] The use of hereditary *atimia* for state debt also cannot be explained as a device to provide for more complete compensation when individual wrongdoers are unable to pay: punishment for public debts did not extend beyond the debtor's direct descendants and therefore did not expand the potential pool of assets subject to confiscation.[80]

I think a different functional explanation probably lies behind the imposition of hereditary *atimia* on state debtors. In the absence of a public prosecutor, it was always uncertain whether a given public debtor who refused to pay despite owning property or who ignored the restrictions of *atimia* would be brought to account by a volunteer prosecutor.[81] A debtor might be tempted to try his luck by not paying, and it appears that some debtors not only remained in Athens without having their property confiscated but continued to participate in political institutions.[82] The prospect that failing to pay would cause one's sons to lose their citizenship rights or at least to live under a similar burden of possible prosecution may have provided an additional inducement to the debtor to find the funds to pay up.

In this way, hereditary *atimia* was a form of direct, rather than indirect, deterrence. Expanding disenfranchisement to the next generation increased the severity of the penalty for the initial wrongdoer, quite apart from the punishment experienced by his descendants.[83] Perhaps just as important, it enhanced the likelihood of punishment, by extending the time frame during which any personal enemy or opportunistic sycophant[84] might bring an enforcement ac-

79. Sons became legally independent at adulthood, but the father typically remained head of the household (*oikos*) and retained ownership and control over the family's property. See MacDowell, *The Law in Classical Athens* (1978) 84–85.

80. In the case of a childless debtor, collateral relatives who chose to claim the estate would similarly suffer *atimia*, but since collateral relatives (unlike the direct descendants) had the option of turning down the estate, this likely rarely happened.

81. As discussed above, there was much less uncertainty surrounding enforcement against debtors who defaulted on contracts with the state. See Hunter, "Policing State Debtors" (2000) 33–34.

82. Hansen, *Apagoge* (1976) 59 n. 22, lists examples; see also Hunter, "Policing State Debtors" (2000) 30–32. This may have been particularly true for well-connected and resourceful citizens, who may have felt that few citizens would want to risk launching a volunteer prosecution against them or even that their higher status might secure a favorable jury verdict despite their factual guilt. The exact opposite might be true, however: it might be that higher-profile citizens were *more* likely to be prosecuted, because they were more likely to have political enemies who might challenge them in court and because the potential financial reward for bringing a prosecution against higher-profile citizens would likely be higher, while lower-status citizens were more likely to be able to avoid prosecution.

83. Posner, *The Economics of Justice* (1981) 220, discusses how making criminal responsibility hereditary increases the costs of misconduct. The importance of the *oikos* in Athenian social and religious life likely made the offender's distress at the punishment of a relative even more acute.

84. On *sycophant* as a legal and ideological term for a vexatious litigant, see Christ, *The Litigious Athenian* (1998) 47–72.

tion. If the original debtor failed to pay in his lifetime despite these incentives, his descendants might be induced to pay, if they did not share their father's confidence that they would not be prosecuted. In this way, imposing *atimia* on the debtor's heirs helped compensate for difficulties of enforcement in a private prosecution system. This instrumental explanation is consistent with the other aspects of the law that seem to be aimed at encouraging payment, such as the doubling of a debt not paid in a reasonable period of time.

What explains the use of hereditary *atimia* for bribery, tyranny, and subverting the democracy? These crimes threatened the very survival of the state. Tyranny and, later, oligarchic revolt were a source of constant concern;[85] the difficulties of enforcing "victimless" crimes made bribery a serious issue.[86] The collective aspect of the punishment for these crimes may have been intended to increase the severity of the penalty experienced by the individual offender, in the interests of both retribution and deterrence. Just as in the case of state debtors, these collective sanctions were likely mechanisms of direct, rather than delegated, deterrence; before committing any of these political crimes, the potential offender had to consider that his children and grandchildren would also be punished.

There may also have been a preemptive aspect to imposing outlawry or disenfranchisement on the offender's sons and descendants. Even apart from deterring the offender, the Athenians may have thought that punishing descendants prevented the *descendants* from committing their *own* crimes. Athenians believed that children tended to be similar in character and political outlook to their father and ancestors.[87] Accordingly, the Athenians believed that descendants of a treasonous offender were more likely than others to pose a danger to the state in the future, and disenfranchising those descendants may have been deemed a prudent safeguard. Here we are getting very close to the cultural, primitivist account of collective sanctions, but there is a subtle difference. According to this view, hereditary *atimia* may have been aimed not at *punishing*

85. See Lanni and Vermeule, "Precautionary Constitutionalism" (2013) 897–901, for a discussion of how key aspects of the Athenian democracy, including the lot, rotation, and collegiality, may have been precautionary measures aimed at preventing tyranny.

86. For a discussion of the evidence that bribery was widespread in Athens and that the Athenians enacted more institutional reforms attempting to address bribery than any other offense, see Conover, *Bribery* (2010) 16–17.

87. For example, court speakers often cite their ancestors' military exploits and other good deeds in an effort to convince the jury of their own virtue. For discussion of the use of character evidence in Athenian courts, see Lanni, *Law and Justice* (2006) 59–64. In addition, some literary examples that initially appear to be simple cases of inherited guilt visited on an innocent descendant are found, on closer inspection, to include an element of the heir committing a mistake similar to that made by his ancestor. The story of Croesus in Herodotus is an example. For discussion, see Sewell-Rutter, *Guilt by Descent* (2007) 5–13; Parker, *Miasma* (1983) 199–200.

the sons for the sins of the father but at *preventing* the sons from committing similar crimes in the future.

Athenian law did not generally employ preemptive punishments, though there are a few passages suggesting that using preemptive punishment for a crime as dire as overthrowing the state was not a completely foreign concept. The speaker in Isocrates' *Against Lochites* urges the jurors to punish the defendant not just for the assault he committed but also as a preemptive measure, because the defendant has the same "character" as those who led the bloody reign of the Thirty Tyrants: "It is better to discover how to avert future crimes than to obtain justice for those already committed. . . . Don't wait until they have banded together and seized upon a crisis in order to harm the entire city, but when they are handed over to you on a pretext, punish them for this in the belief that when you arrest someone demonstrating his complete depravity in a minor incident, you've had a piece of good luck."[88] In the *Laws*, Plato seems ambivalent about the practice of preemptively punishing descendants of those who undermine the state, providing that children of such offenders will be punished with exile only in cases where "not only the father, but his father and grandfather before him have all been condemned on a capital charge."[89] In other words, Plato is careful about imposing a collective punishment only in cases where there is some proof that the tendency to break the law is being handed down across generations.

Collective punishments were not the only approach the Athenians took to protecting the state from internal threats. Many of the alternative approaches to protecting the state exhibit different, but similarly functional, features; there is considerable evidence that the Athenians were also quite thoughtful and deliberate in other legislation aimed at eliminating threats to the state. Another precautionary or preemptive measure was ostracism, the fifth-century practice by which Athenians had the option of voting to expel one citizen per year for a ten-year period.[90] There was no formal charge or accusation made in this procedure, and the ostracized individual could retain his land in Athens and return

88. Isoc. 20.11–12 (trans. Mirhady). Here the speaker seems to have evaluated the defendant's character based not on his ancestors but on his behavior in the incident.

89. Pl. *Laws* 9.865b–d (trans. Bury).

90. Provided a quorum was reached, the citizen with the largest number of votes, however small that number might be, was ostracized. For a basic summary of the practice and discussion of its precautionary features, see Lanni and Vermeule, "Precautionary Constitutionalism" (2013) 897–901, 909–10; for a discussion of ostracism as a form of "prediction market" that aggregated opinions about which individual was the most dangerous to the state, see Ober, *Democracy and Knowledge* (2008) 160–61. For a fascinating account that emphasizes the importance of the *ostrakophoria* as a democratic ritual quite apart from actual expulsion, see Kosmin, "A Phenomenology of Democracy" (2015).

to full citizenship rights at the conclusion of the ten-year period. Forsdyke's interpretation of ostracism[91] suggests that this practice may reflect the opposite approach from that taken in the aforementioned laws against tyranny and subversion of democracy: rather than permanently trying to remove offenders and their potentially dangerous descendants, ostracism promoted the temporary removal and future peaceful reintegration of the destabilizing faction. According to this view, the moderation of ostracism (whereby the ostracized individual retained his property and could return in ten years), in contrast to the aristocratic politics of exile, may have served partly to minimize "the incentives for the exiled individual to seek return by force and destabilize the polis."[92]

The Decree of Demophantos of 410,[93] mentioned earlier, takes yet another instrumental approach. Rather than promoting deterrence solely through the imposition of a penalty on the offender, the decree creates incentives for ordinary Athenians to protect the democracy from potential tyrants. In addition to declaring the offender outlawed, the decree provides for all Athenians to swear an oath to kill anyone subverting the democracy and to reward anyone who kills a potential tyrant by giving him half of the offender's property. The use of such clearly functional penalties to protect the state from subversion in these other contexts bolsters the theory that the use of hereditary *atimia* in cases of crimes threatening the state should be similarly understood in instrumental terms.

It is striking that the Athenians took steps to reward private citizens for punishing the offenses of potential tyrants and state debtors. Because they lacked specific victims, these offenses (as well as other offenses against the state, like bribery)[94] were likely systematically underenforced. The use of hereditary collective sanctions for these offenses may represent a different approach to the problem of underenforcement. The lower probability of prosecution in these public offenses would naturally reduce deterrence. We have seen that collective hereditary punishments boosted deterrence by increasing the severity of the sanction for the offender. It is not surprising that the offenses for which the Athenians continued to use collective sanctions were precisely those for which the usual private enforcement mechanisms were considered inadequate.

91. Forsdyke, "Exile, Ostracism, and the Athenian Democracy" (2000).

92. Forsdyke, "Exile, Ostracism, and the Athenian Democracy" (2000) 233.

93. And. 1.96–98. For an argument of how this decree and other Greek tyrant-killing laws served to overcome coordination problems and facilitate large-scale mobilization in response to internal threats, see Teegarden, *Death to Tyrants* (2014) 15–56.

94. In the case of bribery and corruption, private initiative was supplemented by the special accounting procedures for outgoing magistrates.

Conclusion

The Athenians did occasionally punish the innocent for the crimes of the guilty. In this essay, I have tried to explain how and why. The evidence shows that in one case, the collective liability of a board of magistrates for the malfeasance of any of them, the ancient practice conforms nicely to the modern theory of collective sanctions, that is, that punishment was collective because of the difficulties involved in identifying and deterring the individuals most responsible. But with other offenses, like bribery, tyranny, or the failure to pay state debts, the situation was quite different: the innocent parties subject to punishment were *descendants*—younger or even unborn individuals, who, in the ancient world, would have been remarkable primarily for their helplessness, for their *inability* to take action against the individual wrongdoer. In these punishments meted out to children and grandchildren, some have glimpsed a sort of primitive and irrational quintessence of Athens or Greece as a whole, like Hans Castorp's lurid dream of secret human sacrifice deep within the sunlit temple.[95]

But there was nothing primitive or irrational about Athenian collective sanctions. They were extraordinary responses to extraordinary threats faced by an extraordinary society. Malfeasance, political violence, and failure to pay state debts are not pressing problems for most successful modern societies, but they were continual, existential threats to a participatory democracy that lacked a central enforcement mechanism. And they were the only threats punished by collective sanction. The Athenians quite deliberately decided that the son should be punished for the sins of the father, at least where the sin threatened the operation of the democracy. In so doing, the Athenians gave the father pause from undertaking the offense to begin with and rid themselves of any son inclined to continue the father's political agenda. Even at the time, such a punishment was viewed as troubling, possibly even unfair. But there was nothing irrational about it.[96]

---

95. In Thomas Mann's *The Magic Mountain*, the hero Hans Castorp has a dream in which he imagines witches undertaking a sacrifice of human children inside a classical temple—Mann's suggestion that irrationality, as much as rationality, is an essential part of the Greek gift to Western civilization.

96. I thank Oren Bar-Gill, Glenn Cohen, Sara Forsdyke, Louis Kaplow, Wesley Kelman, David Phillips, Gerald Neuman, Intisar Rabb, Lene Rubinstein, Steven Shavell, Matthew Stephenson, Lloyd Weinreb, Michael Zimm, the participants in the "Ancient Law, Ancient Society" conference, the Harvard Law School Faculty workshop, and the members of the Harvard Law School's Law and Economics Seminar for their helpful suggestions. Cass Luskin provided excellent research assistance.

Bibliography

Bederman, D. J. *International Law in Antiquity*. Cambridge, 2001.

Bers, V., and A. Lanni. "Disqualified Olympians: The Skeptical Greek View of Divine Judges." In A. Mermelstein and S. Holtz, eds., *The Divine Courtroom in Comparative Perspective*, 128–44. Leiden, 2015.

Christ, M. R. *The Litigious Athenian*. Baltimore, 1998.

Connor, W. R. "The Razing of the House in Greek Society." *Transactions of the American Philological Association* 115 (1985): 79–102.

Conover, K. *Bribery in Classical Athens*. PhD diss., Princeton University, 2010.

Daube, D. "Two Notes on Communal Responsibility." *Sociological Review* 36 (1944): 24–42.

de Ste. Croix, G. E. M. "Notes on the Jurisdiction of the Athenian Empire." Part 2. *Classical Quarterly*, n.s., 11 (1961): 268–80.

Dodds, E. R. *The Greeks and the Irrational*. Berkeley, 1951.

Forsdyke, S. "Exile, Ostracism, and the Athenian Democracy." *Classical Antiquity* 19 (2000): 232–63.

Frier, B. W. *Landlords and Tenants in Imperial Rome*. Princeton. 1980.

Frier, B. W. *The Rise of the Roman Jurists: Studies in Cicero's "Pro Caecina."* Princeton, 1985.

Frier, B. W., and D. P. Kehoe. "Law and Economic Institutions." In W. Scheidel, I. Morris, and R. Saller, eds., *The Cambridge Economic History of the Greco-Roman World*, 113–43. Cambridge, 2007.

Gagné, R. *Ancestral Fault in Ancient Greece*. Cambridge, 2013.

Glotz, G. *La solidarité de la famille dans le droit criminel en Grèce*. Paris, 1904.

Hansen, M. H. Apagoge, Endeixis, *and* Ephegesis *against* Kakourgoi, Atimoi, *and* Pheugontes*: A Study in the Athenian Administration of Justice in the Fourth Century B.C.* Odense, 1976.

Hansen, M. H. *The Athenian Democracy in the Age of Demosthenes: Structure, Principles, Ideology*. Norman, 1999.

Hunter, V. "Policing Public Debtors in Classical Athens." *Phoenix* 54 (2000): 21–38.

Johnstone, S. *A History of Trust in Ancient Greece*. Chicago, 2011.

Kahrstedt, U. *Untersuchungen zur Magistratur in Athen*. Stuttgart, 1936.

Kosmin, P. "A Phenomenology of Democracy: Ostracism as Political Ritual." *Classical Antiquity* 34 (2015): 120–60.

Lanni, A. "From Anthropology to Sociology: New Directions in Ancient Greek Law Research." In P. Perlman, ed., *Greek Law in the Twenty-First Century*. Austin, forthcoming.

Lanni, A. "Judicial Review and the Athenian 'Constitution.'" In M. Hansen, ed., *Athenian Demokratia–Modern Democracy: Tradition and Inspiration*, 235–63. Geneva, 2009.

Lanni, A. *Law and Justice in the Courts of Classical Athens*. Cambridge, 2006.

Lanni, A. "The Laws of War in Ancient Greece." *Law and History Review* 26.3 (2008): 469–89.

Lanni, A., and A. Vermeule. "Precautionary Constitutionalism in Ancient Athens." *Cardozo Law Review* 34 (2013): 893–915.

Levinson, D. "Collective Sanctions." *Stanford Law Review* 56 (2003): 345–428.

Levmore, S. "Rethinking Group Responsibility and Strategic Threats in Biblical Texts and Modern Law." *Chicago-Kent Law Review* 71 (1995): 85–121.
Lindgren, J. "Why the Ancients May Not Have Needed a System of Criminal Law." *Boston University Law Review* 76 (1996): 29–57.
MacDowell, D. M. *Athenian Homicide Law in the Age of the Orators*. Manchester, UK, 1963.
MacDowell, D. M. *The Law in Classical Athens*. Ithaca, 1978.
Maine, H. S. *Ancient Law: Its Connection with the Early History of Society and Its Relation to Modern Ideas*. 1861. Reprint, ed. A. Montagu, Tucson, 1986.
Miceli, T., and K. Segerson. "Punishing the Innocent along with the Guilty: The Economics of Individual versus Group Punishment." *Journal of Legal Studies* 36.1 (2007): 81–106.
Ober, J. *Democracy and Knowledge: Innovation and Learning in Classical Athens*. Princeton, 2008.
Parisi, F., and G. Dari-Mattiacci. "The Rise and Fall of Communal Liability in Ancient Law." *International Review of Law and Economics* 24 (2004): 489–505.
Parker, R. *Miasma: Pollution and Purification in Early Greek Religion*. New York, 1983.
Piérart, M. "Les *euthynoi* athéniens." *L'Antiquité Classique* 40 (1971): 526–73.
Phillips, D. *The Law of Ancient Athens*. Ann Arbor, 2013.
Posner, R. A. *The Economics of Justice*. Cambridge, MA, 1981.
Posner, R. A. "A Theory of Primitive Society, with Special Reference to Law." *Journal of Law and Economics* 23 (1980): 1–53.
Rubinstein, L. "Individual and Collective Liabilities of Boards of Officials in the Late Classical and Early Hellenistic Period." In B. Legras and G. Thür, eds., *Symposion 2011: Vorträge zur griechischen und hellenistischen Rechtsgeschichte*, 329–54. Vienna, 2012.
Saunders, T. *Plato's Penal Code: Tradition, Controversy, and Reform in Greek Penology*. Oxford, 1991.
Sewell-Rutter, N. J. *Guilt by Descent: Moral Inheritance and Decision Making in Greek Tragedy*. Oxford, 2007.
Teegarden, D. A. *Death to Tyrants! Ancient Greek Democracy and the Struggle against Tyranny*. Princeton, 2014.
Todd, S. C. *The Shape of Athenian Law*. Oxford, 1993.

CHAPTER 2

An Economic Perspective on Marriage Alliances in Ancient Greece

Michael Leese

A noble man does not mind marrying the base daughter of a base man if she brings him a lot of wealth. Nor does a noble woman refuse to be the wife of a base man who is rich, but rather she wants wealth instead of nobility. They honor wealth. Baseborn people marry nobles, and vice versa. Wealth has mixed the race.

—Theognis, *Elegies* 1.185–90

As Theognis says for sixth-century BCE Megara, many Greeks married for money, and money could also enable upward social mobility through prestigious marriage alliances. In this essay, I argue that there was a marriage market in ancient Greece and that economic calculation occurred within the nonmarket spheres of kinship and marriage.[1] Indeed, so much wealth flowed through marriage transactions that marriage could be the easiest way to add to one's fortune in ancient Greece and could provide the largest single acquisition of wealth in an ancient Greek's life. Choosing a partner was thus potentially the most important economic decision an ancient Greek ever faced.

But money was not enough to gain a marriage alliance among the highest ranks of the elite, where the rules of the marriage market were different from those that governed behavior in the commercial market. The largest financial returns were accessible only to those who were already wealthy enough to invest in the types of cultural and social capital that could be attained only

1. Millett, *Lending and Borrowing* (1991) 115–21, has described the ancient Greeks' approach to social relations as "coolly calculating." Scholars have already demonstrated that marriage alliances were often made for political purposes in ancient Greece: see Blundell, *Women in Ancient Greece* (1995) 67–69; Davies, *Wealth and the Power of Wealth* (1981) 117–20. Economic motivations may have been equally significant.

through a life of opulent leisure. Therefore, once a person was a member of the wealthy leisure class, it was sometimes more profitable to engage in behaviors that per se did not yield any immediate gain but that opened up opportunities for nonmarket transactions that were much more substantial. In other words, avoiding market exchange and focusing instead on nonmarket behaviors, especially investments in cultural and social capital, could secure more lucrative opportunities in rich marriage alliances.

This study therefore sheds new light on the interchange between cultural, economic, and social capital in ancient Greece; I argue here that, rather than a static system in which social and financial interests were largely separate, there was a great deal of fluidity and interchangeability between social and financial capital.[2] More significantly, the fact that economic calculation permeated the realm of social relations also provides a fresh perspective on Karl Polanyi's concept of "embeddedness," the idea that premodern economies were embedded in social relations and did not constitute a separate conceptual realm of activity. Previous scholarship has generally presented a one-sided view of embeddedness, by focusing on how social factors affected economic considerations. But the evidence of ancient Greek marriage alliances demonstrates that the opposite was also true, that money also shaped social relations. The phenomenon of embeddedness is therefore more complex than is often depicted by modern scholars. What is often seen to be a monolithic dichotomy between the social and economic realms was actually a dynamic relationship of interconnected and intertwined interests, the economic and social being inextricably woven together.

Marrying for Money

In the passage of Theognis quoted above, both men and women in archaic Megara saw money as being one of the primary desiderata of marriage. Marriages in ancient Greece were often motivated not by love but by financial considerations,[3] and it seems that marriages were predominantly arranged by the male heads of the bride's family, who frequently chose their future sons- and brothers-in-law. Callias the Rich was said to have given his daughters a great gift: they could all

2. For the concepts of cultural, financial, and social capital, see Bourdieu, "The Forms of Capital" (2001).

3. See, e.g., Aristotle, *Politics* 5.4.6–7 (1304a4–17), for examples of marriages that Aristotle states were motivated primarily by financial interests.

marry whomever they wished.[4] Most Greek fathers were not so generous. Although there were some instances in which ancient Greek women seem to have had some say in the decision, these occurrences seem to have been the exception to the rule.[5] For the most part, marriage was a contract between the groom and the bride's father or family, and brides served to cement economic relationships between men.[6] David Schaps sums up the situation well: "Marriage in Athens was a contract between the bride's father and the groom."[7] Not surprisingly, many of these arranged marriages served financial purposes. Indeed, the transfer of a dowry was central in completing marriage alliances. As Demosthenes says, "If a man together with the lady gives [to her groom] also what is hers [her dowry], he becomes a kinsman and marriage ally."[8] The payment of a dowry, an economic act, sealed the deal between two families.

Marriage was therefore one of the most important economic decisions an ancient Greek faced. Since dowries in ancient Greece were typically paid in cash,[9] they were often the single largest injection of money into a man's pocketbook during his lifetime, usually just at the time when he was starting to control his own household and economic affairs. Husbands were legally permitted to invest and profit from the dowry. This was the case in the Gortyn Law Code, in accordance with which husbands kept all profits from the dowry during marriage and even half of the profits in case of a divorce.[10] At Athens, husbands could keep the dowry even after a divorce, in which case its legal status transformed into that of a loan at the rate of 18 percent a year.[11] Dowries therefore

4. Hdt. 6.122. This passage is often regarded as an interpolation due to un-Herodotean vocabulary (How and Wells, *Commentary on Herodotus* [1912] ad loc.) but nevertheless reveals an important social reality.

5. Blundell, *Women in Ancient Greece* (1995) 67–68. As Bourdieu, "The Forms of Capital" (2001) 104, puts it, "It is quite logical that, in most societies, the preparation and conclusion of marriages should be the business of the whole group, and not of the agents directly involved."

6. For a general discussion of the role women played in cementing alliances between men through the act of marriage, see Von Reden, *Exchange* (1995) 49–55. As explained by Cox, *Household Interests* (1996) 120–21, respective roles of men and women in arranging marriages can be seen in the fact that sisters tended to marry before their brothers: "The earlier marriage of a sister would secure a beneficial alliance for the woman's natal family, and in particular for a late-marrying brother. . . . Epilycus the Philaid and his father gave his sisters in marriage to some of the most powerful politicians of the day: the *strategos* Glaucon, the son of Pericles, and the father of Andocides—these alliances brought the family out of political obscurity." For a similar pattern at Rome, see Saller, "Men's Age at Marriage" (1987).

7. Schaps, *Economic Rights* (1979) 74.

8. *Against Onetor* 30.12.

9. Finley, *Studies* (1951) 45; see also 44–52, for dotal *horoi*. For the ancient Greek dowry in general, see Schaps, *Economic Rights* (1979) 74–88.

10. Gortyn Law Code 2.45.

11. See Dem. 30.7, 18–42. For a general discussion of dowry and marriage law in classical Athens, see Todd, *The Shape of Athenian Law* (1993) 207–31. See also the problematic passage at Dem. 43.54: if the next of kin does not wish to marry an heiress, he must give her away in mar-

provided men with a great deal of cash and, from the legal perspective of both the Gortyn and Athenian law codes, were considered primarily financial, rather than symbolic, transactions.

There seem to have been a number of ancient Greek men who married their wives specifically for their dowry. At least there were Greek thinkers who viewed this as a danger to marriage. Thus Plutarch says that Solon outlawed dowries because he wanted marriage to be pursued not for profit or purchase but for dwelling together and raising children.[12] Marriage for the sake of dowry is not unique to ancient Greece but is a common pattern in societies that practice the institution. For seventeenth-century England, Richard Grassby says that "merchants, like landowners, sought profitable marriages for themselves and their sons" and that "marrying for money was more defensible than marrying for lust because expectations of a dowry could be used as security for commercial credit."[13] In Florence, a dowry of fifteen hundred florins is likely what allowed Cosimo de Medici's father, Giovanni di Bicci, to enter into the partnership in 1385 that would eventually grow into the great bank of the Medici.[14] The timely acquisition of a large dowry could provide great impetus to a successful financial or political career.[15]

In ancient Greece, so much money flowed through dowry transactions that Aristotle believed it was one of the primary causes of wealth inequality at Sparta.[16] Moreover, Phaleas of Chalcedon considered the dowry to be the most significant mechanism whereby wealth remained concentrated in the hands of the upper classes, and he proposed that having the rich only give and the poor only receive dowries would be the quickest way to fix economic inequality in society.[17] Comparative history agrees: the rapid increase in dowry values from fifteenth- to seventeenth-century Florence led to an increasing concentration of wealth among the rich.[18] Therefore, exchanging dowries was one of the primary means by which the wealthy maintained their position, and the dynamics of this system are most clearly visible among the highest classes.

---

riage to someone else with a dowry, along with 500 drachmas (in addition to her property) for the *Pentekosiomedimnoi*, 300 for the *Hippeis*, and 150 for the *Zeugitai*.

12. Plutarch, *Solon* 20.6.

13. Grassby, "English Merchant Capitalism in the Late Seventeenth Century" (1970) 102–3.

14. De Roover, *The Medici Bank* (1968) 36.

15. As a relative proportion of a father's estate, Greek dowries attested from antiquity constituted about 10 percent of the bride's father's estate, which is perhaps lower than the largest dowries in early modern Europe but comparable to those in ancient Rome, where they typically amounted to 5 to 10 percent. See Saller, "Roman Dowry" (1984) 200–202.

16. Aristotle, *Politics* 2.9.15 (1270a15–34).

17. Aristotle, *Politics* 2.7.3 (1266a39–1266b5). For Phaleas of Chalcedon, see Balot, "Aristotle's Critique" (2001).

18. Goldthwaite, *Economy of Renaissance Florence* (2008) 568–69.

During the late 420s, Alcibiades entered into an alliance with the richest man in Greece, Hipponicus, son of Callias the Rich, by marrying Hipponicus' daughter, Hipparete.[19] With this marriage, he received the largest dowry attested from classical Greece, twenty talents.[20] The size of this dowry is believable, as it amounted to 10 percent of Hipponicus' fortune of two hundred talents.[21] This figure is consistent with the attestations from classical Athens, collected by Cheryl Anne Cox, of the relative sizes of dowries in comparison to personal fortunes.[22] The business nature of this alliance can be seen in the fact that the dowry was paid in installments: half up front and the other half with the birth of a child, to seal the deal.[23]

As Thucydides states, Alcibiades needed money to fund his political ambitions,[24] and it seems that he was interested in this marriage mainly for the money. It certainly was not love for his bride-to-be that motivated this marriage. He brought so many mistresses into their house that Hipparete went to the archon to begin divorce proceedings, from which Alcibiades forcibly removed her, and Alcibiades was even accused of plotting to murder his father-in-law Hipponicus to get control of his entire two-hundred-talent fortune.[25] Hipponicus is said to have been so afraid for his life that he offered his entire estate to the Athenian people in case he died under suspicious circumstances without an heir.

Although his family held the hereditary priesthood of *dadouchos*, torch-bearer, in the Eleusinian Mysteries, it was probably not Hipponicus' nobility that primarily attracted Alcibiades. He profited from this alliance, and it seems that he was using this marriage as a stepping-stone to greater ambitions. As John Davies and David Gribble argue,[26] Alcibiades probably used this massive dowry to enter seven chariot teams at the Olympics in 416, at which he won the first, second, and fourth prizes. Thucydides suggests that lavish expenditures

---

19. Isoc. 16.31.

20. Andocides 4.13; Plutarch, *Alcibiades* 8.1–3. For the date, see Davies, *Athenian Propertied Families* (1971) 19.

21. For the figure of two hundred talents, see Lysias 19.48.

22. Cox, *Household Interests* (1996) 118. For an additional listing of dowry amounts, see Schaps, *Economic Rights* (1979) 99.

23. The importance of children in sealing a marriage alliance can be seen in the fact that Pisistratus' care not to have children with Megacles' daughter invalidated their union: see Osborne, *Demos* (1985) 138–39. On the point of marriage being to produce legitimate children, see Dem. 59.122.

24. Thuc. 6.15.

25. Andocides 4.14–15.

26. Gribble, "Alcibiades at the Olympics" (2012) 56, citing Davies, *Athenian Propertied Families* (1971) 19, notes that the daughter of Alcibiades and Hipparete was probably born just before the 416 Olympic Games and that the money for the Olympic chariot teams in those games probably came from Hipponicus.

and victories at Olympia helped Alcibiades to gain the command of the Sicilian expedition, from which he expected to gain even more wealth and honor. Lysias says that Alcibiades made about one hundred talents from his commands as general[27] and that he eventually was accused of aiming at tyranny. Therefore, it seems that Alcibiades saw this marriage as a stepping-stone on the path to Panhellenic glory, and who knows what he might have achieved were it not for the Hermokopidae incident and the defeat at Notium.

If Alcibiades' interests in this marriage can be reasonably inferred, what motivated the family of Hipparete to enter this relationship? Hipponicus also may have been motivated by financial concerns. His entire fortune, which had been built up by his father, was in the silver mining industry, which proved to be a tenuous base. As Davies argues, Hipponicus' wealth seems to have been so concentrated in the mines that the family's fortune was devastated with the collapse of operations in the Laureion region after the Spartan fortification of Deceleia in 412.[28] The fortune dropped so precipitously that Hipponicus' son was said to have been worth only two talents in 387,[29] meaning that 99 percent of Hipponicus' fortune had been lost. With the annual Spartan invasions of Attica in the Archidamian War, perhaps Hipponicus, fearing that his mining interests would be in danger, desired to offset the risks of his high concentration in the silver industry by entering into an alliance with the Alcmaeonidae, whose wealth consisted primarily of land. Hesiod and Cato the Elder both considered agriculture to be much safer than commercial or financial activities,[30] and Paul Christesen has argued convincingly that interest rates on maritime loans were much higher than loans on landed property, because the Greeks understood that the risks inherent in nonagricultural ventures were much higher than in agriculture itself.[31]

In making these choices, Hipponicus may have been following in his father's footsteps. Callias is said to have paid fifty talents, seemingly in lieu of receiving a dowry, to marry the sister of Cimon, Elpinice.[32] This massive sum, the largest single transaction between private individuals from classical Greece as far as I know, was the fine that Cimon inherited from his father, Miltiades, after his failed attack on Paros. The large size of the sum indicates that Callias

27. Lysias 19.52.
28. Davies, *Athenian Propertied Families* (1971) 261.
29. Lysias 19.48.
30. Hesiod, in *Works and Days*, emphasizes at length the dangers of maritime trade (618–94) but nowhere indicates that agriculture is risky. Cato the Elder, in the *praefatio* to his *De agri cultura*, calls maritime trade *periculosum*, "risky," and calls farming *quaestus stabilissimus*, "the safest pursuit."
31. Christesen, "Economic Rationalism" (2003).
32. Plutarch, *Cimon* 4.7.

may have eagerly sought a marriage alliance with this powerful military and political family, whose fortune was also primarily agricultural and therefore more secure than mining.

Both Hipponicus and Callias could have made much cheaper marriage decisions. Hipponicus could have chosen a son-in-law who would have accepted a smaller dowry, and Callias could have *received* a large dowry instead of *paying* for a marriage himself. They seem to have made the choice to transform their wealth into other benefits: social and political capital and perhaps also financial security. Therefore, Hipponicus likely and Callias perhaps made calculated decisions to invest their liquid capital from mining into political and social capital through alliances with the Alcmaeonidae and the Philaidae, two of the most powerful families in Athens.

Scholars have long recognized that social relationships can act as an important economic safety net in a wide variety of historical contexts. As Paul Millett has argued, social connections in ancient Greece acted "as a form of insurance in a world of capricious fortune."[33] Indeed, in *Works and Days*, Hesiod himself advises his brother Perses to invest his material surpluses in the form of favors to foster relationships of reciprocity with his neighbors, social capital as insurance against difficult times.[34] The security that joining forces with a wealthy and powerful family could provide against hardship was some of the best available to a person in ancient Greece.

Thus, in the marriage market of ancient Greece, money could be converted into social and political capital, and vice versa, but money was not enough to allow one to marry into the highest ranks of the Greek elite. Pasion the banker was one of the most successful businessmen of fourth-century Greece, but for all his wealth, he was not able to penetrate the highest ranks of the nobility, since he was born a slave. As Aristotle states, "Distinguished marriages are not for the *nouveaux riches* but for those who are noble in birth."[35]

Indeed, one needed cultural and social capital, in addition to money, to secure a marriage alliance at the highest levels of society. This necessity can be seen in Herodotus' famous account of the process that joined Megacles, son of Alcmaeon, with Cleisthenes, the tyrant of Sicyon, in around 575 BCE.

> Cleisthenes tyrant of Sicyon had a daughter named Agariste, and he wanted to find the best man in Greece to be her husband, so during the

---

33. Millett, *Lending and Borrowing* (1991) 120–21.

34. Hesiod mentions feasting as a way to invest surplus in the security of social capital (342–43), considers neighbors to be a safety net (401), and recommends making voluntary interest payments as investments in future security, "because it will be there for you in the future" (351–52).

35. *Rhetoric* 2.9.11 (1387a29–30).

> Olympic Games (at which he won in the four-horse-chariot race) he had the criers make the following announcement: "Any man who considers himself good enough to become Cleisthenes' son-in-law should come to Sicyon in sixty days' time or sooner, because Cleisthenes will come to a decision about his daughter's marriage within a year. . . ." On the appointed day, Cleisthenes began by finding out where they were from and what each individual's lineage was. Then he kept them with him for a year, while he tested their courage, character, education, and manners by spending time with each of them.[36]

Character, education, and manners—in the end, these were the marks of nobility that allowed Megacles to win the hand of Agariste over Hippocleides, son of Tisander, who had initially been favored because of his descent from the Cypselids, the tyrants of Corinth.

The process whereby Cleisthenes selected his future son-in-law provides an important glimpse into the world of the highest Greek nobility and into the means by which the elite maintained their position at the top of the social ladder. Indeed, proof of nobility was the most important criterion for achieving a marriage alliance with this Greek tyrant. From this perspective, it is useful to turn to institutional economic theorist Thorstein Veblen, who argues that across human societies, cultural capital was a necessary investment to express one's membership in the elite, which he terms the "highest leisure class." He includes in cultural capital "knowledge of dead languages and the occult sciences; of correct spelling . . . of the latest proprieties of dress, furniture . . . games, sport, and fancy-bred animals, such as dogs and race-horses." Veblen states that "refined tastes, manners, and habits of life are a useful evidence of gentility, because good breeding requires time, application, and expense, and can therefore not be compassed by those whose time and energy are taken up with work." He concludes, "It is among this highest leisure class, who have no superiors and few peers, that decorum finds its fullest and maturest expression."[37] The marks of gentility that Veblen emphasizes as being so important for the leisure class in his own time were precisely those that were most instrumental in securing a marriage with the tyrant of Sicyon. As Herodotus states, Cleisthenes spent a year with the suitors to learn their character, education, and manners, in short, their marks of nobility that distinguished them as members of the highest leisure class.

Moreover, Veblen's emphasis on games, sport, and fancy-bred animals, es-

---

36. Hdt. 6.126–28. I have used Robin Waterfield's translation of this passage because of its vividness.

37. Veblen, *The Leisure Class* (1899) 29, 31, 33.

pecially racehorses, brings us back to the way Cleisthenes announced the competition for his daughter's hand. In a world without mass media, what better way was there to advertise his wealth and membership in the highest ranks of the Greek elite than by winning the most expensive and prestigious Olympic event and then offering his daughter to the crowd and his competitors, who were among the wealthiest nobles from the rest of the Greek world? It may not have been by chance that Cleisthenes won the four-horse chariot race at these Olympic Games, just when his daughter was of prime marriageable age; he may have planned it years before. In the end, he chose Megacles of the Alcmaeonidae, who was not only a wealthy man but also the son of Alcmaeon, the first Athenian to win the four-horse chariot race at Olympia.

The four-horse chariot race was the perfect venue for Cleisthenes to demonstrate his wealth and power, in the company of his closest competitors, the other extremely wealthy individuals who could afford to participate in the four-horse chariot race. The participants in this race were precisely the members of the Greek highest leisure class who were most likely to provide a powerful marriage alliance. In Isocrates' speech *On the Team of Horses*, Alcibiades' son explicates the significance of the four-horse chariot race as a means by which the Greek elite demonstrated their wealth and status.

> [My father], seeing that the festival at Olympia was adored and wondered at by all humanity and that in it the Greeks made display of their wealth, strength, and training . . . applied himself to the breeding of racehorses, which is the business of only the wealthiest and which no poor person could do. Not only did he surpass his rivals, but also those who had ever been victorious. Besides this, he was so unsparing and lavish in the sacrifices and in the other expenses regarding the festival that the funds of all the others put together were clearly less than his own private expenditures.[38]

Only the wealthiest could compete in the chariot competition, so winning the four-horse chariot race at Olympia was one of the best ways to advertise one's wealth and nobility in the ancient Greek world. Moreover, as seen with Cleisthenes and Megacles, the ultimate reward from a victory in the four-horse chariot race at Olympia may have been a marriage alliance of the highest rank.

The need to advertise one's membership in this highest class may also explain the massive dedications at the Panhellenic sanctuaries where the major

38. Isocrates 16.32–34.

games were held. Large religious dedications could have served as conspicuous consumption to advertise wealth and simultaneously secure the favor of the gods. All the Greek elite would gather at these sanctuaries, and the networking possibilities would have been substantial.[39] Therefore, the possibility of achieving a wealthy marriage alliance could explain much of the conspicuously consumptive behavior we see in the ancient Greek world—breeding racehorses and making large religious dedications.

The cultural capital needed to secure a marriage at the highest tier could also explain the aristocracy's tendency to avoid commercial, financial, and manufacturing activities. As Veblen has argued, making one's fortune in these activities could be a smear against someone's character among the members of the most extreme upper crust of society, and there are many indications that the ancient Greek leisure class, who were already wealthy, often preferred to invest in cultural capital rather than to concentrate their energies on attaining further success in the market.[40] Although many wealthy ancient Greek individuals participated in commercial, financial, and manufacturing trades, there existed simultaneously a widespread disdain for such activities, particularly among the highest classes;[41] as Aristarchus in Xenophon's *Memorabilia* expresses, many members of the leisure class would have felt it beneath them to engage in manual labor or production for market exchange.[42] In the *Oeconomicus*, Xenophon argues that engaging in the so-called banausic trades was not fit for the *kaloi k'agathoi*, because they ruined one's physique, whereas agriculture provided the type of exercise that was the mark of the true nobility (4.2). The author of the *Oikonomika* attributed to Aristotle agrees: "[Agriculture] contributes greatly to manliness for it does not make bodies worthless like the banausic trades."[43] Not only engaging in manufacturing but also practicing money lending and maritime trade could deprive someone of important cultural capital. In Dem-

39. See, e.g., the discussion of Deinomenid marriage alliances in Mitchell, "The Women of Ruling Families" (2012) 6.

40. This is only the case among the highest leisure class, the aristocracy of the political and social elite. As shown by Kron, *Landed and Commercial Wealth at Classical Athens* (1996), wealthy Athenians engaged in commercial, financial, and manufacturing business activities on a large scale. Moreover, in ancient Rome, though prejudices against commercial activities did exist, even Roman senators still participated widely in maritime trade, so not all members of the leisure class were constrained from participating in profitable commerce: see D'Arms, *Commerce and Social Standing* (1981).

41. Hdt. 2.167.

42. Xen. *Memorabilia* 2.7.6–8. Compare also the words of Eutherus in *Memorabilia* 2.8, who has lost all his property during the Peloponnesian War and must work for a living but is reluctant to engage in any trades that might bring censure on him because they are more suitable for slaves than freemen.

43. *Oikonomika* 1343b3–5.

osthenes' *Against Pantaenetus*, the speaker, Nicobulus, describes the characteristics that made him odious as a moneylender: "The Athenians hate moneylenders. Nicobulus is hateful—he walks quickly, talks loudly, and carries a cane" (52). These sorts of behaviors and visible character traits could attract a negative social stigma based on their association with the exploitative nature of money lending and a life of work that makes one physically weak. The importance of looking physically fit like an aristocrat can be seen in Homer's *Odyssey*, when Euryalus, one of the Phaeacian youths, tells Odysseus that he looks more like a maritime trader than an athlete: "For I do not liken you to a man skilled in games . . . but to one who plies his trade in his many-oared ship, the leader of sailors who are traders. . . . You do not look like an athlete" (8.159–64). Odysseus is insulted and immediately reproaches the youth for being so rash, because Odysseus is proud of his athletic ability as a mark of his nobility.[44] For Veblen, athletics is an important means to demonstrate one's membership in the leisure class, because it shows that someone has the time and wealth to train their bodies in nonproductive sports, since they have no need to engage in moneymaking activities such as maritime trade.

For some, the overall returns would have been higher from behaving like an aristocrat than from engaging in trade and commerce, because the latter activities were viewed as base by the highest leisure class and interfered with the acquisition of the important cultural capital that could only be attained through a life of leisure. Pierre Bourdieu argues that this type of "symbolic capital" is not necessarily noneconomic in its orientation, as it is often interpreted, and that there could be significant financial returns to investing in symbolic capital.

> In a universe characterized by the more or less perfect interconvertibility of economic capital (in the narrow sense) and symbolic capital, the *economic calculation* directing the agents' strategies takes indissociably into account profits and losses which the narrow definition of economy unconsciously rejects as *unthinkable* and *unnameable*, i.e., as economically irrational. In short, contrary to naively idyllic representations of pre-capitalist societies (or of the "cultural" sphere of capitalist societies), practice never ceases to conform to economic calculation even when it gives every appearance of disinterestedness by departing from the logic of interested calculation (in the narrow sense) and playing for stakes that are non-material and not easily quantified.[45]

44. Von Reden, *Exchange* (1995) 59–65.
45. Bourdieu, *Theory of Practice* (1977) 177.

As Bourdieu emphasizes, even when individuals seem to be behaving in ways that appear to be noneconomic in their orientation, they may really be investing in symbolic capital that could yield lucrative economic returns in ways that are unpredictable and difficult to quantify but that are nonetheless impossible to ignore or dismiss as nugatory. When families had built up enough capital and were living as members of the leisure class without pressing financial difficulties, it may have been more profitable to seek a marriage alliance with another wealthy family than to try to seek more money in the open market, which would limit the opportunities for intermarriage with members of the highest leisure class. These types of returns from the interconvertibility between different types of capital, as Bourdieu puts it, are often overlooked in studies of the ancient economy.[46]

From this perspective, Karl Polanyi's notion of "embeddedness," the idea that premodern economies were embedded in social relations and did not constitute a separate conceptual realm of activity, is far more dynamic than Polanyi first argued. Indeed, it seems that the reverse (or perhaps inverse) relationship is also true: social relations were equally embedded in economic concerns, and many behaviors that seem to have served no economic purpose were actually necessary to gain access to some of the most lucrative economic opportunities in the ancient Greek world. Polanyi described the difference between the modern economy and premodern economies as follows: "[In] the market pattern, . . . instead of economy being embedded in social relations, social relations are embedded in the economic system."[47] As I have argued, however, the social relations that were created by marriage alliances were heavily influenced by economic interests. Monetary gain or profit seems to have motivated marriage alliances enough to be able to say that these social relations were shaped by economic concerns. Therefore, the concept of embeddedness, which has been shown to be a characteristic of the modern economy as much as of the premodern economy,[48] also functions in the inverse of the way that Polanyi described. Not only were economic matters embedded in social relations, but social relations were embedded within and manipulated to serve the realm of self-interested economic gain.

Conclusions

It seems that money was one of the most frequent motivations for getting married in ancient Greece, and many individuals could add to their personal wealth

46. An exception, of course, is Kurke, *Traffic in Praise* (1991).
47. Polanyi, *The Great Transformation* (1944) 57.
48. Granovetter, "The Problem of Embeddedness" (1985).

through acquiring dowries, which constituted some of the largest transfers of money in that society. Many ancient Greek property owners sought wealth and security not only in commercial activity but also in profitable and risk-absorbing marriage alliances. Though the returns on these relationships are often difficult or impossible to quantify, it is likely that marital decisions were central to an ancient Greek's personal financial strategies of wealth acquisition and risk management, and more work needs to be done on this important issue.

But to attain a marriage alliance at the highest rank, money was not enough; one also needed the right cultural and social capital to prove one's membership in the highest elite class. Therefore, because a dowry could be such a significant economic transaction, it could be more profitable to accumulate cultural capital, evidence of nobility and gentility, than to engage in commercial moneymaking activities in the market. Access to the highest levels of the elite and to the most expensive dowries could only be attained by avoiding commercial activity and by engaging in the nonindustrial leisure activities that signified one's membership in the Panhellenic aristocracy. Therefore, consumptive expenditures with seemingly no productive use could be transformed into financial capital and could open up otherwise inaccessible and potentially more lucrative opportunities for economic gain that traditionally "productive" activity in the market could not achieve. Sometimes, behaviors that are considered "irrational" from the standpoint of textbook economic rationality could actually produce some of the highest economic gains.

Bibliography

Balot, R. K. "Aristotle's Critique of Phaleas: Justice, Equality, and *Pleonexia*." *Hermes* 129.1 (2001): 32–44.

Blundell, S. *Women in Ancient Greece*. Cambridge, MA, 1995.

Bourdieu, P. "The Forms of Capital." In M. S. Granovetter and R. Swedberg, eds., *The Sociology of Economic Life*, 96–111. Boulder, CO, 2001.

Bourdieu, P. *Outline of a Theory of Practice*. Cambridge, 1977.

Christesen, P. "Economic Rationalism in Fourth-Century BCE Athens." *G&R* 50.1 (2003): 31–56.

Cox, C. A. *Household Interests: Property, Marriage Strategies, and Family Dynamics in Ancient Athens*. Princeton, 1996.

D'Arms, J. H. *Commerce and Social Standing in Ancient Rome*. Cambridge, MA, 1981.

Davies, J. K. *Athenian Propertied Families, 600–300 B.C.* Oxford, 1971.

Davies, J. K. *Wealth and the Power of Wealth in Classical Athens*. New York, 1981.

De Roover, R. *The Rise and Decline of the Medici Bank, 1397–1494*. Cambridge, MA, 1968.

Finley, M. I. *Studies in Land and Credit in Ancient Athens, 500–200 B.C.: The Horos-Inscriptions*. New York, 1951.

Goldthwaite, R. *The Economy of Renaissance Florence*. Baltimore, 2008.
Granovetter, M. "Economic Action and Social Structure: The Problem of Embeddedness." *American Journal of Sociology* 91.3 (1985): 481–510.
Grassby, R. "English Merchant Capitalism in the Late Seventeenth Century: The Composition of Business Fortunes." *Past and Present* 46.1 (1970): 87–107.
Gribble, D. "Alcibiades at the Olympics: Performance, Politics, and Civic Ideology." *CQ* 62.1 (2012): 45–71.
Hargreaves-Heap, S. *Rationality in Economics*. Oxford, 1989.
How, W. W., and J. Wells. *A Commentary on Herodotus*. Oxford, 1912.
Humphreys, S. "Kinship Patterns in Athenian Courts." *GRBS* 27 (1986): 57–91.
Ingalls, W. "Demography and Dowries: Perspectives on Female Infanticide in Classical Greece." *Phoenix* 56.3–4 (2002): 246–54.
Kron, J. G. "Landed and Commercial Wealth at Classical Athens, 500–300 B.C." PhD diss., University of Toronto, 1996.
Kurke, L. *The Traffic in Praise*. Ithaca, NY, 1991.
Millett, P. *Lending and Borrowing in Ancient Athens*. Cambridge, 1991.
Mitchell, L. G. "The Women of Ruling Families in Archaic and Classical Greece." *CQ* 62.1 (2012): 1–21.
Osborne, R. *Demos: The Discovery of Classical Attika*. Cambridge, 1985.
Polanyi, K. *The Great Transformation*. Boston, 1944.
Saller, R. "Men's Age at Marriage and Its Consequences in the Roman Family." *CP* 82 (1987): 21–34.
Saller, R. "Roman Dowry and the Devolution of Property in the Principate." *CQ* 34.1 (1984): 195–205.
Schaps, D. *Economic Rights of Women in Ancient Greece*. Edinburgh, 1979.
Todd, S. C. *The Shape of Athenian Law*. Oxford, 1993.
Veblen, T. *The Theory of the Leisure Class: An Economic Study of Institutions*. New York, 1899.
Von Reden, S. *Exchange in Ancient Greece*. London, 1995.

CHAPTER 3

Assumption of Risk in Athenian Law

David D. Phillips

1. Assumption of Risk in the Law of Draco

Among the clauses of Draco's law on homicide cited in Demosthenes' *Against Aristocrates*, we find the following set of provisions:

> Ἐάν τις ἀποκτείνῃ ἐν ἄθλοις ἄκων ἢ ἐν ὁδῷ καθελὼν ἢ ἐν πολέμῳ ἀγνοήσας, ἢ ἐπὶ δάμαρτι ἢ ἐπὶ μητρὶ ἢ ἐπ' ἀδελφῇ ἢ ἐπὶ θυγατρί, ἢ ἐπὶ παλλακῇ ἣν ἂν ἐπ' ἐλευθέροις παισὶν ἔχῃ, τούτων ἕνεκα μὴ φεύγειν κτείναντα. (Dem. 23.53 [*lex*])

> [If a person kills unintentionally in the games, or having come upon [sc. a highway robber][1] on the road, or in war without recognizing [sc. his victim], or [sc. finding his victim] upon[2] his consort or upon his mother or upon his sister or upon his daughter or upon his concubine whom he keeps for the procreation of free children, for these acts he shall not stand trial as a killer.][3]

1. For this interpretation see, e.g., MacDowell, *Athenian Homicide Law* (1963) 75–76.

2. The preposition could just as well be translated "on" or "with"; the sense is "in immediate carnal proximity to / contact with, *in flagrante* with," irrespective of specific position. See, most recently, Pepe, *Phonos* (2012) 197, 221, including the apposite observation that Lysias and Euphiletus felt no conflict between the law's "*upon* his consort" (**ἐπὶ** δάμαρτι) and Euphiletus' discovery of Eratosthenes "lying *next to* [his] wife" (κατακείμενον **παρὰ** τῇ γυναικί, Lys. 1.24).

3. For φεύγειν as "stand trial," see Pepe, *Phonos* (2012) 192–93; Phillips, *Law of Ancient Athens* (2013) 57; *contra*, e.g., Gagarin, *Drakon* (1981) 114 with n. 8. By the fifth century, the trial venue for lawsuits for homicide (*dikai phonou*) in which the defendant asserted an affirmative defense of lawful killing was the Delphinion. Dem. 23.74: the Delphinion has jurisdiction ἄν τις ὁμολογῇ μὲν κτεῖναι, ἐννόμως δὲ φῇ δεδρακέναι (if a person admits a killing but claims that he acted lawfully); [Arist.] *Ath. pol.* 57.3: ἐὰν δ' ἀποκτεῖναι μέν τις ὁμολογῇ, φῇ δὲ κατὰ τοὺς νόμους, οἷον μοιχὸν λαβὼν ἢ ἐν πολέμῳ ἀγνοήσας ἢ ἐν ἄθλῳ ἀγωνιζόμενος, τούτῳ ἐπὶ Δελφινίῳ δικάζουσιν. (If a person admits a killing but claims that he acted in accordance with the laws (for example, hav-

At first sight, this may appear to be a strange concatenation of cases, as it comprises both unintentional and intentional killings, and in particular, both killings that are justifiable (of the highway robber and the seducer or rapist) and killings that are excusable (in athletics and by friendly fire). For some commentators, the solution to this conundrum has been to privilege one of the latter principles over the other; for Louis Gernet, the unifying principle is excuse,[4] while for Edwin Carawan, it is justification.[5] In the most recent comprehensive treatment of Athenian homicide law, Laura Pepe has correctly stressed the importance of distinguishing among cases with regard to the grounds for immunizing the killer, as indeed Demosthenes does (23.54–56; cf. below, section 4): the man who kills ἐν ἄθλοις ἄκων does no wrong (οὐκ ἀδικεῖν), since his intent (διάνοια) is to defeat a living opponent and not to kill (ζῶντα νικῆσαι καὶ οὐκ ἀποκτεῖναι); the unintentional friendly-fire killer deserves to receive pardon (συγγνώμης τυχεῖν); whereas (comparing Euphiletus' argument in Lysias 1) the *moichos* apprehended *in flagrante* deserves to die.[6] Nonetheless,

ing caught a seducer, or in war without recognizing his victim, or while competing in an athletic contest), they judge his case at the Delphinion.)

4. Humbert and Gernet, *Démosthène* (1959) 191: "Cet article groupe un certain nombre d'espèces où l'homicide est excusé. . . . D'autre part, l'énumération des cas d'excuse attendue ici n'est pas complète (le cas du voleur de nuit, notamment, n'est pas considéré) . . ."

5. Carawan, *Rhetoric* (1998) 92–96, treats these clauses and Demosthenes' interpretation (§§ 54–56) under the heading "The Law of Justifiable Homicide" (92); he suggests that the clauses preserved at Dem. 23.53 come from a post-Draconian addendum governing the jurisdiction of the Delphinion court, but he believes that "the Draconian law of justifiable homicide" (96) contained provisions (not identical to those preserved in our text) concerning athletics, warfare, and "sexual violation." He excludes from Draco's law the clause on highway robbery, on the grounds that Demosthenes does not discuss it; but I think the more likely reason for Demosthenes' omission is that he did not understand what ἐν ὁδῷ καθελών meant. For Carawan, unintentional killing in athletics, *inter alia* (including self-defense), falls under the rubric of justification *qua* justified response to the victim's culpable error (199–215, esp. 200–206; citing Antiphon 3 and 4 and Aristotle in addition to our law[s]). Carawan makes a strong case, but I do not find it convincing. Demosthenes' interpretation of the ἐν ἄθλοις ἄκων clause (23.54: below, section 4 *ad init.*) does not state that (the lawgiver believed that) the victim deserved to die or that the victim committed any error, culpable or otherwise; moreover, as Carawan admits (202), "there is nothing in the wording of the law to suggest that this was the lawgiver's intent." Moreover, I cannot see what "culpable error" has been committed by the soldier who falls victim to friendly fire because—to name just one of the many circumstances of ancient Greek warfare that made it difficult to identify friend from foe—he is so covered in his own blood and others' that he is mistaken for an enemy.

6. Pepe, *Phonos* (2012) 183–227, esp. 191–94, 207–9, 211, 227. Pepe's observations (esp. 193–94) about the language of (lack of) fault in Dem. 23.54–56 can be taken further. Demosthenes begins by summarizing the law as "granting and stating conditions under which *it is permitted* to kill" (διδόντος . . . καὶ λέγοντος ἐφ' οἷς **ἐξεῖναι** κτεῖναι): the value-neutral ἐξεῖναι is appropriate for both excuses and justifications. The reaction of pardon (συγγνώμη)—in other words, excuse—appropriate to the friendly-fire killer should, in my view, be read backward so as also to embrace the killer ἐν ἄθλοις ἄκων (pace Pepe and pace Carawan, *Rhetoric* [1998] 93, Demosthenes' description of the killer's intent as ζῶντα νικῆσαι καὶ οὐκ ἀποκτεῖναι surely indicates that ἄκων was part of the cited—and genuinely Draconian—law): Demosthenes' transitional statement between the two cases (§ 55 *init.*) is πάλιν 'ἂν ἐν πολέμῳ' φησὶν 'ἀγνοήσας,' **καὶ τοῦτον** εἶναι καθαρόν. (Next, the law states that 'if [a person kills] in war without recognizing [his victim],' *this man too* [i.e., just as the killer ἐν ἄθλοις ἄκων] is pure of guilt.) By contrast, in the case of those caught ἐπὶ δάμαρτι κτλ,

there is a unifying principle at work, and I believe it is best understood as assumption of risk.

In the modern American law of torts, the doctrine of assumption of risk holds that a person who voluntarily places himself in a situation of known danger cannot recover for harm he suffers as a consequence; in short, assumption of risk is "voluntary acceptance of the possibility that another person may do one harm."[7] Standard tort cases in which assumption of risk (sometimes expressed by the maxim *volenti non fit injuria*) has been invoked include injuries sustained on rides at amusement parks, as well as those caused to both athletes and spectators by "flying baseballs, hockey pucks, golf balls, wrestlers, or such things as fireworks explosions."[8] In American law, the doctrine of assumption of risk has been on the decline in recent decades, abetted by its partial overlap and not infrequent confusion with the concept of contributory negligence. In essence, contributory negligence is "a negligent act or omission by the plaintiff that 'contributed' by helping to cause the loss on which the plaintiff is suing";[9] "the traditional basis" of distinguishing contributory negligence from assumption of risk "has been that assumption of risk is a matter of knowledge of the danger and voluntary acquiescence in it, while contributory negligence is a matter of some fault or departure from the standard of conduct of the reasonable person, however unaware, unwilling, or even protesting the plaintiff may be."[10]

To be sure, we should not presume that assumption of risk necessarily lies behind provisions on lawful killing in general. For just one counterexample, consider the Roman *ius vitae necisque*, which is not founded on assumption of risk—unless we are to take the very act of being born as constituting an implied assumption of risk, which is philosophically true but legally useless. Yet assumption of risk does underlie not only the clauses cited at Demosthenes 23.53 but also a significant amount of other Athenian legislation, both Draconian and

"the law grants that those who commit the acts of an enemy [τοὺς ἐχθρὰ ποιοῦντας] be punished as enemies [ἐν ἐχθροῦ μέρει κολάζειν]." *Ex hypothesi*—not to mention in Athenian legislation such as the Demophantus decree (below, n. 13), which declares anyone who subverts the democracy or engages in uprising to establish a tyranny to be a public enemy and grants a reward to the killer of such a person (and to his heirs if he dies in the attempt)—the killing of an enemy of the state merits not pardon (excuse) but praise (justification).

7. A classic and influential treatment is Keeton et al., *Torts* (1984) 480–98. The quotation is from Frier, *Roman Law of Delict* (1989) 245 (similarly 90, *ad D.* 9.2.7.4: see below, section 4).

8. Keeton et al., *Torts* (1984) 485–86.

9. Frier, *Roman Law of Delict* (1989) 247. Keeton et al., *Torts* (1984) 451: "Contributory negligence is conduct on the part of the plaintiff, contributing as a legal cause to the harm he has suffered, which falls below the standard to which he is required to conform for his own protection." Cf. American Law Institute, *Restatement Third, Torts* [2010] § 3 with Comment b and Reporters' Note to Comment b.

10. Keeton et al., *Torts* (1984) 482.

later. All the potential victims in Demosthenes 23.53 are (assumed to be) voluntarily engaging in a dangerous activity (athletics, highway robbery, warfare, and seduction or rape). The clause on highway robbery, moreover, is consistent with the right to use lethal force in immediate self-defense that is elsewhere granted by Draco against robbery in general:

> κα[ὶ ἐὰν φέροντα ἒ ἄγοντα βίαι ἀδίκος εὐθὺς] ἀμυνόμενος κτέ[ν]ει, ν[εποινὲ τεθνάναι. (*IG* I³ 104.37–38 = Dem. 23.60 [*lex*])
>
> [And if in immediate self-defense he kills someone carrying or leading away [his property] forcibly and without justification, the death shall be uncompensated.]

In all probability, the same right applied against the ordinary attacker (*IG* I³ 104.33–36).[11] Under Draco's law, then, if you hit me first (whether on the road or anywhere else) or if you try to steal my sheep by force, you assume the risk of death. The same is true if I catch an exiled killer in trespass:

> ἐὰν δ]έ [τ]ις τὸ[ν ἀν]δρ[οφόνον κτένει ἒ αἴτιος ἐ͂ι φόνο, ἀπεχόμενον ἀγορᾶ]ς ἐφορί[α]ς κ[α]ὶ [ἄθλον καὶ ἱερõν Ἀμφικτυονικõν, *h*όσπερ τὸν Ἀθεν]αῖον κ[τένα]ν[τα, ἐν τοῖς αὐτοῖς ἐνέχεσθαι· διαγιγνόσκεν δὲ τὸς] ἐ[φ]έτα[ς. . . . τὸς δ' ἀνδροφόνος ἐξε͂ναι ἀποκτένεν ἐν] τε͂ι ἐμεδ[απε͂ι καὶ ἀπάγεν . . . (*IG* I³ 104.26–31 = Dem. 23.37 [*lex*] + Dem. 23.28 [*lex*])
>
> [And if a person kills the killer or is responsible for his killing, when the killer has stayed away from the border market, games, and Amphictyonic rites, he shall be bound by the same terms as the killer of an Athenian; the *ephetai* shall decide the case. . . . And it shall be permitted to kill or arrest killers in our land . . .][12]

11. These lacunose lines read, . . . [39] . . . ἄρχον]τα χερõν ἀ[δίκον . . . [30] . . . χερ]õν ἀδίκον κτέ[νει . . . [7] . . .]σ [. . . [19] . . . διαγιγνόσκ]εν δὲ τὸς ἐ[φέτ]ας. (. . . starting a fight without justification . . . a fight without justification, he kills . . . the *ephetai* shall decide the case.) The most likely reconstruction of their contents, on the grounds of both economy and position (immediately preceding the robbery clause quoted above), is that the victim of ordinary attack has the same right of lethal response as the victim of specific attack by the robber or highwayman—probably with the proviso, as against the robber, that the responder act in immediate self-defense (εὐθὺς ἀμυνόμενος). Cf. Stroud, *Drakon's Law* (1968) 56 (*ad* vv. 33–36, *sub vocc.* ἄρχοντα χερõν ἀδίκον): "The phrase designates the aggressor in a quarrel and it probably was used here by Drakon as part of a section on justifiable homicide." The provision διαγιγνόσκεν δὲ τὸς ἐφέτας (cf. Gagarin, "Self-Defense" [1978] 119) indicates that Draco mandated trial of the man who claimed response to general attack, as opposed to specific attack, where the responder was declared immune (μὴ φεύγειν κτείναντα, Dem. 23.53 [*lex*]; νεποινὲ τεθνάναι, *IG* I³ 104.38 = Dem. 23.60 [*lex*]).

12. Cf. Dem. 23.44 (*lex*): ἐάν τίς τινα τῶν ἀνδροφόνων τῶν ἐξεληλυθότων, ὧν τὰ χρήματα

Other laws and decrees that either presume or create an assumption of risk include a number of enactments against tyranny and against theft.[13]

A noteworthy feature of all these provisions—which will be of particular relevance in addressing Antiphon's *Second Tetralogy*—is that, with the partial exception of the trespassing exile,[14] and perhaps of the soldier killed by friendly fire, mere negligence on the part of the victim—that is, his failure to appreciate a risk of harm[15]—does not suffice to immunize his killer, at least in the

---

ἐπίτιμα, πέρα ὅρου ἐλαύνῃ ἢ φέρῃ ἢ ἄγῃ, τὰ ἴσα ὀφείλειν ὅσα περ ἂν ἐν τῇ ἡμεδαπῇ δράσῃ. (If, beyond the border, a person drives, carries, or leads [the person and/or property of] one of the killers who have left the country and whose property is unconfiscated, he shall owe the same amount as if he committed the act in our land."); Dem. 23.51 (*lex*): φόνου δὲ δίκας μὴ εἶναι μηδαμοῦ κατὰ τῶν τοὺς φεύγοντας ἐνδεικνύντων, ἐάν τις κατίῃ ὅποι μὴ ἔξεστιν. (There shall be no *dikai phonou* anywhere against those who denounce exiles, if one of them returns where he is not allowed.)

13. [Arist.] *Ath. pol.* 16.10 (*lex*); Andoc. 1.96–98 (*decretum*: the Demophantus decree, 410); *SEG* 12.87 (*lex*: the law of Eucrates on tyranny, subversion of the democracy, and the Council of the Areopagus, 337/6); Dem. 24.113–14 (allegedly Solonian remedies for theft). Note that whereas the various relevant Draconian provisions grant only a license to kill (pace Euphiletus: see below), the compulsory oath included in the Demophantus decree (§ 97) creates a positive duty to kill: "I shall kill <by word and by deed, by vote and> with my own hand, if I am able, anyone who subverts the democracy at Athens, and anyone who, after the democracy has been subverted, thenceforth holds any office, and anyone who engages in uprising to become tyrant or cooperates in establishing a tyrant."

14. Ancient borders being what they were, a person might well be unaware of the exact moment at which he passed from, say, Boeotia into Attica and thereby assumed strict liability for his trespass. But this could hardly be the case with border markets and Amphictyonic games.

15. The definition of negligence adopted here is that of the Model Penal Code (American Law Institute, *Model Penal Code* [1985], § 2.02(d) [emphasis added]): "A person acts negligently with respect to a material element of an offense when *he should be aware of a substantial and unjustifiable risk* that the material element exists or will result from his conduct. The risk must be of such a nature and degree that the actor's failure to perceive it, considering the nature and purpose of his conduct and the circumstances known to him, involves a gross deviation from the standard of care that a reasonable person would observe in the actor's situation." The difference between negligence and recklessness is that the reckless actor "consciously disregards" (MPC § 2.02(c)) such a risk; in short, the negligent actor should be aware of the risk but is not, whereas the reckless actor perceives the risk and ignores it.

For the latitude of *neglegentia* in Roman law, see the summary definition by Berger, *Dictionary* (1953) s.v. *neglegentia*: "In the sources *neglegentia* is tantamount to *culpa*, and similarly graduated (*magna, lata neglegentia*). Precision in terminology is no more to be found here than in the field of *culpa*. One text declares (D. 50.16.226): 'gross negligence (*magna neglegentia*) is *culpa*, *magna culpa* is *dolus*'; another (D. 17.1.29 pr., evidently interpolated) says: 'gross negligence (*dissoluta neglegentia*) is near to *dolus* (*prope dolum*).' In the saying '*lata culpa* is exorbitant (extreme) negligence, i.e., not to understand (*intelligere* [*sic*]) what all understand' (D. 50.16.213.2) *neglegentia* is identified with ignorance." See also Berger's definition s.v. *culpa*: "*Culpa* in criminal offenses or wrongdoings harmful to others is not so problematical [sc. as in the field of contracts]. In some instances it means simply a fault of the guilty wrongdoer for which he is held responsible. As to private wrongs (*crimina privata, delicta*), *culpa* as negligence ('when a man failed to foresee what a careful [*diligens*] man would have foreseen,' D. 9.2.31) it [*sic*] is scarcely conceivable in many cases (theft, robbery). In damage to property (*damnum*) a negligent behavior (carelessness) was taken into consideration and the jurists frequently dealt with cases of this kind. With regard to damage to property . . . Justinian extended the liability of the wrongdoer to the 'slightest negligence' (*culpa levissima*, D. 9.2.44 pr.)."

presumptive default scenario. The athlete in competition, the highway robber who accosts me on the road, the rustler who tries to take my sheep, the ordinary attacker who throws the first punch, the *moichos*—all these actors are fully aware of what they are doing; in none of these cases would a plea of accident be likely to succeed.[16] Hence contributory negligence is insufficient as an organizing principle, while assumption of risk remains. Nonetheless, especially in these cases—athletics, self-defense, and *moicheia*—problems were likely to and did arise, as demonstrated in the Attic orators and elsewhere. It is to these problems that I now turn.

2."Η ἐπὶ δάμαρτι κτλ: Assumption of Risk by the *Moichos*

I begin with Lysias 1, delivered by Euphiletus as the defendant in a *dikê phonou* at the Delphinion (above, n. 3). By his own account, upon learning that one Eratosthenes of Oe was in his house with his wife, Euphiletus gathered a haphazard posse, broke in on the couple *in flagrante*, tied Eratosthenes up, and killed him (Lys. 1.25–27). Euphiletus maintains that the law of Draco[17] (among others) ordered him to kill Eratosthenes, who "met with the treatment that the laws command [οἱ νόμοι κελεύουσι] for people who do such things" (§ 27); the law itself is cited at § 30. Of course, this is not true: Draco's law provided a license, not a mandate; this is the risk assumed by the *moichos* under Draco's law. But what was the actual assumption of risk by a *moichos* around the turn of the fourth century? It has been proposed that the ἐπὶ δάμαρτι clause was a dead letter by this time,[18] and the evidence, though not conclusive, is sugges-

16. The possible exception is the (presumed but not actual) ordinary attacker. While, as Oliver Wendell Holmes famously observed, "even a dog distinguishes between being stumbled over and being kicked" (Holmes, *Common Law* [1881] 3), people are not always as rational as dogs. For example, a slap on the back that is meant to be friendly might—depending on the force of the slap, its unexpected nature, and the general temperament of the slappee—be misinterpreted as an attack from behind.

17. Euphiletus nowhere mentions Draco, presumably because Draco's (supposed) severity (e.g., Demades *ap.* Plut. *Solon* 17.3) made him a problematic figure. Mention of Draco by name is rare in the orators; with the attribution of homicide laws to him at, for example, Dem. 23.51, compare Lyc. 1.64–66, which attributes the (recommended) severity of the Athenians' predecessors to "the intent of the ancient lawgivers" (τὰς τῶν ἀρχαίων νομοθετῶν διανοίας), without specification.

18. Appropriate comparanda might include not only the ἐν ὁδῷ καθελών clause of the very same law (if, as I suspect [above, n. 5], few if any classical Athenians knew what it meant; at any rate, it was arguably rendered redundant by other Draconian [and later] self-defense provisions: above, section 1) but—and here we are on firmer ground—(1) the law, attributed to Solon by Plutarch (Plut. *Sol.* 23.2), that forbade a man to sell his daughter or sister as a slave (alternatively, as a prostitute: McGinn, "Prostitution" [2014] 86) unless she were party to *moicheia* (which is, significantly, omitted from Aeschines' discussion of the repercussions suffered by such a woman [Aeschin. 1.183]) and (2) the law on interference with sacred olive trees that provided for trial by

tive. Euphiletus claims that killing the *moichos* is a recognized remedy not only in Athens but throughout Greece (§ 2), yet he does not cite a single specific precedent, Athenian or other, in his favor—a strong indication that neither he nor Lysias knew of such a case, at least of one in which the killer then won acquittal in a *dikê phonou*.[19] To my knowledge, the only other (alleged) Athenian parallel that we have is king Hippomenes' slaying of the lover of his daughter Leimone by dragging him behind his chariot.[20] Significantly, this is supposed to have happened even before Draco, and Euphiletus had good reason to avoid mentioning it, lest he suffer by comparison to a man who, after so disposing of Leimone's lover, immured Leimone herself with a horse until it ate her.

On the contrary, we know of plenty of *moichoi* who were not killed. Not only is Eratosthenes of Oe (presented as) a repeat offender (§ 16), but we also have Agoratus, the defendant in Lysias 13, who (allegedly) has been caught in the act—and, we are told, the penalty is death! (§ 66)—but nonetheless is still alive to face the present trial by *apagôgê* (summary arrest) for homicide. In Isaeus 8, we hear that the reprehensible Diocles of Phlya "was caught as a *moichos* and suffered what befits people who do such things, but even so has not desisted from the practice" (§ 44). Finally, in Xenophon's *Memorabilia*, Socrates summarizes the risks assumed by the *moichos*—described explicitly as such—as "suffering what the law threatens, and being ambushed, caught, and

---

the Areopagus and death upon conviction, which was no longer enforced by the time of the composition of the *Ath. pol.* ([Arist.] *Ath. pol.* 60.2; cf. Lys. 7, with Todd, *Commentary* [2007] 477–540).

19. Note Lys. 1.30–31: Draco's law expressly forbids the Areopagus to convict a man who kills a *moichos* apprehended *in flagrante*; while Euphiletus clearly means for the principle to extend to the Delphinion, he does not actually say anything about the Delphinion.

20. Heraclid. Lemb. *Epit.* 1; Aeschin. 1.182 with schol. Aeschin. 367b Dilts; Rhodes, *Commentary* (1993) 78–79; Fisher, *Aeschines* (2001) 331–34; Phillips, *Law of Ancient Athens* (2013) 103. Cf. Todd, *Commentary* (2007) 50: "there is no case outside Lysias in which this possibility [i.e., killing a *moichos* caught in the act] is seriously envisaged." Todd (50 n. 31) mentions two other potential cases, attested in Lysias' fragmentary *On the Killing of Achilleides*—more probably, *On Behalf of Achilleides on a Charge of Homicide*: ὑπὲρ Ἀχιλλείδου (φόνου), Lys. frr. 62–64 Carey; the latter interpretation is supported by Sauppe in his preface (the speech is Baiter-Sauppe fragmentary speech XXVI) and by Gernet (Gernet-Bizos fragmentary speech XII) and seems the natural conclusion from Apsines' statement (fr. 62 Carey = fr. 55 Baiter-Sauppe) καὶ Λυσίας ἐν τῷ ὑπὲρ Ἀχιλλείδου τὸ πάθος τὸ τῇ ἀδελφῇ συμβὰν αὐτοῦ· λέγει γὰρ ὡς ἀκρατὴς λύπης γενηθεῖσα αὑτὴν ἀπέκτεινε (Lysias too, in his *On Behalf of Achilleides*, indicates the suffering incurred by his [i.e., presumably, Achilleides'] sister, in stating that she was overcome by grief and killed herself) and *Against Philon on the Killing of Theocleides* (or perhaps *Against Philon on Behalf of Theocleides on a Charge of Homicide)*: πρὸς [not κατὰ, although the source is Pollux (9.39)] Φίλωνα ὑπὲρ Θεοκλείδου φόνου (Lys. fr. 298 Carey). In neither case do the very meager remnants of the speech permit confident conclusion that, as suggested by some commentators (Baiter-Sauppe ad locc.; for the latter speech, which is Baiter-Sauppe fragmentary speech CXXIII [fr. 244], Sauppe cites Hoelscher; likewise Blass, *Attische Beredsamkeit* [1887–98] 1.362, remarks, "Warscheinlich Tödtung eines Ehebrechers"), the *casus litis* was the killing of a *moichos*. More cautious, in addition to Carey and Todd, is Gernet (Gernet and Bizos, *Lysias* [1989] 2.241).

subjected to hubris";[21] there is no mention of the most severe and immediate risk, of instant death at the hands of an outraged *kyrios*.

If the Athenians had long since discarded the immediate self-help killing of the *moichos* in favor of practices such as the use of radishes (and possibly scorpion fish and ax handles) as improvised suppositories, involuntary genital depilation, and ransom,[22] this may well account for Euphiletus' need, in his self-imposed burden of proof, to anticipate and rebut the prosecution's claim that he entrapped his victim and had the actual motive of prior enmity and/or financial gain.[23] It may be this very insecurity that impels Euphiletus to overcompensate, to misrepresent Draco's law as ordering him to kill—an idea that Euphiletus very carefully never makes his own: it is first brought up by his victim, who begs to be ransomed rather than killed (§ 25; cf. § 29), and is then attributed to the law of the city (§ 26); as a law-abiding citizen, Euphiletus has no choice but to obey this law, which, by definition (however tendentious), represents the will of the people, including the present jury (§ 29).[24] If Euphiletus can convince

---

21. X. *Mem.* 2.1.5: "For instance, seducers go into women's quarters knowing that for a seducer there is the risk [κίνδυνος] of suffering what the law threatens, and of being ambushed, caught, and subjected to hubris [ἅ τε ὁ νόμος ἀπειλεῖ παθεῖν καὶ ἐνεδρευθῆναι καὶ ληφθέντα ὑβρισθῆναι]. And given such grave harmful and shameful threats to the seducer, and the availability of means to relieve the desire for sexual pleasures without fear of punishment, is not involving oneself nonetheless in risky acts [τὰ ἐπικίνδυνα] the mark of an absolute madman?" For a summary of the various remedies at law against the *moichos*, see Phillips, "Why Was Lycophron?" (2006) 381–85.

22. Ar. *Nub.* 1083–84 with schol. 1083 (radishing and depilation); *Plut.* 168 (depilation) with schol. (radishing and depilation); *Th.* 536–38 (depilation); *Suda* s.v. ὦ Λακιάδαι (ω 62 Adler) (radishing and ax handles); Lys. 1.25, 29 (see below, n. 24); [Dem.] 59.65–70 (ransom); perhaps Ar. *Ach.* 849 (depilation?); Pl. Com. fr. 189.22 Kassel-Austin (= Ath. 5d), with Catull. 15.17–19; Juv. 10.317 (scorpion fish?). See Kapparis, "Humiliating the Adulterer" (1996); Kapparis, *Against Neaera* (1999) 302–7; Schmitz, "Nomos moicheias" (1997), esp. 91–107; Forsdyke, "Street Theatre and Popular Justice" (2008) 19–22. It tells us something about the canonical status of the radish that—if the *Suda* is correct—Athenians only used ax handles (which surely just about every Athenian owned) in default of radishes (which were presumably not found in every Athenian household).

23. Lys. 1.4: "I believe, gentlemen, that this is what I have to demonstrate: that Eratosthenes seduced my wife . . . ; and that there was no enmity whatsoever between me and him besides this, and that I did not do what I did for money . . . or for any other gain besides punishment according to the laws." The entrapment claim is rebutted at length at Lys. 1.37–46. There is nothing about entrapment in this part of Draco's law (cf. Todd, *Commentary* [2007] 50), so Euphiletus might have interpreted Draco's silence as an argument in his favor. Nonetheless, so strong was the contemporary prejudice against entrapment (cf., e.g., [Dem.] 59.64–70) that Euphiletus proffers the validity of (hypothetical, not actual) entrapment as exclusively his own argument (§ 37: ἐγὼ δέ, ὦ ἄνδρες, δίκαιον μὲν ἂν ποιεῖν ἡγούμην ᾡτινιοῦν τρόπῳ τὸν τὴν γυναῖκα τὴν ἐμὴν διαφθείραντα λαμβάνων (But for my part, gentlemen, I would think I was acting justly in catching by any means whatsoever the man who had corrupted my wife)). Cf. Todd, *Commentary* (2007) 138 with n. 98.

24. §§ 25–26: note especially "but he begged and pleaded with me not to kill him but to exact money from him. But I said, 'It is not I who will kill you but the law of the city [οὐκ ἐγώ σε ἀποκτενῶ ἀλλ' ὁ τῆς πόλεως νόμος]'"; § 29: "he begged and pleaded not to be put to death and offered instead to pay money as recompense. I, however, did not agree with his assessment of the penalty but considered the law of the city to be more authoritative, and I exacted the penalty that you, believing it to be most just, have imposed on those who commit such practices."

his jury that Draco's law really is a mandate, then, even if no one else within living memory has obeyed the mandate, he improves his odds of acquittal, as he decreases the chances of what we might term (in modern parlance) "jury nullification" of the ἐπὶ δάμαρτι clause.[25] On this view, what Lysias is trying to do for his client is to transform a theoretical assumption of risk, grounded in nothing more than an obsolete clause of a law more than two centuries old, into an actual assumption of risk. Hence, perhaps, appears the quite probable allusion to Draco's athletics clause (ἐν ἄθλοις ἄκων)—which, as we shall see, was still very much alive in the classical period—in Euphiletus' concluding public policy argument (§ 47): if Euphiletus is acquitted, then *moichoi*, "seeing of what sort are the prizes that lie before them [οἷα τὰ ἆθλα πρόκειται] for such offenses," will be deterred.

3. Ἄρχειν χειρῶν ἀδίκων: Assumption of Risk by the Ordinary Attacker

Two key cases, one actual and one hypothetical, demonstrate that by the time of the orators, the Draconian right of unlimited response to ordinary attack, which entitled the responder to "stand his ground" regardless of the result, had been compromised by a more modern concept of proportionate response.[26] According to Demosthenes (21.71, 73–75), Euaeon killed his friend Boeotus at a dinner party in response to a single blow and was convicted by a margin of only one vote at his resulting trial—in all probability, a *dikê phonou* at the Delphinion,[27] as was held for Euphiletus. In Demosthenes' analysis, "those who voted to convict did so not because he had defended himself [μὴ ὅτι ἠμύνατο] but because he had done so in such a manner as to kill [ἀλλ' ὅτι τοῦτον τὸν τρόπον ὥστε καὶ ἀποκτεῖναι], while those who voted to acquit allowed even this excess of vengeance" to the victim of hubris (§ 75).[28] This case demon-

25. Jury nullification is "[a] jury's knowing and deliberate rejection of the evidence or refusal to apply the law either because the jury wants to send a message about some social issue that is larger than the case itself or because the result dictated by law is contrary to the jury's sense of justice, morality, or fairness" (Garner, *Black's Law Dictionary* [1999] s.v. "jury nullification"). This will have been a common manifestation and cause of the "legal insecurity" characteristic of Athens in the age of the orators (Lanni, *Law and Justice* [2006] 115–48).

26. See, most recently, Pepe, *Phonos* (2012) 199–210, esp. 209–10.

27. MacDowell, *Demosthenes, "Against Meidias"* (1990) 292–93; *contra* Gagarin, "Self-Defense" (1978) 117–18.

28. About Euaeon's presentation in court, Demosthenes says only that he did not engage in the typical pleas for mercy and gestures of generosity. But, barring incompetence, remorse manifesting in a desire for self-destruction, or both, we may confidently presume that Euaeon based his defense on the initial-aggressor (ἄρχειν χειρῶν ἀδίκων) clauses of Draconian and other laws (including

strates the difficulty raised in any legal system by the concept of reasonable self-defense: once you decide that there is a line separating appropriate from excessive response, it becomes difficult to establish exactly where that line is.[29] This difficulty becomes more serious when, as in an Athenian *dikê phonou*, the court has no latitude whatsoever in sentencing: since Euphiletus and Euaeon intended to harm their victims, regardless of whether they intended to kill them[30] (Euphiletus certainly did; Euaeon will presumably have argued that he did not), they were charged with intentional homicide (*phonos ek pronoias*/*hekousios*), which, when the victim was an Athenian citizen, carried a mandatory penalty of death (Dem. 21.43).

This problem—determining at what precise point the responder becomes liable for intentional homicide, exactly as the initial aggressor would have been had he killed the responder—lies likewise at the heart of Antiphon's *Third Tetralogy*. In this hypothetical case, the defendant argues that since the victim started the fight—ἄρχων χειρῶν ἀδίκων—he got what he deserved (Ant. 4 β 1–4). Here, though, the problem is compounded by the fact that the category of lawful killings does not exist in the hypothetical legal world of the *Tetralogies*: the law prohibits both just and unjust killing (ὁ νόμος εἴργων μήτε δικαίως μήτε ἀδίκως ἀποκτείνειν, 4 β 3).[31] The law of the *Tetralogies* holds every killer liable but penalizes according to intent—intentional killers suffer death (4 α 7); unintentional killers suffer exile (3 α 2, 3 β 10, 3 γ 11). This law lies between

the law of *aikeia*, ordinary battery: Dem. 23.50 [*lex*]; [Dem.] 47.40 *et alibi*) and argued that he did not intend to kill his friend. Immediately before this case (Dem. 21.71), Demosthenes cites another instance of lethal self-defense, the killing, on Samos, of the pancratiast Sophilus by a young man named Euthynus who went on to become a wrestler (on the problems posed by the passage, see MacDowell, *Demosthenes, "Against Meidias"* [1990] 288–89). Demosthenes gives no indication whether Euthynus ever stood trial; the presumption is that he did not, since if he did, he obviously won an acquittal, which would bolster Demosthenes' argument.

29. For example, under the Model Penal Code, the use of deadly force in self-defense is permitted only if "the actor believes that such force is necessary to protect himself against death, serious bodily injury, kidnapping or sexual intercourse compelled by force or threat," unless said "actor, with the purpose of causing death or serious bodily injury, provoked the use of force against himself in the same encounter" or "knows that he can avoid the necessity of using such force with complete safety by retreating or by surrendering possession of a thing to a person asserting a claim of right thereto or by complying with a demand that he abstain from any action that he has no duty to take," with the general exception to this retreat rule that "the actor is not obliged to retreat from his dwelling or place of work, unless he was the initial aggressor or is assailed in his place of work by another person whose place of work the actor knows it to be" (MPC § 3.04(2)(b)). For a critique of these and other contemporary formulations, see Robinson, *Criminal Law* (1997) 440–47.

30. Loomis, "Nature of Premeditation" (1972); Gagarin, *Drakon* (1981) 32–34; Phillips, *Law of Ancient Athens* (2013) 45–46; *contra* Carawan, *Rhetoric* (1998) 223–25; Pepe, *Phonos* (2012) 87–128.

31. Cf. Ant. 3 β 9, 3 γ 7; *recte*, Dittenberger, "Antiphons Tetralogien" (1897) 6: "Gewiss kennt der Tetralogienschreiber keine straflose Tödtung in der Nothwehr, aber einfach desshalb, weil er überhaupt keine straflose Tödtung kennt."

the strict liability in Homer, where the killer's intent may mitigate his moral liability but has no effect on his legal liability,[32] and the actual homicide law of Athens, which not only considers intent but holds some killers blameless. In the *Tetralogies*, the only way for a defendant to escape liability is to establish that, as a matter of fact (as in the *First Tetralogy*) or law (as in the *Second Tetralogy*) or both (as in the *Third Tetralogy*), he did not kill.[33] Already in the *Third Tetralogy*, which precedes Euaeon's killing of Boeotus by at least sixty years,[34] the Draconian defense fails: the defendant is so pessimistic about his chances of acquittal—partly, we may assume, because his victim was elderly and intoxicated, whereas the defendant was merely intoxicated (4 α 6, 4 β 1)—that he absconds into voluntary exile before commencing his second speech.

The fundamental inequity that Antiphon intends to emphasize—an inequity that is as characteristic of Athenian homicide law as of the law of the *Tetralogies* and that I shall revisit in the *Second Tetralogy*—is that neither system recognizes such a thing as contributory fault. Even though the victim started the fight and, moreover, though the most reasonable interpretation of the facts—first conceded, significantly, by the prosecution (4 γ 4)—is that the defendant did not intend to kill, this moral mitigation of fault cannot activate a legal mitigation of fault. In practice, in Antiphon's Athens, the assumption of risk by the ordinary attacker has decreased since the time of Draco, whereas—in exact correspondence—the responder to ordinary attack who employs lethal

32. As in the case of Patroclus (Hom. *Il.* 23.85–90), who killed the son of Amphidamas "as a child, without intent, in anger over a game of dice" (νήπιος, οὐκ ἐθέλων, ἀμφ' ἀστραγάλοισι χολωθείς), but all the same fled into exile from Opus. On homicide in Homer, see Cantarella, *Studi sull'omicidio* (1976) 15–75; Gagarin, *Drakon* (1981) 6–18.

33. In the *First Tetralogy*, the defendant argues that the prosecution has mistakenly identified him as the killer. In the *Second Tetralogy*, the defense admits that the defendant threw the javelin that killed the victim, but it contends that the cause of the victim's death was the victim himself (below, section 4). In the *Third Tetralogy*, the defendant argues that the actual cause of death was the victim's doctor and that even if the defendant's blows were to be considered the proximate cause of death, the legal cause of death would be the victim's precipitating prior blow(s). On issues of fact and law in the *Tetralogies*, cf. Gagarin, *Antiphon the Athenian* (2002) 106–9.

34. The interval may be up to a century, depending on the date of composition of the *Tetralogies*, which I would place early in Antiphon's career (perhaps as early as the 440s). In the *Against Meidias* (347/6), Demosthenes (21.71) speaks of Euaeon's trial as though it were a recent event: ἴσασιν Εὐαίωνα πολλοὶ τὸν Λεωδάμαντος ἀδελφόν, ἀποκτείναντα Βοιωτὸν . . . (Many people know that Euaeon, the brother of Leodamas, killed Boeotus . . .) Boeotus was a rare name at Athens for obvious reasons, including, as noted by Paley and Sandys, *Demosthenes* (1898) 151 n. 1, the currency of the proverb Βοιωτία ὗς (Boeotian sow): Pind. *Ol.* 6.90; cf. Dem. 39.32: νὴ Δία, ἀλλ' ὕβρει καὶ ἐπηρείᾳ τινὶ τοῦτο [sc. τὸ ὄνομα] ἐτέθη σοι. (But, by Zeus, you will respond, the name was given to you out of hubris and spite.) If it is correct to identify the Boeotus in Demosthenes 21 as the namesake and maternal uncle of the Boeotus against whom Demosthenes 39 and [Demosthenes] 40 were delivered (Davies, *Athenian Propertied Families* [1971] 365; MacDowell, *Demosthenes, "Against Meidias"* [1990] 289), then the elder Boeotus, still alive (Dem. 39.32, with Davies, op. cit.; MacDowell, op. cit.) at the date of Demosthenes 39 (349/8?), will have been killed no more than two years before the composition of the *Against Meidias*.

force cannot rely on the protection granted him by Draco but confronts the risk of conviction and execution.[35]

4. Ἐν ἄθλοις ἄκων: Assumption of Risk by Athletes—and Spectators?

Demosthenes interprets the ἐν ἄθλοις ἄκων clause of Draco's law as follows:

> ἄν τις ἐν ἄθλοις ἀποκτείνῃ τινά, τοῦτον ὥρισεν οὐκ ἀδικεῖν. διὰ τί; οὐ τὸ συμβὰν ἐσκέψατο, ἀλλὰ τὴν τοῦ δεδρακότος διάνοιαν. ἔστι δ' αὕτη τίς; ζῶντα νικῆσαι καὶ οὐκ ἀποκτεῖναι. εἰ δ' ἐκεῖνος ἀσθενέστερος ἦν τὸν ὑπὲρ τῆς νίκης ἐνεγκεῖν πόνον, ἑαυτῷ τοῦ πάθους αἴτιον ἡγήσατο, διὸ τιμωρίαν οὐκ ἔδωκεν ὑπὲρ αὐτοῦ. (Dem. 23.54)
>
> [If a person killed someone in the games, [the lawgiver] defined him as doing no wrong. Why? Because he looked not to what happened but to the actor's intent. And what is that? To defeat a living opponent, not to kill. If the victim was too weak to endure the struggle for victory, the lawgiver considered him responsible for his own suffering and therefore granted no retribution on his behalf.]

The orator is presumably correct that the default case envisioned by Draco is competitive combat sports. In ascending order of likely fatalities, these were wrestling, boxing, and pancration. By definition, the athlete assumes the risk of harm upon entering these events; under Draco's law, he assumes the risk of death only if death is unintended. In practice, of course, it will have been difficult to determine, for example, at what point, if any, the intent of a pancratiast who choked out his opponent passed from causing submission or unconsciousness to causing death. If a boxer (or pancratiast) killed a standing and resisting opponent by a punch to the head, such a determination will have been essentially impossible.

35. Athenian litigants very commonly employ the language of risk with regard to dangers facing themselves. Note, in particular, Euphiletus' concluding words at Lysias 1.50: ἐγὼ γὰρ νῦν καὶ περὶ τοῦ σώματος καὶ περὶ τῶν χρημάτων καὶ περὶ τῶν ἄλλων ἁπάντων κινδυνεύω, ὅτι τοῖς τῆς πόλεως νόμοις ἐπειθόμην. (For now I am at risk with regard to my person, my property, and everything else, because I obeyed the laws of the city.) Cf. Lys. 1.45: τί ἂν οὖν βουλόμενος ἐγὼ τοιοῦτον κίνδυνον ἐκινδύνευον, εἰ μὴ τὸ μέγιστον τῶν ἀδικημάτων ἦν ὑπ' αὐτοῦ ἠδικημένος; (What, then, was my intent in taking such a serious risk, unless I had suffered the gravest of offenses at [Eratosthenes'] hands?) It is a fair conjecture that Lysias has Euphiletus apply no such language of risk to Eratosthenes because Eratosthenes' death (upon capture) is presented as automatic, in keeping with the (alleged) mandate of the law (above, section 2).

In fact, though, the difficulties for which we have evidence involve not competitive combat sports but javelin throwing, where the actor lacks not just the intent to kill but the intent to cause any harm whatsoever. According to Plutarch, after a pentathlete's errant javelin killed one Epitimus of Pharsalus, Pericles and the sophist Protagoras spent an entire day examining the problem of who or what should be considered responsible "according to the most correct reasoning": the javelin, the thrower, or the contest officials.[36] If the accident occurred during the games of the Greater Panathenaea, the odds are at least slightly in favor of identifying the victim as a visiting athlete rather than a visiting spectator,[37] which, as we shall see, may have been important.

At any rate, at least the prospect of unintended death by javelin was sufficiently vivid in the Athenian consciousness that Antiphon devoted his *Second Tetralogy* to a variation on the same problem.[38] During javelin practice at the gymnasium, a youth threw a javelin on target, but before it could reach the target, it struck and killed a boy tasked with recovery of the javelins, who ran into its path. The thrower now stands accused of unintentional homicide, as

---

36. Plut. *Per.* 36.5: πεντάθλου γάρ τινος ἀκοντίῳ πατάξαντος Ἐπίτιμον τὸν Φαρσάλιον ἀκουσίως καὶ κτείναντος ἡμέραν ὅλην ἀναλῶσαι μετὰ Πρωταγόρου διαποροῦντα πότερον τὸ ἀκόντιον ἢ τὸν βαλόντα μᾶλλον ἢ τοὺς ἀγωνοθέτας κατὰ τὸν ὀρθότατον λόγον αἰτίους χρὴ τοῦ πάθους ἡγεῖσθαι. (For example, when a pentathlete unintentionally struck and killed Epitimus of Pharsalus with his javelin, [Pericles] spent an entire day with Protagoras examining whether, according to the most correct reasoning, the javelin, the man who threw it, or the contest officials should be considered responsible for the disaster.) Inclusion of the javelin on the list of potentially responsible parties is not idle; under Athenian law, homicidal inanimate objects might be tried at the Prytaneion by the *basileus* and the *phylobasileis* and punished by exile (i.e., thrown over the Attic border: [Arist.] *Ath. pol.* 57.4; Aeschin. 3.244; Dem. 23.76; although, according to Demosthenes, an inanimate object assumed liability only if no human thrower was identified). According to Stadter, *Plutarch's "Pericles"* (1989) 328 (ad loc.), "The parallel [with Antiphon 3: see below] warns us that we are dealing with a standard philosophical example, in which the names may be used for verisimilitude only. It is not good evidence for Pericles' contact with Protagoras." Certainly the latter statement is true, but inclusion of the name of the victim (who is otherwise unknown) is good evidence for the historicity of the event (which, Stadter conjectures, may have occurred at the Panathenaic games), if not the subsequent discussion, and it is more probable that the fatal javelin accident became a "standard philosophical example" because of at least one famous occurrence than that said example originated *ex nihilo* and inspired the invention of fictitious incidents.

37. The Panathenaic games included the pentathlon (*IG* II^2 2311.26, 41); the games of the Greater Panathenaea, unlike those of the Lesser Panathenaea, were Panhellenic (Miller, *Ancient Greek Athletics* [2004] 133). Plutarch writes of Epitimus as someone whom his readers are expected to recognize (Ἐπίτιμον τὸν Φαρσάλιον, "Epitimus of Pharsalus," "Epitimus the Pharsalian," not, e.g., Φαρσάλιόν τινα, Ἐπίτιμον, "a man from Pharsalus, Epitimus [by name]"), which suggests that Epitimus was an athlete (as assumed, without stated grounds, by Dendrinou, Ἀντιφῶντος λόγοι [1939] 129) rather than a spectator (as assumed by MacDowell, *Athenian Homicide Law* [1963] 74), although it is possible that he became famous simply by the manner of his death.

38. Some scholars (e.g., Carawan, *Rhetoric* [1998] 181; cf. Glotz, *Solidarité* [1904] 414 with n. 5) believe that the case of Epitimus inspired the *Second Tetralogy*. But see, *recte*, Gagarin, *Antiphon: The Speeches* [1997] 144: "Speculation on the influence of Protagoras on A[ntiphon] (or vice versa) is futile."

the prosecution stipulates that he intended no harm, let alone death. Since the category of lawful homicide does not exist in the *Tetralogies*, here, as in the *Third Tetralogy*, the defense must argue that the defendant did not kill; in this case, the victim killed himself. In its second speech, the prosecution proposes a compromise of joint liability (Ant. 3 γ 10–11), which the defense must reject (3 δ 6, 10), since, under Tetralogic (and actual Athenian) law, partial responsibility in fact cannot produce partial or mitigated liability in law: the defendant found guilty of unintentional homicide is exiled.

The issue in this case is sometimes compared to the modern claim of contributory negligence,[39] whereby a plaintiff's own negligent behavior constitutes a contributory cause of the harm he suffers (above, section 1). But what we are dealing with here more closely approximates assumption of risk, which, at any rate, is more congenial to the inflexibility of Athenian homicide law, at least insofar as, generally speaking, assumption of risk bars recovery, whereas contributory negligence may bar recovery or simply reduce the damages recovered.[40] The victim in the *Second Tetralogy* is a participant in the exercise, which he knows to be (potentially) dangerous, javelins being specifically engineered to cause death.[41] Moreover, according to the defense, his conduct that furnished the proximate cause of his death was not merely negligent but reckless: he saw people throwing javelins and ran into the line of fire anyway.[42]

Some scholars posit that the actual risk of accidental death by javelin was remote to nonexistent,[43] but even with today's increased safety measures and significant advances in medicine, throwing a javelin with other people within range will occasionally result in a fatality, as in the case of Dieter Strack, an official who was hit in the throat by a javelin thrown by a 15-year-old athlete in

39. E.g., Gagarin, *Antiphon the Athenian* (2002) 121.

40. Keeton et al., *Torts* (1984) 481 n. 14 (cf. the citations in nn. 7–10 above).

41. Compare, in modern tort law, the invocation of assumption of risk to deny liability for harm (to both athletes and spectators) resulting from far less inherently dangerous objects, such as baseballs (Keeton et al., *Torts* [1984] 485–86; Franklin et al., *Tort Law and Alternatives* [2011] 470–75; cf. above with n. 8).

42. Ant. 3 β 4–5: "Because the boy ran under the path of the javelin and put his body in front of it, . . . he was hit because he ran under the javelin; and he has hit us with the responsibility, which is not ours. Since the boy was hit on account of his running under, the youth is not justly charged, since he hit none of those who were standing away from the target. As for the boy, if it is clear to you that he was hit not while standing still but having intentionally gone under the path of the javelin [ἑκουσίως <δ'> ὑπὸ τὴν φορὰν τοῦ ἀκοντίου ὑπελθών], then he is shown even more clearly to have died through his own error"; Ant. 3 δ 7: "And it is not just the error [ἁμάρτημα] that belongs to the boy, but the lack of care [ἀφυλαξία] as well. How could the thrower, seeing no one running across, have taken care not to hit anyone? But the boy, seeing the people throwing javelins, could easily have taken care not to get hit [ὁ δ' ἰδὼν τοὺς ἀκοντίζοντας εὐπετῶς ἂν ἐφυλάξατο μὴ βληθῆναι]: he could have stood still."

43. E.g., Gagarin, *Antiphon the Athenian* (2002) 105 n. 7.

Düsseldorf on August 26, 2012, and died the next day.[44] Even in antiquity, the Athenians were not the only people to consider this prospect. In Roman law, the two cases that present the best parallels are described as follows:[45]

> *Si quis in colluctatione vel in pancratio, vel pugiles dum inter se exercentur alius alium occiderit, si quidem in publico certamine alius alium occiderit, cessat Aquilia, quia gloriae causa et virtutis, non iniuriae gratia videtur damnum datum. Hoc autem in servo non procedit, quoniam ingenui solent certare: in filio familias vulnerato procedit. Plane si cedentem vulneraverit, erit Aquiliae locus, aut si non in certamine servum occidit, nisi si domino committente hoc factum sit: tunc enim Aquilia cessat.* (Ulp. [18 *ad ed.*] *D.* 9.2.7.4)
>
> [If a person kills another in wrestling or in the pancration or one boxer kills another while they are exercising against one another, provided that the one kills the other in a public contest, the *lex Aquilia* does not apply, since the damage is seen as caused for the sake of glory and valor, not for the sake of wrongful behavior. This, however, does not apply in the case of a slave, since only free people are accustomed to compete; it does apply in the case of a wounded *filiusfamilias*. Obviously, if a person wounds a surrendering opponent, the *lex Aquilia* will apply, or if a person kills a slave who is not in the contest, except if this has happened when the slave's master enters him in competition: then the *lex Aquilia* does not apply.]
>
> *Sed si per lusum iaculantibus servus fuerit occisus, Aquiliae locus est; sed si cum alii in campo iacularentur, servus per eum locum transierit, Aquilia cessat, quia non debuit per campum iaculatorium iter intempestive facere. Qui tamen data opera in eum iaculatus est, utique Aquilia tenebitur:* [9.2.10] *nam lusus quoque noxius in culpa est.* (Ulp. [18 *ad ed.*] *D.* 9.2.9.4; Paul. [22 *ad ed.*] *D.* 9.2.10)
>
> [But if, while people are throwing javelins for sport, a slave is killed, the *lex Aquilia* applies. If, though, while others were throwing javelins in a

44. "Javelin Kills Athletics Official Dieter Strack at Youth Meet, German Police Say," *Huffington Post*, August 27, 2012 (http://www.huffingtonpost.com/2012/08/27/javelin-kills-official-dieter-strack-youth-meet-police_n_1832656.html).

45. These are Cases 59 and 60, presented in the sections on assumption of risk and contributory negligence respectively, in Frier, *Roman Law of Delict* (1989). For more on these cases, see Grueber, *Roman Law of Damage to Property* (1886) 21–22, 30–32, 226–29; Valditara, *Damnum iniuria datum* (2005) 22 with n. 149, 36, 40, 41; Corbino, *Il danno qualificato* (2008) 114–16, 169–70, 179.

field, a slave crossed through that place, the *lex Aquilia* does not apply, since the slave should not have made his way at an inopportune time across a field where javelins were being thrown. However, the person who deliberately threw a javelin at him certainly shall be liable under the *lex Aquilia*, since a harmful game falls under the category of fault.]

The key distinction between these cases is that the victim in the first is a participant in the activity[46] who assumes the risk of death[47]—unless he has submitted, in which case the contest is over—while the victim in the second is not a participant, nor is it explicitly stated that he knows he is crossing a field used for javelin throwing; thus the latter may be merely negligent, as opposed to reckless. Nonetheless, under the *lex Aquilia*, on the authority of Ulpian, as ratified in the *Digest*, the two cases are to be treated essentially the same: the Aquilian action fails unless the actor manifests a specific intent to cause undue harm, as by striking an opponent who has submitted or by intentionally aiming his javelin at the victim.

Would this also be the case with regard to an Athenian *dikê phonou*? Specifically, would both the killing of a rival competitor in a combat sport and an accidental death by javelin in training both qualify as ἐν ἄθλοις ἄκων and accordingly go to trial at the Delphinion? The short answer is that we do not know. But this has not inhibited speculation, and in that spirit, I will offer some speculation of my own. Demosthenes' interpretation of the ἐν ἄθλοις ἄκων clause is inherently credible insofar as the standard case envisioned is combat sports; it is entirely probable that Draco as well as Demosthenes considered that athletic mortality rates were highest in boxing and pancration. Moreover, injury inflicted on an opponent who has already submitted would militate against a defense of killing ἐν ἄθλοις **ἄκων**, just as it activates in Roman law an Aquilian action that is otherwise denied.

The javelin case is more problematic, and there has been plenty of debate over where the hypothetical *Second Tetralogy* would take place under actual Athenian law: would trial occur at the Delphinion, on the grounds that the killing occurred ἐν ἄθλοις ἄκων, or at the Palladion, the default venue for uninten-

---

46. This need not be a combat sport: cf. Alfenus (2 *digest.*) *D.* 9.2.52.4 (Frier, *Roman Law of Delict* [1989], Case 58; Grueber, *Roman Law of Damage to Property* [1886] 31, 174, 227; Valditara, *Damnum iniuria datum* [2005] 36; Corbino, *Il danno qualificato* [2008] 169–70): a slave boy participating in a ball game is pushed, falls, and breaks his leg; an Aquilian action against the pusher is denied "since [the damage] appeared to have occurred rather by accident than by fault" (*cum casu magis quam culpa videretur factum*).

47. Cf. Buckland and McNair, *Roman Law and Common Law* (1952) 372 with n. 3: this case illustrates "the rule as to willingness to take the risk" in providing that "where a man engages in a contest he accepts the ordinary consequences."

tional killing?[48] Those who rule out the Delphinion on the grounds that ἆθλα must refer to competition as opposed to training and/or that Demosthenes' interpretation of the law is both complete and correct—that is, that the only ἆθλα covered by the law are combat sports[49]—seem to me to impute to the Athenians a legalism that they did not generally manifest. Assignment of a *dikê phonou* to one of the five dedicated homicide courts (Dem. 23.65–79; [Arist.] *Ath. pol.* 57.2–4) was done by the *basileus* following three preliminary hearings (*prodikasiai*) held in successive months (Ant. 6.42). The *basileus* was not a legal expert, let alone a Roman jurisconsult; in difficult cases, he may have consulted the Areopagus for guidance, including inquiry regarding precedents, but we have no idea as to what those precedents will have been, and, in any event, in Athenian law precedent might be persuasive but had no binding force.[50]

In our hypothetical javelin case, whether it went to the Palladion or the Delphinion, the jury would be the same (the *ephetai*), as would the penalty upon conviction (exile until pardon was granted by the qualified relatives of the victim). But it would be in the interests of the defense to obtain trial at the Delphinion. At the Palladion, with lawful homicide removed from consideration, the defense would be limited to an argument, as in the *Second Tetralogy*, that the victim killed himself. At the Delphinion, the defense would have the additional argument that even if the thrower is the killer, he is excused by Draco's law as having killed ἐν ἄθλοις ἄκων. In the *prodikasiai* and, if necessary, at trial, the prosecution might argue along the same lines as those scholars who insist that this case could not have been heard at the Delphinion: ἆθλα means combat competitions only and does not include javelin throwing (where the risk of death is certainly more remote), let alone javelin practice. The defense might respond that the lawgiver does not specify which ἆθλα are covered and clearly meant to include practice as well as competition,[51] and the defense

48. On the Palladion court, see Dem. 23.71–73; [Arist.] *Ath. pol.* 57.3.

49. Blass, *Attische Beredsamkeit* (1887–98) 3.2.364; MacDowell, *Athenian Homicide Law* (1963) 74; Gagarin, *Antiphon: The Speeches* (1997) 144; Carawan, *Rhetoric* (1998) 180; contra (in my opinion, *recte*) Glotz, *Solidarité* (1904) 506–7 n. 7; Daube, *Roman Law* (1969) 169–70; Decleva Caizzi, *Antiphontis Tetralogiae* (1969) 212. The comparisons drawn by Glotz and Decleva Caizzi with Plato's *Laws* are problematic, as that treatise has no independent probative value for Athenian law. That Plato (*Leg.* 865a) places unintentional killing in javelin practice in the same category as unintentional killing in athletic competition and mistaken-identity friendly-fire killing in war is at best suggestive.

50. Demosthenes and the *Ath. pol.* (above, n. 3) might be taken as evidence that a defendant's request for trial at the Delphinion was sufficient. At the very least, I assume that the defendant had to produce the law(s) that he alleged applied to his case; in instances where such application was not obvious, we simply do not know on what grounds the *basileus* will have decided (and these grounds will presumably have varied as a function of a variety of factors, including the personal opinion of the *basileus*).

51. We might compare Lys. 10.7 (delivered by the prosecutor in a *dikê kakêgorias*, arguing that

might add the argument from equity that youths in training should not be held to a stricter standard than elite athletes in competition.

Of course, this is pure speculation. In the end, though, I suggest that scholars risk missing part of the point of the *Second Tetralogy* if they categorically insist that under Athenian law this case must have gone to the Palladion, or to the Delphinion, and cannot have gone to the other. Antiphon purposely constructs his *Tetralogies* on difficult premises, in order to provoke arguments as well as to demonstrate them, and this is one of the very issues about which he expects his Athenian readers to argue. So it is a fitting tribute to Antiphon—and, I hope, a fitting tribute to the honorand of this volume—that we are still arguing about this issue nearly two and a half millennia later.[52]

Bibliography

American Law Institute. *Model Penal Code: Official Draft and Explanatory Notes; Complete Text of Model Penal Code as Adopted at the 1962 Annual Meeting of the American Law Institute at Washington, D.C., May 24, 1962.* Philadelphia: American Law Institute, 1985.

American Law Institute. *Restatement of the Law Third, Torts: Liability for Physical and Emotional Harm.* St. Paul: American Law Institute, 2010.

Berger, A. *Encyclopedic Dictionary of Roman Law.* Philadelphia: American Philosophical Society, 1953.

Blass, F. *Die attische Beredsamkeit.* Leipzig, 1887–98. Reprint, 3 vols. in 4, Hildesheim: Georg Olms Verlag, 1979.

Buckland, W. W., and A. D. McNair. *Roman Law and Common Law: A Comparison in Outline.* 2nd ed., revised by F. H. Lawson. Cambridge: Cambridge University Press, 1952.

Cantarella, E. *Studi sull'omicidio in diritto greco e romano.* Milan: Dott. A. Giuffrè Editore, 1976.

Carawan, E. *Rhetoric and the Law of Draco.* Oxford: Clarendon, 1998.

Corbino, A. *Il danno qualificato e la lex Aquilia: Corso di diritto romano.* 2nd ed. Padua: CEDAM, 2008.

Daube, D. *Roman Law: Linguistic, Social, and Philosophical Aspects.* Edinburgh: Edinburgh University Press, 1969.

the defendant need not have used the statutory term ἀνδροφόνος, "killer," to be liable for defamation): πολὺ γὰρ <ἂν> ἔργον ἦν τῷ νομοθέτῃ ἅπαντα τὰ ὀνόματα γράφειν ὅσα τὴν αὐτὴν δύναμιν ἔχει· ἀλλὰ περὶ ἑνὸς εἰπὼν περὶ πάντων ἐδήλωσεν. (It would have been a lot of work for the lawgiver to write down all the words that have the same meaning; instead, by mentioning one he made clear his position on all of them.)

52. I am pleased and honored to offer this paper in tribute to Professor Bruce Frier, who taught me Roman law and introduced me to the concept of assumption of risk. I am grateful as well to my fellow participants in the conference in Professor Frier's honor held at the University of Michigan in October 2013 and to Professor Laura Pepe and my audience at the Università degli Studi di Milano in April 2014.

Davies, J. K. *Athenian Propertied Families, 600–300 B.C.* Oxford: Clarendon, 1971.
Decleva Caizzi, F. *Antiphontis Tetralogiae*. Milan: Istituto Editoriale Cisalpino, 1969.
Dendrinou, N. Ἀντιφῶντος λόγοι. Athens: Ἐκδοτικὸς Οἶκος Ἰωάννου καὶ Π. Ζαχαροπούλου, 1939.
Dittenberger, W. "Antiphons Tetralogien und das attische Criminalrecht." Part 2. *Hermes* 32 (1897): 1–41.
Fisher, N. R. E. *Aeschines: "Against Timarchos."* Oxford: Oxford University Press, 2001.
Forsdyke, S. "Street Theatre and Popular Justice in Ancient Greece: Shaming, Stoning and Starving Offenders Inside and Outside the Courts." *Past and Present* 201 (2008): 3–50.
Franklin, M. A., et al. *Tort Law and Alternatives: Cases and Materials*. 9th ed. New York: Foundation Press, 2011.
Frier, B. W. *A Casebook on the Roman Law of Delict*. Atlanta: Scholars Press, 1989.
Gagarin, M. *Antiphon the Athenian: Oratory, Law, and Justice in the Age of the Sophists*. Austin: University of Texas Press, 2002.
Gagarin, M. *Antiphon: The Speeches*. Cambridge: Cambridge University Press, 1997.
Gagarin, M. *Drakon and Early Athenian Homicide Law*. New Haven: Yale University Press, 1981.
Gagarin, M. "Self-Defense in Athenian Homicide Law." *Greek, Roman, and Byzantine Studies* 19 (1978): 111–20.
Garner, B. A., ed. *Black's Law Dictionary*. 7th ed. St. Paul: West, 1999.
Gernet, L., and M. Bizos. *Lysias: Discours*. Paris: Les Belles Lettres, 1989.
Glotz, G. *La solidarité de la famille dans le droit criminel en Grèce*. Paris: Albert Fontemoing, 1904.
Grueber, E. *The Roman Law of Damage to Property: Being a Commentary on the Title of the Digest Ad Legem Aquiliam (IX. 2) with an Introduction to the Study of the Corpus Iuris Civilis*. Oxford: Clarendon, 1886.
Holmes, O. W., Jr. *The Common Law*. Boston: Little, Brown, 1881.
Humbert, J., and L. Gernet. *Démosthène: Plaidoyers politiques*. Vol. 2, *Contre Midias, Contre Aristocrate*. Paris: Les Belles Lettres, 1959.
Kapparis, K. A. *Apollodoros "Against Neaera" [D. 59]*. Berlin: Walter de Gruyter, 1999.
Kapparis, K. A. "Humiliating the Adulterer: The Law and the Practice in Classical Athens." *Revue internationale des droits de l'antiquité*, 3rd ser., 43 (1996): 63–77.
Keeton, W. P., et al. *Prosser and Keeton on the Law of Torts*. 5th ed. St. Paul: West, 1984.
Lanni, A. *Law and Justice in the Courts of Classical Athens*. Cambridge: Cambridge University Press, 2006.
Loomis, W. T. "The Nature of Premeditation in Athenian Homicide Law." *Journal of Hellenic Studies* 92 (1972): 86–95.
MacDowell, D. M. *Athenian Homicide Law in the Age of the Orators*. Manchester: Manchester University Press, 1963.
MacDowell, D. M. *Demosthenes, "Against Meidias" (Oration 21)*. Oxford: Clarendon, 1990.
McGinn, T. A. J. "Prostitution: Controversies and New Approaches." In T. K. Hubbard, ed., *A Companion to Greek and Roman Sexualities*, 83–101. Chichester: Blackwell, 2014.

Miller, S. G. *Ancient Greek Athletics*. New Haven: Yale University Press, 2004.
Paley, F. A., and J. E. Sandys. *Demosthenes: Select Private Orations*. 3rd ed. Part 1. Cambridge: Cambridge University Press, 1898.
Pepe, L. *Phonos: L'omicidio da Draconte all'età degli oratori*. Milan: Giuffrè Editore, 2012.
Phillips, D. D. *The Law of Ancient Athens*. Ann Arbor: University of Michigan Press, 2013.
Phillips, D. D. "*Trauma ek pronoias* in Athenian Law." *Journal of Hellenic Studies* 127 (2007): 74–105.
Phillips, D. D. "Why Was Lycophron Prosecuted by *Eisangelia*?" *Greek, Roman, and Byzantine Studies* 46 (2006): 375–94.
Rhodes, P. J. *A Commentary on the Aristotelian "Athenaion Politeia."* Oxford: Clarendon, 1993.
Robinson, P. H. *Criminal Law*. New York: Aspen, 1997.
Schmitz, W. "Der nomos moicheias – Das athenische Gesetz über den Ehebruch." *Zeitschrift der Savigny-Stiftung für Rechtsgeschichte (Romanistische Abteilung)* 114 (1997): 45–140.
Stadter, P. A. *A Commentary on Plutarch's "Pericles."* Chapel Hill: University of North Carolina Press, 1989.
Stroud, R. S. *Drakon's Law on Homicide*. Berkeley: University of California Press, 1968.
Todd, S. C. *A Commentary on Lysias, Speeches 1–11*. Oxford: Oxford University Press, 2007.
Valditara, G. *Damnum iniuria datum*. 2nd ed. Turin: G. Giappichelli Editore, 2005.

CHAPTER 4

Rivers, Rights, and "Romanization"

Cynthia J. Bannon

Sometime in the middle of the second century, around 161–69 CE, a question about the use of a public river came to the emperors Marcus Aurelius and Lucius Verus, and their reply is reported in Papirius Iustus' collection of imperial constitutions.

> *Imperatores Antoninus et Verus Augusti rescripserunt aquam de flumine publico pro modo possessionum ad irrigandos agros dividi oportere, nisi proprio iure quis plus sibi datum ostenderit. item rescripserunt aquam ita demum permitti duci, si sine iniuria alterius id fiat.* (Papir. [1 *de Const.*] *D.* 8.3.17)
>
> [The emperors Augusti Antoninus and Verus replied that water from a public river for irrigating fields should be divided in proportion to the property holdings, unless someone show that more has been given to him by an individual right. Likewise they wrote that water is only allowed to be channeled if it can be done without harm to another.]

The use of river water should have been uncontroversial, because a public river was common property, with open access for all.[1] Yet the rescript presumes a dispute about the allocation of a public river for irrigation and for other unstated purposes.

The legal doctrine on diverting water from public rivers is not clearly articulated in our sources until the Justinianic period, when a special grant or concession was required for doing so.[2] In the period of classical Roman law,

1. Nerat.-Ulp. *D.* 8.3.3.3, Ulp. *D.* 39.2.24 pr., Paul. *D.* 39.3.17.4, with De Marco, *I loci publici* (2004) 83–86 (cf. 12–29, 71–72, 177–84).

2. On imperial grants for *aquam de publico aquaeductu seu fonte,* see *CJ* 11.43.11. *Fons* seems

to which our rescript belongs, there are no clear rules in the *Digest* and little scholarly consensus, though concessions seem to have been used to balance the various uses of public waterways for such activities as shipping and irrigation.[3] The rescript illustrates these problems without resolving them, yet it is cited regularly in the scholarly debate about public rivers.[4] The rescript and the general problems it raises can be better understood when it is examined in relation to two irrigation decrees, one from Lamasba in North Africa and another from Spain, the still relatively new *lex rivi Hiberiensis*.[5] More broadly, analysis of the rescript contributes to our understanding of Romanization, particularly as expressed through law and the control of natural resources.

The exploitation of natural resources could be an expression of Roman conquest or "Romanization."[6] But, as the quotation marks here suggest, the term *Romanization* means more than the introduction of Roman institutions. In general, the landscape was a key site of "Romanization" where individual communities negotiated with Romans and their culture.[7] In particular, a public river was a "mediating point" where cultural responses to Roman imperialism can be observed because law and practice come together at the river.[8] The regulation of a public river illustrates the negotiation between local and Roman practices, and the rescript in particular belongs to this process, representing the circulation of legal ideas between Rome and the provinces. The emperor and his legal office in Rome could influence legal practice in the provinces through the petition-response process.[9] In this process, local rules and customs played an important—some would say dominant—role, in which local elites used the law to pursue their own interests in much the same way as their Roman counterparts.[10] Nevertheless, this rescript is cited as evidence that the irriga-

to include a natural public source, because it is used generically of a water source on rural land in *C.* 11.63.1 pr.; cf. the interdict *De fonte,* Paul. *D.* 8.3.9, with Grosso, "Sulla servitù" (1932) 402–7, 426–28.

3. Ulp. *D.* 39.3.10.2, Pompon. *D.* 43.12.2, with Fiorentini, *Fiumi e Mari* (2003) 230–43.

4. E.g., Alburquerque, *Protección o defensa* (2002) 287–89; Fiorentini, *Fiumi e Mari* (2003) 239–41.

5. For the text of the *lex rivi Hiberiensis,* see *AE* 1993, 1043 = *HEp* 5 (1995), 911; Beltrán Lloris, "Irrigation Decree" (2006) 153–57, with updates in Beltrán Lloris, "La *lex rivi Hiberiensis*" (2014) 59–63; Maganzani, "Lex rivi Hiberiensis" *FIRA* (2012) 3:171–85. For the text of the Lamasba decree, see *Eph. Epigr.* VII 788 (*CIL* VIII 4440, 18587; *ILS* 5793); *FIRA* (2012) 3.1.195–213. On both, see Maganzani, "Le comunità di irrigazione" (2012) 105–12.

6. For control of water as an expression of conquest, see Purcell, "Rome and the Management of Water" (1996).

7. Terrenato, "Romanization of Italy" (1998) 25. On water technology generally, see Shaw "Water and Society" (1984).

8. For the term *mediating point,* see Woolf, "Formation" (1997) 13.

9. Conolly, *Lives* (2010) 145–47; cf. Millar, *Emperor* (1977) 248–52, 328–41.

10. Tuori, "Legal Pluralism" (2007); Burton, "Long-Term Trend" (1998). See Eich, "Center and Periphery" (2012), on the importance of the perspective from the provinces.

tion rules in both inscriptions conform to Roman practice, on the assumption that proportional allocation was the typical Roman legal arrangement. My argument here challenges this assumption and proposes that the practice of proportional distribution came from the provinces into Roman law. Thus, setting the rescript in the broader context of "Romanization" not only clarifies its interpretation but also illuminates the role of law in building the common culture of the Roman Empire.[11]

Legal Context

The rescript belongs to a collection of imperial constitutions made by Papirius Iustus in the late Antonine period, twenty books from which only few extracts survive.[12] In the *Digest of Justinian*, the rescript appears in book 8, in the chapter on rustic servitudes.[13] In the rescript, a servitude may be involved, if the phrase *proprio iure* indicates a servitude, and there is some evidence to support this interpretation. The general situation of multiple users sharing a source of water is addressed in few other cases concerning servitudes, and two cases offer close parallels. In one case, where several landowners share water from a spring located on private property, the phrase *propium ius* designates the water right, although the use of the adjective may be conditioned by its use to describe the canal itself.[14] In the other case, the method of allocating water among multiple users, in proportion to landholdings, is mentioned in the context of selling property with a servitude. When the property was divided and sold in parcels, the servitude was transferred with each parcel, and the right to water was divided in proportion to the size of the property (*ius aquae ducendae pro modo agri detenti)*.[15] The possibility of dividing a servitude *pro portione* is expressly denied in a third case, in which the rule about servitudes is invoked in an argument concerning an inheritance when the property cannot be divided.[16]

11. The adaptation of Roman law may offer an antidote to the generally pessimistic appraisal of other measures of Romanization in Cherry, *Frontier and Society* (1998) 75–100.

12. The excerpts of Papirius Iustus' writings fill barely three columns in Lenel, *Palingenesia* (2000) 1:947–52. For a "pre-Severan" date, see Schultz, *Roman Legal Science* (1946) 153.

13. Book 8 includes one other extract from Papirius' *Constitutiones*, regarding freedom of construction in the absence of a servitude, Papir. Iust. *D.* 8.2.14.

14. *Ita ut suo quisque die a capite duceret primo per eundem rivum eumque communem, deinde ut quisque inferior erat, suo quisque proprio rivo* (Procul. *D.* 8.6.16, discussed below). Cases relating to the *Interdict on Daily and Summer Water* presume multiple users: see, e.g., Iul. *D.* 43.20.4 and 5 pr.–1, with Bannon, *Gardens and Neighbors* (2009) 83–99; Fiorentini, *Fiumi e Mari* (2003) 241–43.

15. Pompon. *D.* 8.3.25. When land was divided and sold in parcels, servitudes attached to the property were transferred with each parcel; see Paul. *D.* 8.3.23.3.

16. Paul. *D.* 45.1.4.1. According to this argument, all heirs must pay a penalty incurred by the

While the circumstances of the rescript are generally consistent with servitudes, interpreting the *proprium ius* as a servitude is problematic because no servitude was needed to divert water from a public river.[17] The simple fact of diverting water from a public source onto private property, even through a man-made canal, did not convert the water into private property, the type of property governed by servitudes.[18] If a servitude had been involved in the rescript, it would have involved not the diversion of water but a right to channel water across riverside property to fields farther from the river or to cross private property along the river either on foot or with a canal.[19] The difficulty in construing the *proprium ius* as a servitude led to some suspicion that the entire clause *nisi proprio iure quis plus sibi datum ostenderit* was interpolated or revised by Justinian's compilers to reflect the law of that era, in which a formal grant was required to use any public source of water.[20] Yet interpolation is not the most likely explanation.[21] Instead, the difficulty may reflect the patchwork treatment of the diversion of public rivers in the legal sources, particularly the interdicts relating to the water supply.

The use of public rivers was addressed in several of the praetorian interdicts, of which three are expressly directed at public rivers.

> *De fluminibus. ne quid in flumine publico ripave eius fiat, quo peius navigetur* (*D.* 43.12)
>
> [On Rivers: that nothing be done in a public river or on its bank to hinder sailing]

---

estate through a *cautio*: *ab omnibus, si id factum, de quo cautum est, individuum sit, veluti 'iter fieri', quia quod in partes dividi non potest, ab omnibus quodammodo factum videretur.* Paul quotes Cato here, so the rule for servitudes was well established in the classical period.

17. Ulp. *D.* 39.2.24 pr., Pompon. *D.* 43.12.2 and 43.20.3.2, with De Marco, *I loci publici* (2004) 83. For free diversion with some limits, see Fiorentini, *Fiumi e Mari* (2003) 231; for an argument, to the contrary, for administrative grants, see Alburquerque, *Protección o Defensa* (2002) 284–89. None of the scholars cited here considers all three cases together.

18. Ulp. *D.* 43.12.1.8.

19. Nerat.-Ulp. *D.* 8.3.3.3, Paul. *D.* 39.3.17.4.

20. The verb *permitti* was added by compilers to reflect the regime of concessions in postclassical law, according to Albertario, 'Le derivazioni" (1930). Longo, "Sull'uso delle acque" (1933) 158–59, attributes to the compilers both *permitti* and the clause *nisi . . . ostenderit*. Solazzi, "Usus Proprius" (1941) 393–94, emends *iure* to *usu* on the grounds that *ius* is not properly used of rights to public water.

21. No interpolations are recorded for the rescript in Levy and Rabel, *Index Interpolationum* (1929) 1:106. Arguments for interpolation, such as those by Albertario and Longo, tend to be influenced by the author's view of the question about free derivation or concession in classical law.

Ne quid in flumine publico fiat, quo aliter aqua fluat, atque uti priore aestate fluxit (*D.* 43.13)

[That nothing be done in a public river to make it flow other than it did in the previous summer]

Ut in flumine publico navigare liceat (*D.* 43.14)

[That it be possible to sail in a public river]

These interdicts primarily protected boat traffic on public rivers, as indicated in two of the titles; the third is interpreted to have had the same intent.[22] While these interdicts may have protected only navigable rivers at first, they were broadened over time to cover nonnavigable rivers and apparently also activities other than navigation.[23] The use of public rivers was also addressed by the interdicts "on daily and summer water" (*De aqua cottidiana et aestiva*, *D.* 43.20) and "on streams" (*De rivis*, *D.* 43.21).[24] These interdicts concern uses other than navigation, especially the problem of allocating water among multiple users, explicitly in the interdict *De aqua cottidiana et aestiva,* whose title refers to daily or seasonal schedules for water use, and implicitly in the interdict *De rivis*, which promoted maintenance of canals; maintenance was often a source of contention in shared canal systems.[25] All of these interdicts dealt with

22. Fiorentini, *Fiumi e Mari* (2003) 239–41.

23. The interdict *De fluminibus* was broadened by Labeo to protect various uses: see Labeo-Ulp. (68 *ad ed.*) *D.* 43.12.1.12, with Fiorentini, *Fiumi e Mari* (2003) 161–62. The interdict *Ne quid in flumine publico fiat* (*D.* 43.13) may have had a broader scope from the start, according to Alburquerque, *Protección o defensa* (2002) 267–69. On the origins of the interdicts, see Kaser and Hackl, *Zivilprozessrecht* (1996) 411–12. Public and private rivers were not distinguished on the basis of boat traffic. Cassius' definition of a public river as perennial is generally accepted: see Ulp. *D.* 43.12.1.3, with Fiorentini, Fiumi e Mari (2003) 75, 86–98.

24. These interdicts applied to both public and private sources,: e.g., the interdict *De aqua cottidiana et aestiva* applied to water rights generally, (Ulp. *D.* 43.20.1.9), and specifically to public sources, (Ulp. *D.* 43.20.1.38–44). The application of the interdict *De rivis* to both public and private canals is explicit: *hoc interdictum ad omnes rivos pertinet, sive in publico sive in privato sint constituti,* (Ulp. *D.* 43.21.3.4, with De Marco, *I loci publici* ([2004)] 100–101).

25. For multiple users of a river and the interdict *De aqua cottidiana et aestiva,* see Paul. *D.* 43.20.3.1–2. For the interdict *De rivis,* a reservoir (*lacus*), not a river, is the source in the only case that specifies multiple users, Ulp. *D.* 43.21.3.3; cf. *D.* 43.21.1 pr., where the purpose of the interdict is explained as keeping the canals clear *aquae ducendae causa.* See also Ulp. *D.* 43.20.5.1, on use of the interdict *De aqua cottidiana et aestiva* in a case about two individuals who share a canal (*rivus*). For other cases on interdicts in which water is diverted from a river, see Ulp. *D.* 39.3.10.2, 43.12.1.15, 43.13.1.1 and 5, 43.20.1.8, 43.21.1.4–5. The interests of those living around the river are most often invoked in decisions about the interdict *Ne quid . . . quo aliter aqua fluat* (Ulp. *D.* 43.13.1.1, 3, 4, 6, 7; cf. Pompon. *D.* 43.20.3.1).

situations analogous to the rescript, that is, a conflict of interest among those who shared a public river. Although none of the cases on the interdicts mentions proportional distribution, they raise the same questions as the rescript, that is, to what extent open access to a public river was limited, by what legal mechanisms, and on what legal grounds. As noted above, the cases on the interdict provide no clear answers.

Since contextualizing the rescript within the *Digest* does not clarify the nature of the water rights, other contexts should be considered, particularly law in the provinces. Some support for a provincial context for the rescript can be gleaned from its transmission: Papirius Iustus' first book, to which our rescript belongs, addressed law in the provinces, and his second book was about municipal law (*de iure municipali*).[26] If the rescript belongs with the praetorian interdicts, this legal context is also suggestive, because praetorian law on rivers informed the formula in one of the inscriptions from the provinces that will be discussed shortly.[27] Before examining the inscriptions, it is helpful to consider an historical case that illustrates both the potential and the limitations of legal analysis of conflict over a public river.

The River Darias, a Historical Example

Around 100 BCE, the Romans drove the Salassi out of the Po valley into the highlands and founded Eporedia as a garrison to hold the territory.[28] The region was hardly pacified, as the Salassi were continually fighting with their downstream neighbors over the water of the river Darias. Because the Salassi controlled the mountains, they also controlled the river, and they diverted its water into secondary canals to process gold, thereby depriving the people in the plains of water for irrigation. Although the Romans seized the gold mines and contracted them out to the *publicani*, the Salassi maintained control of the mountains and the river, turning a profit from both: they charged tolls to all who crossed the Alps and sold the river water to the *publicani*.[29] Conflicts over

26. Half the excerpts in Papirius Iustus' first book concern law in the provinces, but they are few overall, eight only: see *D.* 18.1.71, 48.12.3, 49.1.21, plus the rescript in 8.3.17.

27. The *quidquid paret* formula (*lrH* para. 15, III.39–43) is similar to an old praetorian formula for a claim against a contractor tasked with cutting brush that hangs over a public river, *qui flumina retanda*: see Gell. 11.17.2, with Nörr, "Prozessuales (und mehr)" (2008) 141.

28. Strabo 4.205 (4.6.7). For the foundation of Eporedia, see Vell. 1.15.5, with Broadhead, "Migration and Transformation" (2000) 153.

29. *Publicani* could be contracted to collect fees from users of private water connections: see Vitr. 8.6.2, with Bruun (2003), 307.

access to river water provided a ready pretext for repeated Roman military intervention, which culminated with Augustus' foundation of the veteran colony Augusta Praetoria in 25 BCE.[30]

At first glance, the river Darias may seem rather far from our rescript both geographically and historically. But the essential problem—how multiple users arranged access to a public river—is the same. In both situations, a group of irrigators came into conflict with others who used the river. In the rescript, the others claimed the water by individual right, *proprio iure.* On the Darias, the upstream Salassi or the *publicani,* who bought water from them, could have made a similar claim. Although Strabo does not mention law, beyond a vague notice of "selling" the river, it is not unlikely that Roman legal institutions of some sort were used, since there was a history of cultural and commercial exchange between the Transpadane region and the rest of Italy starting in the third century BCE.[31] Caesar granted the Transpadanes citizenship in 49 BCE, and the Salassi were integrated into the community at Augusta Praetoria.[32] No colonial charter from Augusta Praetoria is known, but extant charters outline a legal framework for both public and private water resources, and Roman legal practices were regularly adopted in the provinces.[33] More detailed information about this process can be found in the irrigation decrees from Spain and Africa.

Two Inscriptions

Two long inscriptions describe arrangements for multiple users to share a common water supply. The *lex rivi Hiberiensis* (*lrH*) records regulations for an irrigation community that diverted water from the Ebro River into a main canal, the *rivus Hiberiensis,* as it is called in the inscription (*lrH* para. 1, I.1). The water was then distributed by gravity flow to subsidiary canals serving individual parcels of land along the main canal.[34] The Lamasba decree from North Africa

30. Pliny, *NH* 3.123.

31. Broadhead, "Migration and Transformation" (2000) esp. 149–50 and, in relation to mines, 162–63.

32. On the grant of citizenship, see Dio 51.36. On the community at Augusta Praetoria, see Keppie, *Colonisation* (1983) 205–6; Williams, "Roman Intentions" (2001) 98.

33. Frederiksen, "Municipal Laws" (1965) 196.

34. In the *lrH*, the shared canal is called *rivus Hiberiensis,* "Ebro Canal" (e.g., paras. 1a, I.1 and 2; 2b I.21–22; 5, II.12; reconstructed in paras. 6bis, II.25; 15, III.40), and "judging by its name," it "would have been fed by the waters of this river or run parallel to it," according to Beltrán Lloris, "Irrigation Decree" (2006) 149, cf. 167–70; see 149–53 on the discovery of the decree. On the canal system, see *lrH* paras. 1a, I.1–2; 3a, I.27–31; 3c, I. 42–44. On Roman irrigation works in the Ebro River basin, see Arenillas and Castillo, "Dams" (2003); Beltrán Lloris and Willi, "Estado de la Cuestión" (2011) 23–31.

governed a community of landowners in the territory of a town.[35] In both cases, topography and infrastructure were the same: water was distributed by gravity flow through a main canal by gravity flow, to subsidiary canals serving individual properties along the main canal. Also, both inscriptions address the same problem, a conflict among users of the shared canal, a situation similar to that in our rescript and thus helpful in its interpretation. The main difference between these two irrigation communities is the type of water sources (a spring at Lamasba and the Ebro River in Spain), but there is no explicit evidence for the legal status of these sources, whether they were private property or public, like the river in the rescript. Both similarities and differences between the inscriptions are instructive in understanding water rights generally and interpreting the rescript in particular.

The *lex rivi Hiberiensis* (*lrH*) was enacted during the reign of Hadrian, under the auspices of the provincial governor or his *legatus iuridicus*, whose sanction authorizing the decree appears at the end of the inscription (*lrH* paras. 15–16, III.44–48). The *lrH* reports the settlement of a dispute between upstream and downstream irrigators who belonged to two local communities, both Roman *municipia*.[36] The *lex* unites them in an irrigation community and prescribes the rules for its operation (e.g., monetary contributions, maintenance, assemblies of the irrigators) as well as legal remedies for their enforcement, including a formula and procedures for *pignoris capio* and for prosecuting misconduct on the part of a magistrate.[37] The legal mechanisms and administrative structure are recognizably Roman. The irrigation community is identified as a *pagus*, a flexible administrative framework used in various areas of the western Roman Empire.[38] In addition, the *lrH's* legal remedies draw on Roman civil procedure extensively and skillfully.[39] The *lrH* has a Roman character at least partly because the Roman authorities were involved in its drafting, probably invited by the downstream community to support its claim for a share of the water. Ro-

35. The system at Lamasba was fed by a spring named the *aqua Claudiana*, according to Shaw, "Lamasba" (1982) 68–69, 72–86.

36. On the status of the two communities, see Pliny, *NH* 3.24. On the dispute, its cause, and its resolution, see Beltrán Lloris, "An Irrigation Decree" (2006) 160–63, 178–79, 186–87, 189–90. See, similarly, Nörr, "Prozessuales (und mehr)" (2008) 119–20.

37. In the *lrH,* duties of the participants included contributions of money and labor (para. 1a–b I.1–15), cleaning and repairs (paras. 3a, I.27–38; 6, II.18–25), and assemblies to determine the schedule and allocation (para. 3c–4, I.38–II.2). Local magistrates supervised, giving notice of these duties to individual participants (para. 2a, I.16–20) and imposing fines for noncompliance (paras. 1b, I.9–15; 4, II.2–11, 6bis, III.25–34), with help from the *publicani* in collecting fines and seizing pledges (*pignoris capio)* (paras. 8–9, II.43–III.7). Also included was the legal procedure for prosecuting magistrates' misconduct in implementing the *lex* (paras. 13–15, III.23–43).

38. Beltrán Lloris, "An Irrigation Decree" (2006) 195–97; Tarpin, *Vici et Pagi* (2002) 232–33.

39. Nörr, "Prozessuales (und mehr)" (2008) 111, 124.

man intervention may have been needed because the irrigators belonged to different political communities.[40]

The Lamasba decree, like the Ebro *lex*, records the settlement of a dispute about the allocation of water. Unlike the *lex*, the Lamasba decree has little connected prose, little law, and little or no express role for Roman authorities. A short preamble, only partially preserved, begins with imperial titles that date the inscription to the reign of Elagabalus in 218–22 CE. At Lamasba, the irrigation community did not use Roman law to establish an autonomous institutional framework. Instead, it was integrated into the local political structure: a decree of the local town council appointed a commission of probably three arbiters to negotiate allocation of water, according to the preamble, *ex decreto ordinis et colonorum*.[41] The bulk of the Lamasba decree (in several columns) consists of lists with uniform entries that give (1) name of the landowner, (2) size of the property, (3) time of day when the plot is watered, and (4) total time of watering for this property.[42]

Both irrigation decrees reflect a degree of "Romanization," since both were created by Romanized communities under the leadership of a local, Romanized elite. In the Ebro decree, the two groups that made up the irrigation community belonged to Roman towns, Caesaraugusta and Cascantium, Augustan veteran colonies, though the Roman presence in the Ebro valley is older, dating to the time of the Second Punic War.[43] The irrigation community included Romans, some of them veterans: one of the dykes on the canal is located "at the villa of Rectus the centurion" (*ad Recti centurionis*, para. 2b, I.24), and one of the assemblies was held at a villa belonging to the Valerii Aveniae (para. 4, I.47–52). Similarly, the territory of Lamasba had long been under Roman administration when the irrigation decree was made, although the status of the town is uncertain. Lamasba is identified in other inscriptions as a *municipium* but may have attained the rank of *colonia*. The decree itself was authorized by the local government, described as *ordo* and *coloni*. While these terms point to some definition of the community as Roman, they are not precise enough to establish the

40. Beltrán Lloris, "An Irrigation Decree" (2006) 160–62; see 165 and 189 on the downstream party inviting Roman aid. Cf. Nörr, "Prozessuales (und mehr)" (2008) 124. On the role of the provincial governor in adapting Roman law to local conditions, see Maganzani, "Juridiction romaine" (2007).

41. *Eph. Epigr.* VII 788 (*CIL* VIII 4440, 18587; *ILS* 5793).

42. Shaw, "Lamasba" (1982) 72, 82.

43. Strabo 3.2.15 (Caesaraugusta); Pliny, *NH* 3.24 (Cascantium); Beltrán Lloris, "An Irrigation Decree" (2006) 160–62, 178–79, 189–90. On the Ebro treaty, see App. *Ib.* 7.25–27, with Richardson, *Romans in Spain* (1996) 20–22; on second-century BCE Roman settlements, see Livy, *Per.* 41.2 (Gracchurris); App. *Hisp.* 43 (Ilturgi); Beltrán Lloris, "Latin Colonies" (2011) 133–34.

status of either Lamasba itself or its residents.[44] In view of the decree's date, the members of the irrigation community were Roman citizens. Some were Roman veterans who were married to local women.[45] Of the men on the commission, only one name is preserved, a "Valentinus," who probably belongs to the same family as one of the irrigators named in the decree. Because this family was of middling wealth compared to the other irrigators, he was probably seen as a good mediator, able to represent both the wealthy and the less-wealthy members of the irrigation community. If this differentiation in local society exacerbated the conflict over water, the Romanized elite played a role in both causing and resolving the dispute. A similar dynamic seems to have been at work in the Ebro community, where the locals invited help from the Roman authorities and where local institutions had jurisdiction over enforcement of the *lex*.[46] The example of the river Darias also suggests the pattern in which a Romanized elite used Roman authority to negotiate access to water.[47] The Romans may have intended to exploit the conflict over the Darias for their own purposes, but their intervention effectively empowered the local communities.[48]

In Spain and Africa, both communities used Roman cultural practices to formalize their irrigation arrangements, but in different ways and to differing degrees. Both adopted the so-called epigraphic habit to record the resolution of their dispute.[49] Both also used law, though in different ways. The Lamasba decree does not mention legal institutions at all, although it assumes some kind of property rights, perhaps more local than Roman in form, as the basis for allocation of water.[50] In contrast, the *lrH* is full of detailed Roman legal procedure. The difference may result from choices about what to inscribe, or it could be that Lamasba's recourse to the Roman legal system was so "normal" that there

44. On the status of Lamasba, see Kehoe, *Economics of Agriculture* (1988) 107 n. 71; on centuriation in the territory of Lamasba, indirect evidence for Romanization, see Chevallier, "Essai de chronologie" (1958) 115. Shaw, "Lamasba" (1982) 70, refers to *decuriones* and *possessores*, but the decree mentions only *ordo* and *coloni*.

45. Shaw, "Lamasba" (1982) 66–67, 9, and 88–89, on the Roman community generally, the identification and role of Valentinus, and the role of the Romanized elite in the irrigation dispute. For a less generous estimate, see Cherry, *Frontier and Society* (1998) 98.

46. Beltrán Lloris, "An Irrigation Decree" (2006) 165; Nörr, "Prozessuales (und mehr)" (2008) 128. For Spain generally, see Mackie, *Local Administration* (1983) 41–42.

47. The irrigation community on the Darias may have included former members of the praetorian cohorts, who received the best land in the colony. On the allocation of land, see Dio (53.25.5), with Keppie, *Colonisation* (1983) 206; Broadhead, "Migration and Transformation" (2000) 155.

48. For the Romans' motives concerning the Darias, see Strabo IV.205 (4.6.7).

49. Woolf, "Formation" (1997) 39; Edmondson, "*Instrumenta Imperii*" (1993) 171–73 (on Italy), 175–80 (on the Greek cities); Beltrán Lloris, "Irrigation Decree" (2006) 188; Beltrán Lloris, "Writing" (1999) 140.

50. Shaw, "Lamasba" (1982) 89, detects Semitic models of inheritance practice in the property arrangements; he assumes a type of property right (see 74, 81–83, 88).

was no need of mention. The Ebro community explicitly adapted Roman law as a means of asserting control over the water supply and, at the same time, maintaining its own economic and social status, much as the Roman elite did.[51] The more extensive use of law in Spain may be characteristic of the region: already in 87 BCE, two local communities in the Ebro valley, not even Roman citizens, had used Roman law to settle a dispute about a public water supply, conducted through a *rivus*, as recorded on the *Tabula Contrebiensis*.[52]

While both communities adopted elements of Roman culture, they used this Romanizing framework to formalize and reinforce local practices. In the Ebro community, Roman law enforced long-standing local arrangements for water sharing.[53] For example, the irrigators met to decide the irrigation schedule in an assembly, or *concilium*, held at a private estate, not in a civic center.[54] In addition, the irrigators' rights and duties were assigned in proportion to the amount of water that they derived from the canal, repairs and maintenance *pro parte* (*lrH* para. 2b, I.24–26 with BL 173), and their participation in the assembly, speaking and voting, was also in proportion to their share of the water (*pro modo aquationis*, I.47–51; *pro portione quantum quique aquae ius habent sententiam dicant*, I.7–8).[55] The water itself was allocated in proportion to landholdings, another feature of local practice.[56] Despite the *lrH's* extensive use of Roman law, the method of allocating water follows local practice, and the only parallel for this practice in the Roman era—aside from the rescript—is found

51. B. W. Frier, *Rise of the Roman Jurists* (1985) 74–75. For the phenomenon in the provinces, see Fournier, "L'apport de Cicéron" (2010); Humfress, "Law's Empire" (2013) 80–81. Cf., with particular emphasis on water, Horden and Purcell, *Corrupting Sea* (2000) 242: "In all of these cases, hydraulic technology served the interests of a recognizably powerful section of society, concerned with lucrative redistribution rather than prudence."

52. *AE* 1979, 377, with Richardson, "*Tabula Contrebiensis*" (1983).

53. Colonial laws such as the *lex Colonia Iuliae Genitivae* from Urso may have provided a model, since that law recognizes preexisting water rights in the rural territory of the colony: *itemque iis, qui eum agrum habent possident ha/bebunt possidebunt, itineris aquarum lex ius/que esto* (chap. 79). Cf. Beltrán Lloris, "Irrigation Decree" (2006) 188: "In view of the immense importance attached to tradition in irrigation communities clearly acknowledged by Roman jurisprudence, the regulations, arising from an agreement between the *pagani* themselves, would have matched local customs, of which, unfortunately, only some are contained in the *lex*. . . . [T]he work of the provincial authority would have been limited to registering and shaping the local traditions that the *pagani* agreed to abide by." Typically, the adaptation of Roman law is influenced by existing social structures and practices, according to Humfress, "Law's Empire" (2013) 84–85.

54. *LrH* para. 4, I.47–II.5; the end of the description of this assembly is lost because the text at the top of column II is fragmentary. Compare local responsibility for finance and *munera: see* Mackie, *Local Administration* (1983) 42–43.

55. *LrH* paras. 2b, I.25 (*pro parte*); 4, I.50–51 (*pro modo aquationis*); 1a, I.7–8 (*pro portione quantum quique aquae ius habent sententiam dicant*). See also Beltrán Lloris, "Irrigation Decree" (2006) 183, 188–89.

56. Beltrán Lloris, "Irrigation Decree" (2006) 166 n. 68, 170, 204. Cf. Butzer et al., "Irrigation Agrosystems" (1985) 490, 497–79.

in the Lamasba decree. In the Lamasba community, water was allocated to each landowner in "direct proportion to the amount of property he holds."[57]

For both Lamasba and the Ebro, comparative evidence suggests that proportional allocation was a local practice, yet discussions of both inscriptions cite our rescript as proof of congruence between these local practices and Roman law.[58] As argued above, in Roman private law, proportional allocation of water was the exception, not the rule. It is mentioned in the *Digest* only in connection with sale of land, and sale does not seem to be involved in either inscription. While, as noted above, there is a private law case about an irrigation community similar to those in the inscriptions (*D.* 8.6.16), this is a common water-sharing arrangement that is not exclusively connected with proportional allocation. This very legal case specifies allocation by time, not in proportion to land: each landowner channels the water "on his own day" (*suo die*). In fact, allocation by time or volume is typical of practices in Italy, as documented in inscriptions and Frontinus' description of allocation of the Aqua Crabra at Tusculum.[59] Time schedules and proportional allocation need not be mutually exclusive, however. In both the Ebro community and in Lamasba, for example, proportional allocation was combined with a time schedule.[60] In servitudes and the other evidence for Italy, water was allocated by time, with no reference to the size of the land it irrigated. Moreover, water use could be unlimited in servitudes, whereas the *lrH* specifies that the right to water is limited by proportional allocation. Conceptually, water rights in the *lrH* cannot be identified with servitudes, and the proportional allocation of water distinguishes these two types of legal right.

When the rescript is read in a provincial context, the difficulty in interpreting the phrase *proprio iure* can be resolved, although neither the *lrH* nor the Lamasba decree provides a parallel for the term *ius proprium* that is used

57. Shaw, "Lamasba" (1982) 81–87, infers proportional allocation from his interpretation of the unit "K" in the inscription: K represents the number of trees on the land, which is an indirect measure of area. The parallel between the Ebro community and Lamasba is noted by Beltrán Lloris, "Irrigation Decree" (2006) 194 and n. 228; he questions Shaw's argument that the practices at Lamasba were local. See Shaw, "Water and Society" (1984) esp. 167–69; similarly, with a broader perspective, Cherry, *Frontier and Society* (1998) 146.

58. Cf. Shaw, "Lamasba" (1982) 83 n. 2: "a principle also enshrined in Roman law, see *D.* 8.3.17 and 8.3.25." See also Beltrán Lloris, "Irrigation Decree" (2006) 170.

59. Front. *Aq.* 9.4–5. See, similarly, *CIL* XIV 3676 (Tusculum) and VI 1261 (Rome), with Bannon, *Gardens and Neighbors* (2009) 78–79.

60. A schedule is inferred from the instructions for annual maintenance of the *rivus Hiberiensis*, according to which the canal is to be emptied for cleaning not before the ides of July and not before the last irrigation turn (*imam sortem aquationis*): *see lrH* para. 3c, I.44, with Beltrán Lloris, "Irrigation Decree" (2006) 176–77. A schedule is explicit in the entries in the Lamasba decree: see, Shaw, "Lamasba" (1982) 72.

in the rescript. As noted above, in the rescript, the phrase *proprio iure* appears to refer to a servitude, a private property right, which cannot be established on a public resource. The same phrase does designate a servitude in the case about multiple users of a spring on private property (Procul. *D.* 8.6.16), a situation similar to what is described in the Lamasba decree. There, a number of landowners shared water from a spring that is identified only as the *aqua Claudiana* in the inscription, with no further information about its status as public or private.[61] The water from the *Aqua Claudiana* was probably treated as a common resource, like the water in the Ebro community.[62] If Roman categories had been applied, the Ebro would have been classified as a public river in Roman law, because it flowed all year round.[63] Like a servitude, the water right in the *lrH* was attached to the land, but unlike a servitude, it did not create a relationship between two parcels of land. Instead, it was a right to use a public or common resource. Similar arrangements are described in the charter for Caesar's colony at Urso in Spain, where the water sources would also have been public, not private property.[64] The writings of the Roman surveyors attest to the same practice of endorsing local arrangements for water rights (Hygin. *Agrim.* 83.12–18 T).[65] In such provincial communities, water rights were more similar to servitudes than to administrative grants, but they do not fall into either category. Instead, the inscriptions show that there was

61. On the identification of the *aqua Claudiana* as a spring, see Shaw, "Lamasba" (1982) 72–73, where Shaw does not directly address the legal status of the water. In "Water and Society" (1984) 168–69, he assimilates the system to servitudes (citing *D.* 8.3.20.3 and 8.3.36) and asserts that "ownership of the water, like its division, is personal and individual."

62. There is no evidence for a pre-Roman property regime in Africa; there may have been a mix of private and communal ownership, according to Cherry, *Frontier and Society* (1998) 18 with scholarship cited in n. 66.

63. Although the *lrH* does not expressly label the Ebro as public, it fits the definition of a public river in Roman law because it flowed year-round, or perennially: see Fiorentini, *Fiumi e Mari* (2003) 68–99; Zoz, *Riflessioni* (1999), 110. On seasonal flow in the Ebro, see Al-Mudayna, *Historia de los regadíos* (1991) 15–16. The Ebro appears to have been perennial, based on the need to close the canal for annual cleaning: see *lrH* para. 3c, I.38–46, with Beltrán Lloris, "Irrigation Decree" (2006) 176–77.

64. *Lex Colonia Iuliae Genitivae*, chap. 79 (*CIL* II^{2} 5, cols. 2.39–3.6): *qui fluui riui fontes lacus aquae stagna paludes / sunt in agro, qui colon(is) h[ui]usc(e) colon(iae) diuisus / erit, ad eos riuos fontes lacus aquasque sta / gna paludes itus actus aquae haustus iis item / esto, qui eum agrum habebunt possidebunt, uti / iis fuit, qui eum agrum habuerunt possederunt. / itemque iis, qui eum agrum habent possident ha / bebunt possidebunt, itineris aquarum lex ius / que esto*. These water rights were similar to an early form of servitudes, according to Capogrossi Colognesi, *Ricerche* (1966) 116–21, esp. 119–20, and, more recently, "La *lex rivi Hiberiensis*" (2014) esp. 88–89.

65. Cf. Campbell, *Roman Land Surveyors* (2000) 86.35–36, 88.1. See, similarly, Hygin. *Agrim.* 112.4–8 T; Hygin. *Grom.* 365.31–366.6 L; Campbell, *Roman Land Surveyors* (2000) 114.8–10, 268.17–22. Augustus may have articulated this policy in edicts that are known only from a paraphrase that does not mention rivers or other water sources (Front. *Agrim.* 7.1–8.6 T; Campbell, *Roman Land Surveyors* [2000] 6.7–20 with 323 n. 18). The surveyors knew that servitudes were an institution of the *ius civile*: see Hygin. *Agrim.* 97.23–98.5 T; Campbell, *Roman Land Surveyors* (2000) 98.37–99.3.

a third type of water rights, specific to the provinces and probably defined by local, rather than Roman, law.[66]

The availability of an alternative to servitudes and administrative grants is suggested by usage of the phrase *proprium ius* in the *Digest*. *Proprium ius* designates a person's right as an individual under the law in contrast to that person's rights in a particular legal role, such as heir or ward.[67] Most often the phrase is used when the jurists classify types of law, for example, *ius civile, ius naturale*, and *ius proprium* as the particular law of a civic community.[68] Two cases involve situations analogous to the rescript, in which an individual uses public property—albeit of different kinds, as one case concerns the sea while the other concerns public places generally. In writing about the interdict on public places, Ulpian asserts that individuals have a right to use them based in civic, not individual, rights: *iure scilicet civitatis, non quasi propria cuiusque* (*D.* 43.8.2.2). Similarly, Paul describes an individual's right to use the sea as *proprium ius* when approving the use of the interdict *uti possidetis* (*D.* 47.10.14). In neither case can the *proprium ius* be identified as a property right or servitude; in both, it designates a vague and broad right of an individual to use public property.[69] Although Paul suggests an analogy with usufruct (*utpote cum de iure fruendo agatur*), no legal mechanism, such as an administrative grant, is mentioned. In these cases, as in the provincial inscriptions, an alternative type of right is assumed and defined in relation to local practice. In the rescript, the term *proprium ius* is similarly vague and should also be interpreted as local practice, confirmed by the emperor.[70] In any case, the right to use a public water supply was not limited to servitudes or administrative grants but could be defined by local practice and formulated as *proprium ius*.

Conclusion

Rescripts were a means of communication between center and periphery, and in the rescript under discussion here, the communication was a two-way dia-

66. In the rescript, the right to water may have been explicitly treated as a possession, if Mommsen's emendation (*possessionem* to *possessionum*) is rejected and if the text from manuscript F is restored: *rescripserunt aquam . . . pro modo possessionum . . . dividi oportere*. ("They wrote that the water as possession . . . should be divided in proportion to the size of land-holdings.")

67. Paul. *D.* 21.2.73 (heir), Papin. *D.* 31.69.2 (ward).

68. Ulp. *D.* 1.1.6 pr., Gaius *D.* 1.1.9, Ulp. *D.* 50.16.195.2. Roman private law, the *ius civile*, can be one instance of *ius proprium*: see Pompon. *D.* 1.2.2.12, Gaius *D.* 1.6.3, Gaius *D.* 41.1.1 pr.

69. Solazzi, "Usus Proprius" (1941) 384–85; Alburquerque, *Protección o Defensa* (2002) 49.

70. For similar confirmation of local practice by Constantine, see Kehoe, *Law and the Rural Economy (2007)* 144–46; generally, Burton, "Long-Term Trend" (1998) 13–16 (on continuity in the administration of public land).

logue between the emperor's office and the provinces. The irrigation inscriptions show that law was being made in the provinces both by the simple fact of inscribing local practice on stone and by skillful adaptation of the *ius civile*. When the *ius civile* was adapted to local practices in the provinces, however, the legal categories were only partly shaped by Roman law. In the case of public rivers at least, legal practice was more varied than the *Digest* alone attests. Thus water rights represent a dynamic process of "Romanization."[71] Instead of assuming that the rescript involves *ius civile*, the rescript should be interpreted in terms of law in the provinces, particularly where proportional distribution was usual.

Legal concepts and practices were cultural artifacts that circulated around the empire with imperial officials who used law to one extent or another in governing. The process was operating already in the late second century BCE, when the *Tabula Contrebiensis* was inscribed. Its legal sophistication has been credited to the Roman commander at the time, C. Valerius Flaccus, whose expertise has been traced to his tenure as urban praetor (Cic. *Balb.* 24).[72] For the *lrH*, Hadrian's legate Alpinus may have served the same function. For the rescript or, generally, for proportional distribution, no individual stands out, but one has an intriguing profile, a certain Sextus Julius Possessor. African by origin, he was an equestrian official in the reign of Marcus Aurelius. His career is known from inscriptions from Roman Spain, where he served as procurator on the banks of the Baetis River.[73] He also spent time in Rome as assistant to the prefect of the grain supply: his job was to keep account of Spanish and African oil, transporting supplies and paying the shippers. Possessor is just the sort of person who could have brought the idea of proportional allocation from Africa or Spain, where it was an indigenous custom that suited the climate, to the emperor's legal office at Rome at about the time that the rescript was issued. Attractive as this story may be, it can be only hypothetical, yet it illustrates the potential for circulation of ideas around the empire and the multidimensional process of Romanization.

71. On the variable forms of Romanization with a focus on Gaul, see Williams, "Roman Intentions" (2001) 97; in the eastern provinces, Edmondson, "*Instrumenta Imperii*" (1993).

72. For the source of Flaccus' legal expertise, see Richardson, *Tabula Contrebiensis* (1983) 40.

73. Inscriptions about Julius Possessor are collected in Campbell, *Rivers* (2012) 260–61. In one inscription, Possessor is praised by the boatmen of Hispalis in Spain "because of his exceptional honesty and integrity" (*ob innocentiam iustitiam / que eius singularem*, *CIL* II 1180 = *ILS* 1403).

Bibliography

Al-Mudayna. *Historia de los regadíos en España (. . . a.c.–1931).* Madrid, 1991.

Albertario, E. "Le derivazioni d'acqua dai fiumi pubblici in diritto romano." *BIDR* 38 (1930): 197–214.

Alburquerque, J. M. *La protección o defensa del uso colectivo de las cosas de dominio público: Especial referencia a los interdictos "« de publicis locis»."* Madrid, 2002.

Al-Mudayna. *Historia de los regadíos en España (. . . a.c.–1931).* Madrid, 1991.

Arenillas, M., and J. C. Castillo. "Dams from the Roman Era in Spain: Analysis of Design Forms." In *Proceedings of the First International Congress on Construction History, Madrid 20th^th^-—24th^th^ January 2003,* 1.243–57. Madrid: Instituto Juan de Herrera, 2003. http://www.sedhc.es/biblioteca/acta.php?id_act=6&id_cng=4

Bannon, C. J. *Gardens and Neighbors: Private Water Rights in Roman Italy.* Ann Arbor, 2009.

Beltrán Lloris, F. "An Irrigation Decree from Roman Spain: The *lex rivi Hiberiensis*." *JRS* 96 (2006): 147–97.

Beltrán Lloris, F. "La *lex rivi Hiberiensis* nel suo contesto: I pagi e l'organizzazione dell'irrigazione in Caesar Augusta." In L. Maganzani and C. Buzzacchi, eds., *Lex rivi Hiberiensis: Diritto e tecnica in una comunità di irrigazione della Spagna romana,* 55–74. Naples, 2014.

Beltrán Lloris, F. "Les colonies latines d'Hispanie (IIe siècle av. n. É.): Émigration italique et intégration politique." In N. Barrandon and F. Kirbihler, eds., *Les gouverneurs et les provinciaux sous la République romaine,* 131–44. Rennes, 2011.

Beltrán Lloris, F. "Writing, Language, and Society: Iberians, Celts, and Romans in Northeastern Spain in the 2nd and 1st Centuries B.C." *BICS Studies* 43 (1999): 131–51.

Beltrán Lloris, F., and A. Willi. "El regadío en la Hispania Romana: Estado de la Cuestión." *Cuadernos de Prehistoria y Arqueología de la Universidad de Granada (CPAG)* 21 (2011): 9–56.

Broadhead, W. "Migration and Transformation in North Italy." *BICS* 44 (2000): 145–66.

Bruun, C. "The Roman World." In O. Wikander, ed., *Handbook of Ancient Water Technology,* 575–604. Leiden, 2000.

Bruun, C. "Roman Water Supply." In J.-J. Aubert, ed. *Tâches publiques et entreprise privée dans le monde romain,* 305-25. Geneva, 2003.

Burton, G. "Was There a Long-Term Trend to Centralisation of Authority in the Roman Empire?" *RPh* 72 (1998): 7–24.

Butzer, K. W., et al. "Irrigation Agrosystems in Eastern Spain: Roman or Islamic Origins?" *Annals of the Association of American Geographers* 75.4 (1985): 479–509.

Campbell, B. *Rivers and the Power of Ancient Rome.* Chapel Hill, 2012.

Capogrossi Colognesi, L. "La *lex rivi Hiberiensis* e gli schemi delle servitù d'acqua in diritto romano." In L. Maganzani and C. Buzzacchi, eds., *Lex rivi Hiberiensis: Diritto e tecnica in una comunità di irrigazione della Spagna romana,* 75–91. Naples, 2014.

Capogrossi Colognesi, L. *Ricerche sulla struttura delle servitù d'acqua in diritto romano.* Milan, 1966.

Cherry, D. *Frontier and Society in Roman North Africa.* Oxford, 1998.

Chevallier, R. "Essai de chronologie des centuriations romaines de Tunisie." *MEFRA* 70 (1958): 61–128.

Conolly, S. *Lives behind the Laws: The World of the "Codex Hermogenianus."* Bloomington, 2010.
Costa, E. *Le acque nel diritto romano*. Bologna, 1919.
De Marco, N. *I loci publici dal I al III secolo: Le identificazioni dottrinali, il ruolo dell'usus, gli strumenti di tutela*. Naples, 2004.
Edmondson, J. "*Instrumenta Imperii*: Law and Imperialism in Republican Rome." In B. Halpern and D. W. Hobson, eds., *Law, Politics, and Society in the Ancient Mediterranean World*, 156–92. Sheffield, 1993.
Eich, P. "Centre and Periphery: Administrative Communication in Roman Imperial Times." In S. Benoist, ed., *Rome, a City and Its Empire in Perspective: The Impact of the Roman World through Fergus Millar's Research*, 85–108. Leiden, 2012.
Fiorentini, M. *Fiumi e mari nell'esperienza giuridica romana*. Milan, 2003.
Fournier, J. "L'apport de l'oeuvre de Cicéron à la connaissance du système judiciaire provincial au 1er siècle av. J.-C." In N. Barrandon and F. Kirbihiler, eds., *Administrer les provinces de la République romaine*, 181–94. Rennes, 2010.
Frederiksen, M. W. "The Republican Municipal Laws: Errors and Drafts." *JRS* 55 (1965): 183–98.
Glick, T. F. *Irrigation and Society in Medieval Valencia*. Cambridge, 1970.
Horden, P., and N. Purcell. *The Corrupting Sea: A Study of Mediterranean History*. Oxford, 2000.
Humfress, C. "Law's Empire: Roman Universalism and Legal Practice." In P. J. du Plessis, ed., *New Frontiers: Law and Society in the Roman World*, 73–101. Edinburgh, 2013.
Kaser, M. *Das römische Privatrecht*. 2nd ed. 2 vols. Munich, 1971.
Kaser, M., and K. Hackl. *Das römische Zivilprozessrecht*. 2nd ed. Munich, 1996.
Kehoe, D. P. *The Economics of Agriculture on Roman Imperial Estates in North Africa*. Göttingen, 1988.
Kehoe, D. P. *Law and the Rural Economy in the Roman Empire*. Ann Arbor, 2007.
Keppie, L. *Colonisation and Veteran Settlement in Italy, 47–14 B.C.* London, 1983.
Lenel, O. *Palingenesia Iuris Civilis*. 2 vols. Leipzig, 1889. Reprint, Rome, 2000.
Levy, E., and E. Rabel. *Index Interpolationum*. 4 vols. Weimar, 1929–35.
Longo, G. "Sull'uso delle acque pubbliche in diritto romano." In *Richerche romanistiche, 149–77. Milan,* 1966. Originally published in E. Albertario, ed., *Studia in memoria di Umberto Ratti* (Milan, 1934), 51–96.
Mackie, N. *Local Administration in Roman Spain, A.D. 14–212*. Oxford, 1983.
Maganzani, L. "Juridiction romaine et autonomie locale dans les provinces au dernier siècle de la République." *RD* 85 (2007): 353–73.
Maganzani, L. "Le comunità di irrigazione nel mondo romano: Appunti sulla documentazione epigrafica, giuridica, letteraria." In G. Purpura, ed., *Revisione ed integrazione dei Fontes Iuris romani Anteiustiniani (FIRA), studi preparatori, vol. 1, Leges*, 103–19. Turin, 2012.
Maganzani, L. "Lex rivi Hiberiensis." In In G. Purpura, ed., *Revisione ed integrazione dei Fontes Iuris romani Anteiustiniani (FIRA), studi preparatori, vol. 1, Leges*, 171–85. Turin, 2012.
Millar, F. *The Emperor in the Roman World (31 BC–AD 337)*. Ithaca, 1977.
Nörr, D. "Prozessuales (und mehr) in der *lex rivi Hiberiensis*." *ZRG* 125 (2008): 108–88.
Purcell, N. "Rome and the Management of Water: Environment, Culture, and Power." In

G. Shipley and J. Salmon, eds., *Human Landscapes in Classical Antiquity: Environment and Culture*, 180–212. London, 1996.
Purpura, G., ed. *Revisione ed integrazione dei Fontes Iuris romani Anteiustiniani (FIRA), studi preparatori*. 2 vols. Turin, 2012.
Richardson, J. S. *The Romans in Spain*. Oxford, 1996.
Richardson, J. S. "The *Tabula Contrebiensis*: Roman Law in Spain in the Early First Century B.C.." Part 1. *JRS* 73 (1983): 33–41.
Riera, S., et al. "Variabilité climatique, occupation du sol et paysage en Espagne de l'Âge du fer à l'époque médiévale: intégration des donnés paléoenvironnementales et de l'archéologie du paysage." In E. Herman, ed., *Société et climats dans l'empire romain: Pour une perspective historique et systémique de la gestion des ressources en eau dans l'empire romain*, 251–80. Naples, 2009.
Saliou, C. *Les lois des bâtiments: Voisinage et habitat urbain dans l'empire romain; Recherches sur les rapports entre le droit et la construction privée du siècle d'Auguste au siècle de Justinien*. Beirut: Institut français d'archéologie du Proche-Orient, 1994.
Schulz, F. *History of Roman Legal Science*. Oxford, 1946.
Shaw, B. D. "Lamasba: An Ancient Irrigation Community." *AntAfr* 18 (1982): 61–103.
Shaw, B. D. "Water and Society in the Ancient Maghrib: Technology, Property, and Development." *AntAfr* 20 (1984): 121–73.
Solazzi, S. "Usus proprius." *SDHI* 7 (1941): 373–420.
Tarpin, M. *Vici et Pagi dans l'occident romain*. Rome: École française de Rome, 2002.
Terrenato, N. "The Romanization of Italy: Global Acculturation or Cultural Bricolage?" In C. Forcey et al., eds., *TRAC 97: Proceedings of the Seventh Annual Theoretical Roman Archaeology Conference*, 20–27. Oxford, 1998.
Tuori, K. "Legal Pluralism and the Roman Empires." In J. W. Cairns and P. J. du Plessis, eds., *Beyond Dogmatics: Law and Society in the Roman World*, 39–52. Edinburgh, 2007.
Williams, J. H. C. "Roman Intentions and Romanization: Republican Northern Italy." In S. Keay and N. Terrenato, eds., *Italy and the West: Comparative Issues in Romanization*, 91–101. Oxford, 2001.
Woolf, G. "The Formation of Roman Provincial Cultures." In J. Metzler, ed., *Integration in the Early Roman West: The Role of Culture and Ideology*. Luxembourg, 1997.
Zoz, M. G. *Riflessioni in tema di res publicae*. Turin, 1999.

CHAPTER 5

Justice in Aelian's *Miscellaneous History*

Lauren Caldwell

This essay considers how imperial Romans thought about nature and justice, with special attention to Aelian, a writer who made contributions to intellectual life in the Severan Age with the production of two large-scale texts, *On Animals* and *Miscellaneous History*. These texts are multibook collections that offer hundreds of quasi-historical and informational anecdotes about the natural world, the human world, and interactions between the two.[1] Despite the lack of structure in these "miscellaneous" texts, order emerges there as an issue of concern to Aelian, and this essay explores this seemingly paradoxical aspect of his work.[2] Aelian's interest in order, I will argue, is reflected in his anecdotal depictions of the natural and human worlds, especially when these worlds are shown to act reciprocally in a way that promotes justice, balance, and tranquility.

Aelian's project is part of a long tradition of Greco-Roman literary works—beginning with Hesiod's *Works and Days* in the seventh century BC—that represent the natural world as somehow reinforcing morality in the human realm. Educated readers may have noticed ways in which Aelian's understanding of nature and order also aligned with accounts of Stoic beliefs found in Cicero and Diogenes Laertius, although Aelian asserts, at more than one point in his work, that he is not embarking on a philosophical project.[3] In their interest in morality and proper conduct, Aelian's anecdotes may be placed alongside other stories and sayings concerning ethical virtues that circulated widely in imperial

1. For what is known of Aelian's life and writings, see Kindstrand, "Claudius Aelianus und sein Werk" (1998).

2. For discussion of whether miscellanies can be defined as their own genre, see Vardi, "Genre, Conventions, and Cultural Programme" (2004); König and Whitmarsh, "Ordering Knowledge" (2007).

3. For these assertions, see Aelian, *HA* 5.1, 6.60. Smith, *Man and Animal in Severan Rome* (2014) 100–120, identifies a variety of philosophical influences on Aelian's work, including Stoicism. On the Severan jurists and Stoic thought, see Honoré, "Ulpian, Natural Law, and Stoic Influence" (2010). See also García Valdés, "Ciencia y moral" (2003) 13–19, 25–39.

society in a range of forms, both oral and written. The written forms of these stories included the genres of fables, *gnomai*, proverbs, and anecdotal *exempla* along the lines of those found in both the *Miscellaneous History* and *On Animals*. Such *exempla* were a traditional Roman form for conveying ethical messages to educated audiences and served as an entertaining alternative to formal philosophical writings.[4] As Teresa Morgan has shown, when such moralizing texts take up the issue of justice (δίκη or *iustitia*), they generally consider it as it has to do (1) with the gods, (2) with the law, or (3) with political or social harmony.[5] Aelian is engaged particularly with the third range of meaning and to some extent with the second.

Aelian treats nature's authority in human affairs also within the context of political tensions and difficulties during his lifetime. Recent political events were uppermost in Aelian's mind, as is suggested by his contemporary Philostratus, whose *Lives of the Sophists* records in 222 CE that Aelian wrote an "indictment of 'Gynnis,'" criticizing the tyranny of the emperor Elagabalus after his death.[6] One task in examining the anecdotes in *On Animals* and *Miscellaneous History*, then, is to ask to what extent they contain a politicizing message that might be linked with contemporary concerns. Concentrating on this aspect of Aelian's project helps us better understand the intellectual atmosphere of the Severan Age, when the great jurists Ulpian, Papinian, and Paul worked at Rome in the service of the emperor.[7] Justice, of course, was an ideal that was central to juristic thinking and to the development of Roman law, and questions about the extent to which the institution of the law could be an effective means of achieving justice were relevant not only to experts but also to the lives of ordinary citizens. Aelian pursued his research at Rome, but he explicitly disavowed any desire to pursue "power and reputation" at the imperial court and asserted the independence of his intellectual project.[8]

In this essay's examination of how Aelian envisions the relationship between nature, human beings, and justice, I focus primarily on four consecutive anecdotes in book 1 of the *Miscellaneous History*. In these anecdotes, Aelian takes an interest in the relationship between the flourishing of agriculture and the use of authority or power by humans. The sequence of anecdotes begins by offer-

4. Morgan, *Popular Morality* (2007) 6–8, 122–59.

5. Morgan, *Popular Morality* (2007) 109–11.

6. *VS* 2.31: καὶ ὅς "ἐκπεπόνηταί μοι" ἔφη "κατηγορία τοῦ Γύννιδος, καλῶ γὰρ οὕτω τὸν ἄρτι καθῃρημένον τύραννον, ἐπειδὴ ἀσελγείᾳ πάσῃ τὰ Ῥωμαίων ᾔσχυνε." (And he said, "I have finished off an accusation of the 'Gynnis,' for this is what I call the recently overthrown tyrant, since he dishonored the Romans with every manner of licentiousness.")

7. On the benefits of placing the writings of the jurists in the wider historical context of the third-century empire, see Schiavone, *The Invention of Law in the West* (2012).

8. Aelian, *HA* epil.; Whitmarsh, "Prose Literature and the Severan Dynasty" (2007) 47–49.

ing what appears to be an unproblematic message that the natural and human worlds reinforce each other harmoniously, but it ends on a note of some skepticism about how humans are capable of invoking nature in a more self-serving way to justify their own use of power. In the final anecdote in the sequence, he takes up an issue debated by the Roman jurists: the extent to which fathers should be permitted to exercise power over their children. Paternal power was a legal right that was acknowledged by the jurists as a cultural choice, not as something dictated by nature—although, as Aelian shows, a father could be tempted to justify his power by characterizing his actions as natural.[9]

With the contention that the four anecdotes in book 1 of the *Miscellaneous History* form a sequence that conveys a coherent message about nature, law, and justice, I follow a line of inquiry in recent scholarship that finds patterns and meanings, not simply haphazard arrangement, in imperial compilations of texts such as miscellanies.[10] With their wide range of topics, miscellaneous texts such as *On Animals* and *Miscellaneous History* could be selectively consulted by imperial readers for individual stories or pieces of information, but they could also be read straight through, with the reader detecting thematic links between consecutive passages.[11]

Good Rulers and Natural Justice

Before beginning the analysis of the *Miscellaneous History*, it is worth considering two examples of Aelian's thinking about kingship and justice, the first from *On Animals* and the second from one of Aelian's fictional literary letters from farmers. Lying behind Aelian's use of nature to send a moral message is the question of how, within these short stories, he establishes values—such as justice and moderation—in nature. In *On Animals*, Aelian takes an interest in the third range of meaning of the manifestation of justice described above, the achievement of political or social equilibrium—in this case, within nature.

For example, in *On Animals* 5.11, Aelian describes the order found in bee society. The king, he says, is concerned to regulate the hive, while the bee subjects are moderate, despising luxury and softness.

> Μέλει τῷ βασιλεῖ τῶν μελιττῶν κεκοσμῆσθαι τὸ σμῆνος τὸν τρόπον τοῦτον. τὰς μὲν προστάττει ὑδροφορεῖν, τὰς δὲ ἔνδον κηρία

9. Gaius, *Inst.* 1.55.
10. König and Whitmarsh, "Ordering Knowledge" (2007).
11. Morgan, "The Miscellany and Plutarch" (2011) 69–70.

διαπλάττειν, τὴν γε μὴν τρίτην μοῖραν ἐπὶ τὴν νομὴν προϊέναι. . . . ἕως μὲν οὖν περίεστιν ὁ βασιλεύς, εὐθενεῖται τὸ σμῆνος, καὶ ἀταξία πᾶσα ἠφανίσθη. . . . ἔστι δὲ καὶ σωφροσύνη ἀκροτάτη. χλιδὴν γοῦν καὶ θρύψιν μεμίσηκε. καὶ τὸ μαρτύριον, τὸν χρισάμενον μύρῳ διώκει τε καὶ ἐλαύνει ὡς πολέμιον ἀνήκεστα δράσαντα. οἶδε δὲ καὶ τὸν ἐλθόντα ἐξ ἀκολάστου ὁμιλίας, καὶ διώκει καὶ ἐκεῖνον οἷα δήπου ἔχθιστον.[12]

Aelian is explicit here in defining the moderate conduct that is appropriate for the bee king and his subjects: the king knows how to apportion a single essential task to individual groups, who work for the benefit of the community, and Aelian draws attention to the order in the community that results from this effort. By focusing on the ability of the bee monarch to rule moderately, with disdain for excess, which leads the monarch to drive away any "perfumed" man he encounters, Aelian is also able both to present the natural world as furnishing an example for good relations in the Greco-Roman human world and, notably, to present the political convention of kingship as part of the natural order. In the same text, he acknowledges, however, that humans often fail to live up to the ideals exemplified by nature. In book 1 of *On Animals*, the reader has already learned from Aelian that, in his view, the "benevolent" conduct of bee kings contrasts with that of the Persian kings Cyrus the Great and Darius, who achieved greatness in building their palaces and gardens only by inflicting harm on many people.[13]

Aelian was not the first Greco-Roman author to employ bees as an example of an orderly society: for Hesiod, Aristophanes, Aristotle, Plato, Xenophon, and Vergil, bees provided an ideal model.[14] The hive was an effective image for moralizing authors to invoke, as it allowed the reader to envision a small-scale, ordered, productive community where members work toward a common goal.[15] The behavior of bees was a topic of interest to other Severan thinkers, too, in-

12. Aelian, *NA* 5.11, my trans., following Scholfield, *On Animals* (1958): "It is the concern of the King Bee that his hive should be regulated in the following manner. To some bees he assigns the bringing of water, to others the fashioning of honeycombs within the hive, while a third lot must go abroad to gather food. . . . Now so long as the King survives, the swarm flourishes and all disorder is suppressed. . . . The bee is in the highest degree moderate; it loathes luxury and soft living. Witness the fact that it pursues and drives away a man who has perfumed himself, as if he were some enemy who has perpetrated actions past all remedy."

13. Aelian, *NA* 1.59.

14. Hes. *Op.* 303–6; Aristoph. *Wasps* 1102–21; Plat. *Rep.* 552c–3; Verg. *Aen.* 1.430–36. In the Cyropaideia, Xenophon has Artabazus link Cyrus with the king bee, making the point that both are born to rule. See van Overmeire, "The Perfect King Bee" (2011).

15. Allen, "Burning *The Fable of the Bees*" (2004) 74: "The principal attraction of the beehive in the history of Western political thinking has been precisely its utility as a way of imagining society: compact and surveyable, the hive serves as an exemplar for the integration of parts into a whole."

cluding Aelian's contemporary, the jurist Ulpian. In legal texts, though, bees appear more as rebellious and unpredictable than as calm and obedient creatures, and they furnish little in the way of a model for just or moderate governance in the human world. In fact, legal debate centered on whether bees should be considered domesticated animals or wild, given their tendency to fly away in swarms from their owner's property.[16] Aelian's observations are the result of the way he has formulated his project. Observations about the virtuous behavior of bees are in keeping with the larger aim of *On Animals*, which, as Aelian states in his prologue, is to demonstrate that animals, by nature, share various human qualities, including justice.[17]

In one of his few surviving fictional letters, *Letters of Farmers* 20, Aelian explores the relationship between nature and human conduct in a way that picks up on the comment in *On Animals* about the contrast between the benevolent conduct of bee kings and that of Cyrus the Great and Darius. The focus of the letter is not on kings and governance but on interactions between a farmer and the agricultural world, as the character of Phaedrias, working as a farmer in the Attic countryside, defends the wisdom of farming. In this scheme, the earth, under the eyes of the gods, sees to the growth of all that is good and beautiful, and farmers, through their close contact with the earth, are in the best position to benefit from it.

> φύεται μὲν ἐν τοῖς ἀγροῖς καλὰ πάντα, κεκόσμηταί τε ἡ γῆ τούτοις καὶ τρέφει πάντας. . . . φύεται δὲ καὶ δικαιοσύνη καὶ σωφροσύνη καὶ ταῦτα ἐν τοῖς ἀγροῖς, δένδρων τὰ κάλλιστα, καρπῶν τὰ χρησιμώτατα, μὴ τοίνυν γεωργῶν καταφρόνει· ἔστι γάρ τις καὶ ἐνταῦθα σοφία· γλώττῃ μὲν οὐ πεποικιλμένη οὐδὲ καλλωπιζομένη λόγων δυνάμει, σιγῶσα δὲ εὖ μάλα καὶ δι' αὐτοῦ τοῦ βίου τὴν ἀρετὴν ὁμολογοῦσα.[18]

The verb φύεται (grow) opens the letter and is repeated when Aelian shifts from the discussion of physical produce to the mention of abstract qualities. The letter serves to make another point about nature's moral authority that is not

16. Ulpian, *D.* 9.2.27.11, 9.2.49 pr., 10.2.8.1. See Frier, "Bees and Lawyers" (1982); Frier, "Why Did the Jurists Change Roman Law?" (1994).

17. Aelian, *HA* prooim. As Aelian illustrates throughout *On Animals*, the fact that animals can have a share in these qualities means that, even though they lack the capacity for reason, they are comparable to humans.

18. Aelian, *Letters of Farmers* 20: "All beautiful things grow in the country; the earth is adorned by them and nourishes everything. . . . And justice and moderation, these also, grow in the country, the most beautiful of trees, the most profitable of fruits. So do not be disdainful of farmers; for there is also a kind of wisdom in them, one not adorned by speech or made pretty by the art of rhetoric, but conspicuous by its silence and acknowledging excellence through its life alone."

stated explicitly in the description of bees: just human behavior is in harmony with flourishing in nature and can serve to promote it.

Letters of Farmers 20 makes explicit that virtues, including δικαιοσύνη (justice) and σωφροσύνη (moderation), grow in nature and must be encouraged and assisted by the hands of the farmer, whose labor promotes their flourishing. The farmer also emerges as a figure who embodies justice and moderation and is simultaneously "silent," much like the bees in *On Animals*, whose actions demonstrate the virtue of their conduct. Although the farmer cannot make a crafted speech, Aelian notes, the farmer's cultivation of a place where all that is beautiful grows is a testament to his virtue. Unlike the bee king, of course, the farmer is not a monarch ruling over subjects. His promotion of justice and moderation is undertaken differently because he is not a figure of authority at the top of a hierarchy: he performs the labor himself, instead of assigning it to subjects.[19] Nevertheless, the farmer participates in the same world of ethical standards presented in *On Animals*, as he promotes the ideals of justice and moderation. We might compare Aelian's depiction of the farmer and his work to that found in Hesiod's *Works and Days*, in which, as Laura Slatkin has noted, nature is "represented by characteristics and processes of 'the earth'—through which Hesiod figures questions of morality and social order."[20] To sum up, then, in Aelian's *Letters of Farmers* 20, natural processes produce growth; this growth includes justice and other virtues; and the farmer's work, by enhancing the physical produce of the land, augments and strengthens virtues.

On Animals and *Letters of Farmers* 20 help us begin to answer the question of how Aelian envisions such stories about justice as useful and valuable for his readers. As we will see, Aelian continues to emphasize that nature gives "gifts" to humans and to animals, which they, in turn, are responsible for using appropriately. Justice, for example, is a product of nature in Aelian's stories, but humans or animals may use it and its gifts well or badly. These stories form a picture of nature's moral authority, and that picture is enhanced by the four anecdotes on kingship found in book 1 of the *Miscellaneous History.*

Justice in *Miscellaneous History* 1.31–34

In *Miscellaneous History* 1.31–34, Aelian develops the theme of justice to show that proper human conduct, particularly on the part of a ruler, is in harmony

19. Costa, *Greek Fictional Letters* (2001) 128.
20. Slatkin, "Measuring Authority, Authoritative Measures" (2004).

with nature. Rather than establishing justice and moderation in nature by providing an illustration from the animal world, or by idealizing an unnamed farmer, however, Aelian here appeals to the reader's historical imagination, focusing on the exemplary conduct of the Persian king Artaxerxes. Stories about a king from the distant past allow Aelian to present an ideal physical landscape in which nature appears to promote harmonious human relations. Through the use of a historical place and time at a far remove from Aelian's own day, these short narratives work to frame the relationship between the present and the past and to create a profile of the ruler who is just, while treating the issue of monarchy obliquely, in a way that would have suited Aelian's concerns in the aftermath of Elagabalus' reign. The first three anecdotes, 1.31–33, show that the natural landscape enables a king and his subjects to establish a just relationship.[21] In turn, this imagery of careful productivity and cultivation is used to suggest, particularly in 1.33 and 1.34, that the king is like a good farmer or gardener, encouraging the growth of his state in the proper places and pruning overgrowth that could prove harmful, although always doing so in a way that remains moderate and just. In contrast, as shown in an anecdote in *Miscellaneous History* 2 examined below, the ruler who does not promote justice fails in his relationship to humans and to the natural landscape.

The surviving text of the *Miscellaneous History* lacks a prologue or epilogue, in which Aelian might have made a programmatic statement to help frame these anecdotes about justice and kingship. The prologue to *On Animals* provides some orientation for the reader. While making clear that his interest is in examining the human capacities for wisdom, justice, and care, Aelian also mentions that one of man's "gifts of nature" is his ability to "protect himself against plots."

> ἄνθρωπον μὲν εἶναι σοφὸν καὶ δίκαιον καὶ τῶν οἰκείων παίδων προμηθέστατον, καὶ τῶν γειναμένων ποιεῖσθαι τὴν προσήκουσαν φροντίδα, καὶ τροφὴν ἑαυτῷ μαστεύειν καὶ ἐπιβουλὰς φυλάττεσθαι καὶ τὰ λοιπὰ ὅσα αὐτῷ σύνεστι δῶρα φύσεως, παράδοξον ἴσως οὐδέν.[22]

Aelian does not elaborate on what he identifies as man's ability to protect himself from plots, but his labeling of this ability as a gift of nature demonstrates Aelian's interest in the notion of nature as giving gifts to humans. This theme

21. For discussion of the links between agriculture and virtue in Xenophon, Varro, and Vergil, see Kronenberg, *Allegories of Farming from Greece and Rome* (2009).

22. Aelian, *NA* prooim, trans. Scholfield, *On Animals* (1958): "There is perhaps nothing extraordinary in the fact that man is wise and just, takes great care to provide for his own children, shows due consideration for his parents, seeks sustenance for himself, protects himself against plots, and possesses all the other gifts of nature that are his."

runs through *Miscellaneous History* 1.31–34, which concern the Persian king Artaxerxes, and also appears in an anecdote in book 2, about the Persian king Xerxes. In these short vignettes, the natural landscape and its products serve as the means by which the king and his subjects sustain an orderly and just relationship. In turn, this imagery is used to suggest a king who is a good farmer or gardener; in contrast, the ruler who does not promote justice fails in his relationship to the natural landscape.

More specifically, Aelian connects the four anecdotes about Artaxerxes to make a claim that social balance and political stability are achieved through reciprocal gift giving between ruler and subject, which, in turn, promotes growth and flourishing, both in the natural world and in the civic setting. In his exposition of the relationship between nature, justice, and power, Aelian aligns with those authors from classical antiquity to the eighteenth century who were interested not only in the theme of human labor in the agricultural world but also in its implications, including how this labor could serve the purpose of ensuring political order and how political power rests on the labor of subjects.[23]

In the first story, *Miscellaneous History* 1.31, Aelian relates how Persian *nomos*—custom or law—calls for a king who is traveling to receive offerings of agricultural produce from his subjects.

> νόμος οὗτος Περσικὸς ἐν τοῖς μάλιστα ὑπ' αὐτῶν φυλαττόμενος. ὅταν εἰς Πέρσας ἐλαύνῃ βασιλεύς, πάντες αὐτῷ Πέρσαι κατὰ τὴν ἑαυτοῦ δύναμιν ἕκαστός <τι> προσκομίζει. ἅτε δὲ ὄντες ἐν γεωργίᾳ καὶ περὶ γῆν πονούμενοι καὶ αὐτουργοὶ πεφυκότες οὐδὲν τῶν ὑβρισμένων οὐδὲ τῶν ἄγαν πολυτελῶν προσφέρουσιν, ἀλλ' ἢ βοῦς ἢ ὄϊς, οἱ δὲ σῖτον, καὶ οἶνον ἄλλοι. παρεξιόντι δ'αὐτῷ καὶ παρελαύνοντι ταῦτα ὑπὸ ἑκάστου πρόκειται καὶ ὀνομάζεται δῶρα καὶ δοκεῖ τούτῳ. οἱ δὲ ἔτι τούτων ἐνδεέστεροι τὸν βίον καὶ γάλα καὶ φοίνικας αὐτῷ καὶ τυρὸν προσφέρουσι καὶ τρωκτὰ ὡραῖα καὶ τὰς ἄλλας ἀπαρχὰς τῶν ἐπιχωρίων.[24]

23. For the argument that agricultural writers such as Varro satirized the Greco-Roman tradition of using the natural landscape to support ideologies, see Kronenberg, *Allegories of Farming from Greece and Rome* (2009) 1–3. Allen, "Burning *The Fable of the Bees*" (2004), discusses how Bernard Mandeville's *Fable of the Bees*, an eighteenth-century text, brings out the problematic nature of labor as necessary for reinforcing political order.

24. Aelian, *VH* 1.31, trans. Wilson, *Historical Miscellany* (1997): "A custom most carefully maintained by the Persians, when the king drives to Persepolis, is that each and every one of them, according to his means, brings an offering. Since they are engaged in farming and toil on the land, living by what they produce, they bring no pretentious or unduly expensive gifts, but rather oxen, sheep, or corn, or in other instances wine. As the king passes and drives on his way, these objects are laid out by each man, and are termed gifts; the king treats them as such. Men who are even poorer than these farmers bring him milk and dates and cheese, with ripe fruit and other first fruits of local produce."

In Aelian's account, the offerings are gifts, not tribute produced under compulsion. They are the product of cultivation, but they are simple and unadorned; they are not luxury products, nor are they described as ingredients for an elaborate royal meal. In other words, Aelian does not use this anecdote to criticize the Persian court for extravagance, nor does he echo his comment, noted above, that the harshness of Persian kingship compares unfavorably to the moderation of monarchy in bee society. As it emerges from the four tales, the behavior of this ruler is mild and balanced, as a king bee. His actions tend to occur in a landscape of cultivation and abundance, and his virtues are demonstrated in conjunction with the actions of farmers in the countryside who are his subjects. This use of the Persians for both positive and negative examples suggests that Aelian takes a mixed view of the Persians. As for kingship, Aelian's positive take on gift giving is different from that found in collections of proverbs from the early Roman Empire. In these examples, gifts are one thing that can corrupt the justice of kings.[25] In presenting agricultural produce as a form of gift, Aelian's perspective is similar to that of Hesiod in the *Works and Days*, in which the productivity of the land is a gift granted to the just.[26]

Aelian's choice to portray a Persian king in a favorable light in this context defies reader expectation to some extent, since the theme of food in connection with a Persian king would seem to invite disapproval, at least if other imperial authors' depictions are any guide. For example, Athenaeus, Aelian's contemporary, uses this trope in his *Deipnosophistae*, where he cites Xenophon's *Agesilaus* on the luxury of Persian kings: the king's servants are made to scour the land in search of pleasing drinks, and a large kitchen staff prepares sumptuous meals.[27] In another anecdote in the *Miscellaneous History*, Aelian too offers a critique of Persian customs, recounting the story of how a deposed pharaoh fell ill and died after exchanging his native Egyptian moderation for the luxury and rich diet of Persia.[28] This example falls in with other anecdotes appearing in the *Miscellaneous History* that are disdainful of luxury, in which the usual suspects—women, Sybarites, and tyrants—are held up as negative examples.

Why does Aelian avoid associations with luxury and indulgence in his story

25. Morgan, *Popular Morality* (2007) 40, cites proverbs about justice and kingship found in the collections of Zenobius and Ps.-Diogenianus.

26. Slatkin, "Measuring Authority, Authoritative Measures" (2004).

27. Athenaeus, *Deip.* 4.144b.

28. Aelian, *VH* 5.1: Ταχὼς ὁ Αἰγύπτιος ἕως μὲν ἐχρῆτο τῇ ἐπιχωρίῳ διαίτῃ καὶ εὐτελῶς διεβίω, ὑγιεινότατα ἀνθρώπων διῆγεν· ἐπει δὲ εἰς Πέρσας ἀφίκετο καὶ εἰς τὴν ἐκείνων τρυφὴν ἐξέπεσε, τὸ ἄηθες τῶν σιτίων οὐκ ἐνεγκών, ὑπὸ δυσεντερίας τὸν βίον κατέστρεψε, τῆς τρυφῆς ἀλλαξάμενος θάνατον. (The Egyptian Tachos enjoyed the best of health as long as he adhered to the customs of his country and lived modestly. But when he moved to Persia and lapsed into its luxurious habits, he could not tolerate the unaccustomed diet and died of dysentery, exchanging luxury for death.)

of the Persian king who receives food offerings from his subjects? His text does not offer a straightforward conclusion here, but the subsequent stories, including *Miscellaneous History* 1.32, make it easier to analyze 1.31. In 1.32, it becomes more clear that Aelian's interest is in using the Persian king to illustrate moderation and reciprocity, rather than coercive power, which appears to be the focus in Athenaeus' *Deipnosophistae*. In 1.32, Aelian introduces another example of the Persian custom of agricultural gift giving, whose story he goes on to report in indirect discourse. (This suggests, perhaps, that we are dealing with a change of source in Aelian's text.) In this story, the Persian Sinaetes is away from his farmstead and is said to be "unprepared" when he meets Artaxerxes. He is described as afraid because of the custom,[29] by which Aelian appears to be referring to the previously mentioned tradition of presenting the traveling king with a gift. Fortunately, because the Cyrus River is nearby, Sinaetes is able to draw water to present to Artaxerxes, along with a promise of more worthy gifts later. The king accepts the humble gift and later dispatches from the staging post a golden cup and money for Sinaetes, along with a speech of praise for his gift of honor and reverence.

Here, a product of the natural world is used properly by a subject of the king, and the king responds favorably, in a show of reciprocity. The king responds to the humble gift, however, with a much more lavish and nonnatural gift than what his subject Sinaetes has provided. The differing character of the two gifts brings out that harmony and order—but also hierarchy—is sustained through this exchange, although the king does not act in a way that is harsh. The king's power, it could be said, is more effective because it is subtle: instead of being forced into submission to the king, Sinaetes is rewarded and praised by him, making it more likely that he will accept his authority. Juxtaposing 1.32 with a similar version of the story found in Plutarch's *Life of Artaxerxes* shows that Aelian places special emphasis on the combination of nature, gifts, and political authority in the *Miscellaneous History*. In Plutarch's *Life of Artaxerxes*, the story is presented briefly, as an unnamed person, caught short, runs to a river, cups water in his hands, and offers it to Artaxerxes. Aelian's version is distinctive in connecting Artaxerxes with the practice of a Persian custom that involves gifts freely given and returned between persons of unequal status—the king and his subject.

Adding to the picture, *Miscellaneous History* 1.33, the third anecdote, again concerns the theme of the Persian king who is on the road and encounters a gift-giving subject, but it expands the scope of this theme to consider growth

29. Aelian, *VH* 1.32.

from the agricultural world as facilitating the interaction between subject and king. This time, the subject of the king, Omises, produces a remarkable gift for Artaxerxes, a giant pomegranate supported on a winnowing fan. The story concludes by pointing up its moral, which appears to be Aelian's own creation.

> ῥοιὰν ἐπὶ λίκνου μεγίστην Ὠμίσης Ἀρταξέρξῃ τῷ βασιλεῖ ἐλαύνοντι τὴν Περσίδα προσεκόμισε. τὸ μέγεθος οὖν αὐτῆς ὑπερεκπλαγεὶς ὁ βασιλεὺς "ἐκ ποίου παραδείσου" φησὶ "λαβὼν φέρεις μοι τὸ δῶρον τοῦτο;" τοῦ δὲ εἰπόντος ὅτι οἴκοθεν καὶ ἐκ τῆς αὐτοῦ γεωργίας, ὑπερήσθη καὶ δῶρα μὲν αὐτῷ βασιλικὰ ἔπεμψε καὶ ἐπεῖπε "νὴ τὸν Μίθραν, ἀνὴρ οὗτος ἐκ τῆς ἐπιμελείας ταύτης δυνήσεται καὶ πόλιν κατά γε τὴν ἐμὴν κρίσιν ἐκ μικρᾶς μεγάλην ποιῆσαι." ἔοικε δὲ ὁ λόγος ὁμολογεῖν οὗτος ὅτι πάντα ἐκ τῆς ἐπιμελείας καὶ τῆς διαρκοῦς φροντίδος καὶ τῆς σπουδῆς τῆς ἀνελλιποῦς καὶ τῶν κατὰ φύσιν δύναιτο ἂν κρείττονα γενέσθαι.[30]

Here, Artaxerxes has assumed that the bountiful agricultural produce is from a royal estate, and he is pleased to see his subjects capable of growing such remarkable fruit on their own. The theme of this story resonates with that of Aelian's letter on farming, where the good farmer encourages the right kind of growth. However, in *Miscellaneous History* 1.33, Artaxerxes extends this notion of the "right kind of growth" into the political sphere, asserting that Omises has the potential to be a successful civic leader, given his success growing pomegranates. What holds true in farming holds true for the family and the city; nature is used to support a particular model of moral and political authority. As in *Miscellaneous History* 1.32, the humble gift of the ruled and the extravagant gift of the ruler are set against each other. One message that emerges from this vignette is that an imbalance of power is always present in a relationship between the ruler and the ruled, even in a setting of harmony and balance. The farmer who grows the large pomegranate expends great effort to maintain his harmonious relationship with the king.

By drawing together the agricultural and the civic worlds in this anecdote, Aelian sends a two-part moral message about the polity as a whole and its in-

30. Aelian, *VH* 1.33, trans. Wilson, *Historical Miscellany* (1997): "As king Artaxerxes was traveling through Persia, Omises brought him a very large pomegranate on a winnowing fan. The size of it caused the king great amazement, and he asked, 'From what estate do you come with this offering?' When the other replied, 'From my home, from my own farm,' he was quite delighted and sent the man royal gifts, adding: 'By Mithras, with care such as he displays, this man will even be capable, as far as I can judge, of making a small city into a great one.' This remark seems to acknowledge that with care, continuous thought, and relentless enthusiasm, anything may be improved beyond its natural state."

habitants. First, each person has something to contribute to the growth and flourishing of the city, according to his own station. Second, a good ruler not only observes a custom such as gift giving but is also like the good farmer or gardener: he encourages growth in the right places, by picking out a prime citizen who can be promoted and do his part for the community. The imagery of careful selection and pruning as encouraging controlled growth is as relevant in the civic sphere as in the agricultural one. Notably, in this model, individuals make a contribution to the overall well-being of the city. Ultimately, despite the effort that Omises must expend to impress the king, Artaxerxes comes across as moderate, not as one who will exploit his power over the weak. Relations between Artaxerxes and Omises are not marked by hostility or fear.

This emphasis in Aelian on a ruler's use of moderation is brought out by the parallel in Plutarch's *Life of Artaxerxes*. There, too, Omises gives a large pomegranate to Artaxerxes, which prompts the king to swear by Mithras that Omises could make a small city great. But the purposes of the two anecdotes diverge. Plutarch uses the Omises story to illustrate the gentle character of Artaxerxes; by emphasizing that Omises offered only a single pomegranate to the king, Plutarch makes clear that the king made no extraordinary demands. Aelian, however, uses this anecdote, along with his previous two, to define, illustrate, and praise a Persian custom. This explains the presence of care in the king's oath in Aelian, something that is not found in Plutarch.[31] For Plutarch, Omises' care is not a necessary detail for making the point that Artaxerxes was a gracious recipient of gifts.

In these anecdotes, Artaxerxes emerges as a model of ethical behavior, acting in harmony with his subjects, who take part in a flourishing agricultural world. Aelian has complicated this message, however, by showing that the abundance of nature is achieved only by human work—namely, the work of farmers.[32] They provide the king with gifts that are the fruit of their efforts. This theme of the "gift" in *Miscellaneous History* 1.31–33 draws attention to the work that must be expended to bring out nature's full potential and the political stability that follows. Even though Aelian appeals to the reader's imagination by glossing over the labor that is involved in the production and cultivation of agricultural produce, the very theme of the "gift" in each anecdote draws attention to the work that must be expended to bring out nature's full potential and, in turn, to stabilize household and political hierarchy. This is a different message from that Aelian conveyed by *Letters of Farmers* 20, in which the farmer

31. Stamm, *Vergangenheitsbezug in der Zweiten Sophistik* (2003) 121, 130–32.
32. See Allen, "Burning *The Fable of the Bees*" (2007).

is presented as working alone, not as a participant in a hierarchical political structure.

The final anecdote to be considered, *Miscellaneous History* 1.34, suggests a mutually beneficial relationship between proper law giving and nature, and it places justice front and center. In this anecdote, more than the others, the good king appears as a figure who puts law into practice to the benefit of his subjects. This time, the main character in the story is Rhacoces, a member of the Mardian people, who are subject to the Persians. The moral of the story is found in the outcome of Rhacoces' interaction with the king Artaxerxes. The plot, involving a decision about whether a father should put his son to death, is one that Roman imperial readers would have found vaguely familiar from rhetorical exercises.[33] The tale is distinctive in showing justice to be involved with the institution of the law, with local judges and ultimately the king summoned to adjudicate the case that is presented. Aelian uses the encounter to complicate his previous treatment of order as an ideal achieved in the human world by the exchange of gifts grown in nature.

As the story in *Miscellaneous History* 1.34 runs, Rhacoces has six children, and his son Cartomes persistently causes trouble for the others. After attempting unsuccessfully to correct Cartomes' behavior, Rhacoces eventually calls local judges to his house and asks them to execute his son. Considering such a case to fall beyond their capacity, the officials take Cartomes and Rhacoces to the king, Artaxerxes, who asks Rhacoces whether he could endure seeing his son killed. Rhacoces responds with a comparison based on his experience with gardening.

> ἀμφοτέρους δὲ ἐπὶ τὸν βασιλέα τῶν Περσῶν τὸν Ἀρταξέρξην ἤγαγον. τὰ αὐτὰ δὲ λέγοντος τοῦ Μάρδου ὑπολαβὼν ὁ βασιλεὺς ἔφη "εἶτα τολμήσεις τοῖς ὀφθαλμοῖς τοῖς σεαυτοῦ τὸν υἱὸν ἀποθνήσκοντα ὑπομεῖναι;" ὃ δὲ ἔφη "πάντων μάλιστα· ἐπεὶ καὶ ἐν τῷ κήπῳ ὅταν τῶν φυομένων θριδακινῶν τὰς ἐκφύσεις τὰς πικρὰς ἀποκλῶ καὶ ἀφαιρῶ, οὐδὲν ἡ μήτηρ αὐτῶν λυπεῖται, ἀλλὰ θάλλει μᾶλλον καὶ μείζων καὶ γλυκίων γίνεται. οὕτω καὶ ἐγώ, ὦ βασιλεῦ, τὸν βλάπτοντα τὴν ἐμὴν οἰκίαν καὶ τὸν τῶν ἀδελφῶν βίον θεωρῶν ἀπολλύμενον καὶ τῆς κακουργίας τῆς εἰς αὐτοὺς παυόμενον καὶ αὐτὸς αὐξηθήσομαι καὶ τοῖς λοιποῖς τοῖς κατὰ γένος συνέσομαι τὰ αὐτὰ ἐμοὶ εὖ πάσχουσιν." ὧν ἀκούσας Ἀρταξέρξης ἐπῄνεσε μὲν τὸν Ῥακώκην καὶ τῶν βασιλικῶν δικαστῶν ἐποίησεν ἕνα, εἰπὼν πρὸς τοὺς παρόντας ὅτι ὁ περὶ τῶν ἰδίων

33. Stamm, *Vergangenheitsbezug in der Zweiten Sophistik* (2003) 132.

παίδων οὕτω δικαίως ἀποφαινόμενος πάντως καὶ ἐν τοῖς ἀλλοτρίοις ἀκριβὴς ἔσται δικαστὴς καὶ ἀδέκαστος.[34]

At a moment of difficulty in decision making, it is an analogy from nature, rather than a carefully structured legal argument, that helps Rhacoces justify a particular behavior on the part of a father and a ruler. Natural flourishing, though completely external to the human world and to human will, here provides an instructive parallel for a human's good judgment. Justice, in the form of the adverb δικαίως (justly), here makes its first explicit appearance in the four anecdotes in book 1. Artaxerxes praises Rhacoces for giving evidence of justice (or, rather, impartiality)—which, notably, includes a willingness to use force—when it comes to dealing with his children. But Artaxerxes sees as just not only a father's willingness to kill his son but also a father's interest in the flourishing of his household. The good head of household, then, displays the qualities that Aelian praised at the end of *Miscellaneous History* 1.33. Meanwhile, the reader is prompted to consider that the Persian custom of gift giving introduced in *Miscellaneous History* 1.31 is, in fact, concerned with more than food and drink. Notably, the anecdote makes no mention of Rhacoces as offering food and drink to the king. Instead, the moral of 1.33, too, seems to be confirmed, as Rhacoces shows the qualities of fair-mindedness and ability to take action to make his family greater.

These qualities have a potentially darker side that Aelian brings out in this story: the balance or moderation within the family is often maintained only by a father's wielding of force, which can quickly verge on unjust behavior. When presented in agricultural terms, the exercise of authority comes across as the virtuous act of a good farmer, but Rhacoces benefits from the king's gift of wisdom and moderation in deterring Rhacoces from "pruning," which would be the most severe exercise of his paternal power. Thus, in *Miscellaneous History* 1.34, Aelian raises the prospect that the maintenance of household order comes at a cost to its members. It is significant, however, that the story concludes on

34. Aelian, *VH* 1.34, trans. Wilson, *Historical Miscellany* (1997): "They brought both [Cartomes and Rhacoces] before Artaxerxes, the king of Persia. When the Mardian repeated his statement, the king replied: 'Have you really the courage to witness with your own eyes the death of your son?' 'Quite certainly,' said the man, 'because in my garden, when I tear off and throw away the bitter shoots which grow on the lettuces, the mother lettuce shows no grief and flourishes all the more, becoming larger and sweeter. In the same way I too, your majesty,' he said, "seeing the destruction of one who ruins my home and the lives of his brothers, seeing an end to the damage done to them, I myself shall be the gainer, and I shall witness the other members of my family enjoying the same good fortune as myself.' Upon hearing this, Artaxerxes commended Rhacoces and made him one of the royal magistrates, observing to the assembled company that a man who showed himself so fair-minded in the case of his own children would certainly be accurate and incorruptible in his treatment of other people's affairs."

a lighter note, with a confirmation of justice and moderation as Artaxerxes annuls the death sentence of Cartomes, replacing it with a stern warning.[35] If we imagine that the ending of the story is intended to inform or educate the reader about the problem of paternal authority, the message might be that such power is less effective when it is exercised coercively. To improve the flourishing of the household, it is better to make a father's power at least less harsh, if not undetectable to those weaker than he is. Notably, the story leaves open the question of whether Cartomes would have had access to the more lenient punishment without the intervention of Artaxerxes. As a consequence, the reader comes away with an unsettled sense that a father may be able to appeal to nature to justify overly harsh wielding of his power within the household.

Aelian was hardly alone among third-century intellectuals in considering the issue of paternal power and its limits. The issue was raised by the Roman jurists, too, who were concerned about what type of human conduct or human authority was natural or in harmony with nature. Debates among the classical jurists of the first, second, and third centuries CE centered on the traditional authority of the *paterfamilias* over the members of his family and focused on its scope and its limits. In their discussions of aspects of *patria potestas* and in urging moderation in the exercise of the power of life and death over descendants, the jurists in fact acknowledged that there was nothing inevitable or particularly natural about a father's control. For example, the Severan jurists Ulpian and Papinian expressed a desire to restrict the right of a father to kill a daughter who committed adultery, and Ulpian urged a father to bring his son before the prefect of Rome or the provincial governor for a hearing before punishing him with death.[36] Ulpian and Paul note that a father should be constrained from breaking up his child's happy marriage and that the emperor Antoninus Pius, as well as Septimius Severus and Caracalla, took steps to prevent this.[37] Although it may not be possible to detect a direct conversation between Aelian's anecdotes and contemporary legal debate, Aelian is clearly interested in the consequences of unchecked paternal power.

Aelian has ended these four anecdotes, then, by inviting his readers to find moral unity, rather than endless ambiguity, in the individual stories, on two grounds. First, proper gift exchange between king and subject, facilitated by the abundance of nature, can foster harmony beyond the relationship of the

35. Aelian, *VH* 1.34.

36. For the case of adultery, see Ulpian, *D.* 48.5.24 pr., 4, 48.5.2.8; Papinian, *D.* 48.5.23.4. For the case of the father bringing his son before the prefect or governor, see *D.* 48.8.2. For discussion of the power of life and death as treated by the jurists, see Frier and McGinn, *A Casebook on Roman Family Law* (2004) 191–210.

37. *PS.* 5.6.15; cf. 2.19.2; Ulpian, *D.* 24.1.32.19–20.

ruler and the ruled. Second, households of the kingdom operate harmoniously and justly under a father who emulates the example of the king and also takes a lesson from the example of natural processes. Cartomes is unjust in that he inhibits the growth of the family, which is discussed in the same terms as physical growth of plants. In this case, the good father and the just ruler are presented as figures who demonstrate skill in recognizing both what to "prune" when the time is appropriate and how to go about it. The good father and the just ruler also perceive the larger advantages and guidance that nature offers. The father is willing to give up (or "trim") his son for the good of the family (the "garden"), just as the ruler, when acting as impartial but benevolent judge, possesses the ability to know when to trim and when not to, as is dramatically demonstrated in his last-minute sparing of Cartomes' life.

The father who is ready to sacrifice his son for the well-being of the family in *Miscellaneous History* 1.34 also uses the language of agricultural labor in describing his task, and only the king is able to relieve him of this burden. The overall message about political order that emerges from 1.31–34 is similar to the message about household order. In short, the stability that results from hierarchy is good, but it is not without potential costs, including, in 1.34, an uncertainty for weaker parties about whether they will receive a just outcome in a conflict. As for Aelian's treatment of the relationship between man-made law and justice in 1.34, it seems significant that the judges who are summoned by Rhacoces are unable to resolve his conflict with his son. They are not hostile forces, but they do little to improve the situation. In conveying some doubt or skepticism in 1.34 about the law as an effective instrument for achieving justice, Aelian's perspective seems aligned not so much with that of the Roman jurists as with that of proverbs, *gnomai*, and fables—genres from the early empire that appear to express ethical views for a cross section of society.[38]

Injustice and Nature in *Miscellaneous History* 2.14

Stories that depict unjust behavior by kings help to complete the picture created by the anecdotes about Artaxerxes, by using the image of nature, again, to promote a model of enlightened rule. In an anecdote in book 2 of the *Miscellaneous History*, the Persian king Xerxes is presented as failing to interact properly with

38. Morgan, *Popular Morality* (2007) 169, notes that the lack of trust in the law that characterizes proverbs, *gnomai*, and fables gives the impression for the early empire that "the institution of the law, which exists to mediate conflicts, has developed faster than the public belief and confidence in institutions which it needs in order to function well."

the agricultural world, although in a way that differs from the flawed conduct of Rhacoces in 1.34. Instead of misguidedly invoking an analogy from nature in an attempt to rationalize his use of power, Xerxes inappropriately responds to the beauty of the agricultural world, engaging in a form of gift giving that cannot be reciprocal and thus cannot encourage the kind of justice and moderation we have seen in previous depictions.

That the story will be disapproving of Xerxes is clear from its first word, which labels the king a γελοῖος (laughingstock).

> γελοῖος ἐκεῖνος ὁ Ξέρξης ἦν . . . ἐν Λυδίᾳ γοῦν φασιν ἰδὼν φυτὸν εὐμέγεθες πλατάνου, τὴν ἡμέραν ἐκείνην κατέμεινεν οὐδέν τι δεόμενος, καὶ ἐχρήσατο σταθμῷ τῇ ἐρημίᾳ τῇ περὶ τὴν πλάτανον. ἀλλὰ καὶ ἐξῆψεν αὐτῆς κόσμον πολυτελῆ, στρεπτοῖς καὶ ψελίοις τιμῶν τοὺς κλάδους, καὶ μελεδωνὸν αὐτῇ κατέλιπεν, ὥσπερ ἐρωμένῃ φύλακα καὶ φρουρόν. ἐκ δὲ τούτων τί τῷ δένδρῳ καλὸν ἀπήντησεν; ὁ μὲν γὰρ κόσμος ὁ ἐπίκτητος καὶ μηδὲν αὐτῷ προσήκων ἄλλως ἐκρέματο, καὶ συνεμάχετο ἐς ὥραν οὐδέν· ἐπεὶ τοῦ φυτοῦ κάλλος ἐκεῖνό ἐστιν, εὐγενεῖς οἱ κλάδοι καὶ ἡ κόμη πολλὴ καὶ στερεὸν τὸ πρέμνον καὶ αἱ ῥίζαι ἐν βάθει καὶ διασείοντες οἱ ἄνεμοι καὶ ἀμφιλαφὴς ἡ ἐξ αὐτοῦ σκιὰ καὶ ἀναστρέφουσαι αἱ ὧραι καὶ ὕδωρ τὸ μὲν διὰ τῶν ὀχετῶν ἐκτρέφον, τὸ δὲ ἐξ οὐρανοῦ ἐπάρδον· χλαμύδες δὲ αἱ Ξέρξου καὶ χρυσὸς ὁ τοῦ βαρβάρου καὶ τὰ ἄλλα δῶρα οὔτε πρὸς τὴν πλάτανον οὔτε πρὸς ἄλλο δένδρον εὐγενὲς ἦν.[39]

The reader who is familiar with the anecdotes about Artaxerxes in book 1 is primed to notice that even as Xerxes offers gifts to the tree, no gift is given to the king in return. As Aelian makes clear, there is no agricultural abundance encouraged in this interaction, and Xerxes seems to be the opposite of the good farmer from *Letters of Farmers* 20 or the capable farmers subject to Artaxerxes. Moreover, in contrast to the previous scenarios in book 1 of the *Miscellaneous History*, there is no human being in this anecdote who can engage in mutually

39. Aelian, *VH* 2.14, trans. Wilson, *Historical Miscellany* (1997): "The famous king Xerxes was a laughingstock, if it is true that he despised sea and land, the handiwork of Zeus, manufactured for himself novel roads and abnormal sea routes, and yet was the devotee of a plane tree, which he admired. In Lydia, they say, he saw a large specimen of a plane tree, and stopped for that day without any need. He made the wilderness around the tree his camp, and attached to it expensive ornaments, paying homage to the branches with necklaces and bracelets. He left a caretaker for it, like a guard to provide security, as if it were a woman he loved. What benefit accrued to the tree as a result? The ornaments it had acquired, which were quite inappropriate to it, hung on it without serving any purpose and made no contribution to its appearance, since the beauty of a tree consists of fine branches, abundant leaves, a sturdy trunk, deep roots, movement in the wind, shadow spreading all around, change in accordance with the passing of seasons, with irrigation channels to support it and rain water to sustain it."

beneficial gift giving with the king. We recall from earlier anecdotes that responding properly to the natural world is a way that order and harmony in governance can be maintained by a monarch: in 1.32, Sinaetes was rewarded for bringing the king a gift from nature; in 1.33, Omises was recognized as a prime citizen for his good farming; in 1.34, Rhacoces was made magistrate when he showed his wisdom partly by way of an analogy with the world of farming. In *Letters of Farmers* 20, Aelian described justice and moderation as beautiful trees growing in the country. In *Miscellaneous History* 2.14, we might expect an action by Xerxes or by another human being that can prompt the kind of pruning that can result in agricultural or civic growth, but it is not found here.

A shorter version of the story of Xerxes appears in Herodotus' *Histories* as an episode in Xerxes' journey to the Hellespont, and the differences between the two versions suggest that Aelian has shaped the story to convey a message about the relationship between nature and enlightened or unenlightened rule.[40] In Herodotus' account, Xerxes is said to be on the road to Sardis when he sees the plane tree; but the story provides no further elaboration on Xerxes' actions. Aelian, however, chooses to emphasize that Xerxes fails in all of his interactions with nature, including his choice of abnormal routes on land and on sea and his decision to adorn the tree in a way that suggests a basic inability to distinguish between the agricultural and human worlds. Aelian's story concludes with censure of Xerxes for supplying the tree only with unsuitable ornaments that hang pointlessly, providing no enhancement to its appearance or flourishing. With Aelian's description of what sustains a tree's beauty (i.e., proper attention to the health of its branches, leaves, trunk, and roots), the reader sees that Xerxes has been an unsuccessful guardian of the natural environment.

Miscellaneous History 2.14 is not a story of nature's revenge against an unjust or troublemaking ruler, for nature does not retaliate against Xerxes for not promoting its flourishing. Aelian nevertheless makes the point that neither human nor natural flourishing is being maximized in this scenario. Missing from this narrative is the figure of the farmer, whose skill would make up for Xerxes' inadequate sense of what is appropriate. With 2.14, then, we are brought back around to the moral message of 1.31–34, where harmonious interactions between the king and the farmers subject to him are in balance with nature. Ultimately, we are also brought back to the idealization of the farmer's relationship with nature and virtue entirely outside the political world, as depicted in *Letters of Farmers* 20.

40. Hdt. 7.31: ταύτην ἰὼν ὁ Ξέρξης τὴν ὁδὸν εὗρε πλατάνιστον, τὴν κάλλεος εἵνεκα δωρησάμενος κόσμῳ χρυσέῳ. (As Xerxes went on his way [i.e., to Sardis], he found a plane tree, and, on account of its beauty, he presented it with golden decoration.)

Conclusion

While Aelian shows how the interaction between the natural and human worlds can promote the ideal of justice, we have seen that he also complicates this message, particularly in *Miscellaneous History* 1.34, where he makes his clearest statement that within the human world, the definition of what is "natural" can be used to serve the interests of the powerful in a way that disadvantages the weak. The fact that a father is the figure whose deployment of nature is the most problematic in these anecdotes suggests, perhaps, that there was some anxiety among third-century readers about the ability of a father to keep his impulses in check—a concern that occupied the attention of the jurists as well. Moreover, in highlighting the influence of the king Artaxerxes in resolving a crisis in an individual citizen's household, Aelian evokes the figure of the Roman emperor as ultimate judge—a connection that would not have been lost on the third-century reader.

Although sometimes offering an explicit moralizing message, Aelian largely prefers to be indirect, and he left his contemporary reader free to draw conclusions about the relevance of his anecdotes to the ethical concerns of the early empire. For the modern reader, Aelian's works offer a distinctive take on ethics that can help to fill in our picture of third-century intellectual life. The capacity of the anecdotal form to respond to imperial concerns offers a way of understanding Aelian as politically and socially engaged as he imaginatively treats the topic of justice.[41]

Bibliography

Editions

De Natura Animalium. Ed. M. García Valdés, L. A. Llera Fueyo, and L. Rodríguez Noriega Guillén. Berlin, 2006.
The "Digest" of Justinian. Ed. and trans. A. Watson, T. Mommsen, and P. Krueger. Philadelphia, 1985.
Epistulae et Fragmenta. Ed. D. Domingo-Forasté. Stuttgart, 1994.
Historical Miscellany. Ed. and trans. N. G. Wilson. Cambridge, MA, 1997.
The Letters of Alciphron, Aelian, and Philostratus. Ed. and trans. A. R. Benner and F. H. Forbes. Cambridge, MA, 1949.
On Animals. Ed. and trans. A. F. Scholfield. 3 vols. Cambridge, MA, 1958–72.
Varia Historia. Ed. M. R. Dilts. Leipzig, 1974.

41. I am grateful for the opportunity to contribute to this volume in honor of Bruce Frier, my adviser and mentor, and also for the helpful comments of the editors, which have improved this essay.

Secondary Literature

Allen, D. "Burning *The Fable of the Bees*: Cultural Poetics and the Incendiary Authority of Nature." In L. Daston and F. Vidal, eds., *The Moral Authority of Nature*, 74–99. Chicago, 2004.

Costa, C., ed. *Greek Fictional Letters*. Oxford, 2001.

Daston, L. and F. Vidal, eds. *The Moral Authority of Nature*. Chicago, 2004.

French, R. *Ancient Natural History: Histories of Nature*. New York, 1994.

Frier, B. W. "Bees and Lawyers." *CJ* 78 (1982–83): 105–14.

Frier, B. W. "Why Did the Jurists Change Roman Law? Bees and Lawyers Revisited." *Index: Quaderni camerti di studi romanistici* 22 (1994): 135–49.

Frier, B. W., and T. A. J. McGinn. *A Casebook on Roman Family Law*. Oxford, 2004.

García Valdés, M. "Ciencia y moral: Eliano desde Aristóteles y a la luz del estoicismo y la 'zoofilia' moderna." *Emerita* 71 (2003): 1–50.

Holford-Strevens, L., and A. Vardi, eds. *Aulus Gellius: An Antonine Scholar and His Achievement*. Oxford, 2004.

Honoré, T. "Ulpian, Natural Law, and Stoic Influence." *Legal History Review* 78 (2010): 199–208.

Kindstrand, J. "Claudius Aelianus und sein Werk." *ANRW* 2.34.4: 2954–96.

König, J. "Fragmentation and Coherence in Plutarch's *Sympotic Questions*." In J. König and T. Whitmarsh, eds., *Ordering Knowledge in the Roman Empire*, 43–68. Cambridge, 2007.

König, J., and T. Whitmarsh. "Ordering Knowledge." In J. König and T. Whitmarsh, eds., *Ordering Knowledge in the Roman Empire*, 3–42. Cambridge, 2007.

König, J., and T. Whitmarsh, eds. *Ordering Knowledge in the Roman Empire*. Cambridge, 2007.

Kronenberg, L. *Allegories of Farming from Greece and Rome: Philosophical Satire in Xenophon, Varro, and Virgil*. Cambridge, 2009.

Morgan, T. "The Miscellany and Plutarch." In F. Klotz and K. Oikonomopoulou, eds., *The Philosopher's Banquet: Plutarch's "Table Talk" in the Intellectual Culture of the Roman Empire*, 54–73. Oxford, 2011.

Morgan, T. *Popular Morality in the Early Roman Empire*. Cambridge, 2007.

Potter, D. *The Roman Empire at Bay, AD 180–395*. New York, 2014.

Prandi, L. *Memorie storiche dei greci in Claudio Eliano*. Rome, 2005.

Schettino, M. "Il passato e il presente di Roma nell' opera di Eliano." In L. Troiani and G. Zecchini, eds., *La cultura storica nei primi due secoli dell' impero romano*, 283–307. Rome, 2005.

Schiavone, A. *The Invention of Law in the West*. Trans. J. Carden and A. Shugaar. Cambridge, MA, 2012.

Slatkin, L. "Measuring Authority, Authoritative Measures: Hesiod's *Works and Days*." In L. Daston and F. Vidal, eds., *The Moral Authority of Nature*, 25–49. Chicago, 2004.

Smith, S. *Man and Animal in Severan Rome: The Literary Imagination of Claudius Aelianus*. Cambridge, 2014.

Stamm, C. *Vergangenheitsbezug in der Zweiten Sophistik? Die Varia Historia des Claudius Aelianus*. Frankfurt am Main, 2003.

van Overmeire, S. "The Perfect King Bee: Visions of Kingship in Classical Antiquity." *Akroterion* 56 (2011): 31–46.
Vardi, A. "Genre, Conventions, and Cultural Programme in Gellius' *Noctes Atticae*." In L. Holford-Strevens and A. Vardi, eds., *Aulus Gellius: An Antonine Scholar and His Achievement*, 159–86. Oxford, 2004.
Whitmarsh, T. "Prose Literature and the Severan Dynasty." In S. Swain, S. Harrison, and J. Elsner, eds., *Severan Culture*, 24–51. Cambridge, 2007.
Wilkins, J. "Galen and Athenaeus in the Hellenistic Library." In J. König and T. Whitmarsh, eds., *Ordering Knowledge in the Roman Empire*, 69–87. Cambridge, 2007.

CHAPTER 6

Agency, Roman Law, and Roman Social Values

Dennis P. Kehoe[1]

Inspired by Bruce Frier's scholarship in Roman law, I have sought, in my own work, to come to a better understanding of the relationship between Roman law and the economy of the Roman Empire. In doing so, I have drawn on methodologies from the modern debate in the fields of law and economics and from the "new institutional economics," to assess the economic implications of legal rules in areas of the law involving private property crucial to the Roman agrarian economy, namely, those involving investment in land and land tenure. In this essay, I seek to reconsider and ultimately to defend the usefulness of this approach, by studying another area of the law significant for the economy, agency in commercial and financial relationships.[2] I focus on mandate, a contractual relationship that remained central to Roman economic life throughout the classical period of Roman law and beyond. This essay forms part of a broader project of analyzing mandate as a social institution in the Roman world. In a separate, companion essay, I have focused on explaining an implicit reciprocity in mandate in economic terms.[3] Here, I address, more specifically, the policy considerations of the Roman legal authorities, including those of the jurists in developing legal doctrines surrounding mandate, and those of the chancery in responding to petitions.

Analyzing the legal rules underpinning economic institutions in the Roman Empire helps us to understand better the possibilities for economic change and even growth. Ideally, the law contributed to economic life by facilitating productive contractual arrangements that would foster economic activity. It is cer-

1. All translations of legal texts are my own; those from book 4 of the *Code of Justinian* are as in Frier, *The "Codex" of Justinian* (2016).

2. For general theoretical discussion of the problem of agency, see Furubotn and Richter, *Institutions and Economic Theory* (2005) 162–70.

3. Kehoe, "Mandate and the Management of Business in the Roman Empire" (forthcoming).

tainly possible to make the case that law and legal institutions only played a peripheral role in areas of the economy in which actors used other institutions to organize their activities and resolve disputes. However, if law and legal institutions did play a central role in the economy, they could have served chiefly to benefit well-connected groups, even at a cost to society as a whole.[4] Agency in commercial and financial relationships is an appropriate testing ground for the role of law in the Roman economy, since property owners relied on agents of various types to carry out significant transactions on their behalf. Agency relationships existed in virtually all sectors of the Roman economy, including more familiar forms of agency, such as a slave's or freedman's management of a business on behalf of a slave owner or patron (often at a location far away from where the owner or patron resided) or a bailiff's or procurator's management of estates for an absentee landowner. To cite a less obvious example, a tutor administering the property on behalf of a ward (a pupil, i.e., an orphaned minor) can be analyzed as an agent.[5] As is widely recognized, in contrast to the modern world, Rome had no provision for direct agency, since Roman law did not make it possible for one person to create obligations between a principal and a third party. This apparent gap in Roman private law has often been regarded as a major impediment to the development of complex forms of business organization in the Roman world, with the implication that, in this respect at least, Roman law provided a significant barrier to potential economic growth.[6]

Even so, it is clear that complex agency relationships did exist in the Roman Empire, and in recent years, scholars have used increasingly sophisticated methodologies to examine how property owners worked around the apparent limitations in Roman law in order to create forms of agency.[7] The crucial issue in agency relationships involves aligning the interests of the agent sufficiently with those of the principal so that the latter will benefit from the agent's actions, while preserving for the principal sufficient enforcement mechanisms to protect him from opportunistic behavior on the part of the agent. Much of the current research on agency in the Roman world has focused on the use of slaves

4. This theme is emphasized by Ogilvie, "Whatever Is, Is Right?" (2007), in an analysis of the role of legal institutions in the medieval European economy. For the "instrumental" aspect of institutions, see also Greif, *Institutions and the Path to the Modern Economy* (2006) 40–41. For the tendency of institutions, once established to perpetuate themselves, see Hodgson, *Evolution and Institutions* (1999).

5. For agency in tutorship, see Kehoe, "Law, Agency, and Growth in the Roman Economy" (2013); Kehoe, "Agency, Tutorship, and the Protection of Pupils in Roman Law" (2017).

6. For agency in Roman law, see Plescia, "The Development of Agency in Roman Law" (1984); Kaser, *Das römische Privatrecht* (1971) 605–9; Kirschenbaum, *Sons, Slaves, and Freedmen* (1987); Frier and Kehoe, "Law and Economic Institutions" (2007) 127–34.

7. See especially Wacke, "Die adjektizischen Klagen im Überblick" (1994), finding the "seeds" of modern forms of agency in the *actio institoria*.

and freedmen as agents, as well as on the related legal remedies, the so-called *actiones adiecticiae qualitatis*, by which third parties entering into contracts with slave agents could recover from their owners.[8] To be sure, the use of slaves as agents was rooted in the fundamental role that slavery played in Roman society. Roman property owners had little choice but to adapt the institution of slavery to their financial needs. Thus a major focus of current scholarship has been to analyze the rewards and penalties that are intrinsic to the Roman slave system and that would make it possible for property owners to make profitable use of social dependents as agents.[9] The primary reward that property owners could provide to a slave agent was liberty, along with continued financial support. Withholding such rewards would represent a major sanction, along with other, more drastic means by which slaves could be punished. The ways in which owners and slaves reacted to these incentives helped to shape the institution of slavery.

There were limits, however, on the services that slaves or freedmen serving as agents could provide property owners, since there were some transactions, especially those involving substantial financial outlays, for which slaves would not be suitable agents. Instead, Roman property owners often relied on social equals to perform such services.[10] This type of agency—rooted in reciprocal relationships among social equals that originated in Roman concepts of *fides*, *officium*, and *amicitia*—was defined in the law under the contract of mandate, or *mandatum*.[11] In mandate, a principal, the *mandator*, requested or commanded that an agent, the *mandatarius*, undertake some business on his or her behalf.[12] Mandate was a consensual contract involving the good faith of both parties. The person asked to take up a mandate could refuse to do so, but once accepted, a mandate had to be performed in terms of the good-faith obligations imposed on the agent. The mandator was obligated to compensate the agent for

8. See, e.g., Aubert, *Business Managers in Ancient Rome* (1994) 46–91; de Ligt, "Legal History and Economic History" (1999).

9. For a survey, see Frier and Kehoe, "Law and Economic Institutions" (2007) 126–34. See also Morley, "Slavery under the Principate" (2011) 279–84; Bodel, "Slave Labour and Roman Society" (2011); Broekaert, "Freedmen and Agency in Roman Business" (2016).

10. For this theme in general, see Verboven, *The Economy of Friends* (2002); Kirschenbaum, *Sons, Slaves, and Freedmen* (1987) 148–99. Kirschenbaum emphasizes that many upper-class financial transactions were carried out by friends without any contractual relationship with the principal.

11. Randazzo, *Mandare* (2005). For general discussion of the role of *amicitia* in shaping Roman private law, see Finazzi, "Amicitia e doveri giuridici" (2010). For reciprocity implicit in Roman contractual relationships, especially those involving credit, see Bürge, "Vertrag und personale Abhängigkeiten" (1980) 130–43.

12. Zimmermann, *The Law of Obligations* (1996) 413–32; Kaser, *Das römische Privatrecht* (1971) 577–83.

any expenses that he undertook or losses that he might have suffered as a result of his service. Unlike other consensual contracts, however, mandate was not, in and of itself, reciprocal; the agent's service for the mandator was supposed to be gratuitous (accordingly, it was distinguished from an employment contract; see below); any benefit arising from the business that the mandator performed accrued to the mandator.

From an economic perspective, as I have argued in my companion essay, mandate provided a useful legal definition to cover forms of agency that involved considerable financial stakes for the principal and potentially catastrophic liability for the agent.[13] The types of financial activities with which mandate seems most commonly to have been associated included purchasing property on behalf of another, standing surety in credit arrangements, and providing credit. These were activities in which the use of slaves or other social dependents as agents was unsuitable, since the principal would have little capacity to compensate himself for the possible losses resulting from the agent's failure. Mandate was especially important in the credit market, since it provided a means to overcome information problems and link creditors with suitable borrowers. In a trading community, such as the one at Puteoli analyzed by Taco Terpstra in his recent book, creditors and borrowers themselves formed a community, and mandate could provide a legal definition for the mutual services that members of such communities exchanged.[14] A related institution was "unauthorized administration," *negotia gesta*, which defined the rights and obligations of parties when an agent performed some business on behalf of another without the latter's knowledge, often when that person was absent and not able to take a direct hand in his or her affairs.[15] Unauthorized administration proved to be a versatile remedy, covering many different situations that might arise in the ordinary business of managing property. To cite several representative examples, unauthorized administration provided a way for a person managing the property in an undistributed succession to recover expenses from his or her coheirs. Someone who paid taxes on behalf of another could recover under unauthorized administration (*C.* 2.18.16, 252). When magistrates disposed of funds belonging to a municipality, their actions would be governed by this remedy (Paul. *D.* 3.5.36.1; *C.* 2.18.18, 293). A person who plead a case on behalf

13. Kehoe, "Mandate and the Management of Business in the Roman Empire" (forthcoming). On the importance of mandate to credit, see Wolf, "Lo stigma dell'ignominia" (2010) 548–49.

14. Terpstra, *Trading Communities in the Roman World* (2013) 9–49; Wolff, "Der neue pompejanische Urkundenfund" (2001); Camodeca, *Tabulae Pompeianae Sulpiciorum* (1999), discussed in Kehoe, Ratzan, and Yiftach, "Transaction Costs, Ancient History, and the Law" (2015) 20–27.

15. Zimmermann, *The Law of Obligations* (1996) 433–50; Kaser, *Das römische Privatrecht* (1971) 586–90; Finazzi, "Amicitia e doveri giuridici" (2010) 807–25.

of a community's communal rights to water resources had an action under unauthorized administration, to recover expenses from the other people with an interest in the water (Papin. *D.* 3.5.30.7). In addition, unauthorized administration came to be applied to other agency relationships for which no other means of recovery existed. Thus it defined the relationship between a procurator administering all of the property of a principal, the *procurator omnium bonorum*, as well as various curators administering other people's property, including the *curator furiosi*, who was responsible for the property of an insane person, and the *curator minoris*, who administered the property of an adult under the age of twenty-five (tutors and pupils, by contrast, were liable to one another in the actions on tutorship).[16] Similar good-faith obligations bound both the principal and the agent in this relationship. In this essay, I seek to build on the conclusions in the companion essay mentioned above, to analyze more closely the extent to which the Roman legal authorities responded to social needs in formulating rules for mandate and unauthorized administration.

Methodological Issues

As mentioned previously, the contract of mandate provided a legal definition for reciprocal relationships among social equals that originated in Roman aristocratic values. The seeming discrepancy between the lack of incentives for the agent in mandate and the importance of the contract for Roman commercial life raises methodological questions that are often the focal point in the debate about the Roman economy and the role of legal institutions in it. If the person performing the mandate was not supposed to profit from his service, under what conditions would it be advantageous to accept the responsibility to perform a mandate? In my own analysis of the economic aspects of mandate, I make use of the contemporary debate about the relationship between law and economics, to argue that mandate involved an implicit reciprocity between economic actors, who likely sometimes performed mandates and sometimes depended on the services of others acting under a mandate. The contract of mandate facilitated such reciprocity by defining precisely the rights and duties of both mandator and agent, which provided guidelines for how the two parties were to perform their respective roles, as well as a way to resolve disputes. However, a very different take on this approach is offered by Francesco Boldizonni, a historian of early modern Europe. In his provocative book *The*

16. Kaser, *Das römische Privatrecht* (1971) 586–90.

Poverty of Clio (2011), Boldizzoni undertakes a forceful attack on approaches to analyzing the ancient economy that involve application of modern economic theory. In Boldizzoni's judgment, premodern economic arrangements can only be analyzed usefully from the point of view of the historical factors that shaped them. Economic institutions, as M. I. Finley argued in *The Ancient Economy*, are firmly embedded in social values. In the Roman Empire, the social values that shaped economic activity included, among other things, the prestige of owning land and slaves, which were valued in terms of the honor that they provided, rather than any economic gain that might result in comparison to other forms of investing wealth. For Boldizonni, the assumption underlying modern economic analysis, that actors seek to maximize their own wealth, is a choice embedded in our society's values and cannot be assumed to be relevant to the analysis of other societies, especially premodern ones. The type of approach that Boldizzoni questions can be seen in the recently published collection of essays by MIT economist Peter Temin, *The Roman Market Economy* (Princeton, 2013), which analyzes major economic issues in the Roman Empire in terms of modern economic theory. To take Boldizzoni's approach to its logical conclusion, any investigation of the Roman economy that uses the analytical tools of law and economics and of the new institutional economics is bound to produce results that obscure, rather than illuminate, historical relationships.

Boldizzoni makes an indisputable point about the importance of recognizing the ways in which historical factors intrinsic to every society shape economic institutions and the choices of economic actors. Certainly, such an approach informs a rich tradition of scholarship in Roman law, exemplified by the work of Alfons Bürge, whose profound knowledge of Roman social institutions informs his analysis of many areas of Roman law, such as, notably, the enforcement of contractual obligations.[17] Boldizzoni's observation, however, does not invalidate modern theoretical approaches that allow us to understand better how economic actors react to incentives in pursuing their welfare within the broader constraints established by social and legal institutions. The fruitfulness of combining approaches based on historical factors and modern economic analysis can be seen in efforts to understand the use of social dependents, particularly slaves and freedmen, as agents in business, a topic that has been the focal point of a great deal of research in recent years. One of the most important contributions in this area is the recent book by Henrik Mouritsen on freedmen in Roman society.[18] In his study, Mouritsen demonstrates the crucial role that

17. Bürge, "Vertrag und personale Abhängigkeiten" (1980).

18. Mouritsen, *The Freedman in the Roman World* (2011), discussed in Kehoe, "Contracts, Agency, and Transaction Costs" (2015) 246–48.

freedmen played in Roman economic life, particularly in performing duties for upper-class patrons that required skill and discretion but that also allowed the freedman to act quite independently from his patron. Mouritsen emphasizes that despite the scope for independent action that many freedmen enjoyed (particularly when they were conducting the patron's business at considerable geographical distance), patrons still exercised considerable means of enforcement against freedmen. As Mouritsen suggests, the passage to liberty often meant that a freedman carried out functions similar to the ones he performed while a slave, and many freedmen remained dependent on their patrons for financial and social support. Thus a freedman who performed unsatisfactorily could face the potentially ruinous sanction of being cut off from his patron's backing. At the same time, the patron's authority was buttressed by an aristocratic ideology that privileged such values as loyalty and dutifulness, *fides* and *officium*, to define how freedmen should conduct themselves. This ideology was crucial precisely because, in many situations, patrons had little control over or even knowledge of their freedmen's actions. Mouritsen's approach to understanding the role of freedmen in the social and economic life of the Roman world is fully grounded in a rich understanding of Roman social values, not to mention a mastery of the ancient literary, legal, and epigraphical sources.

As important as Mouritsen's analysis is, his approach does not tell the whole story about the organization of business in the Roman world. From a quite different perspective, Giuseppe Dari-Mattiacci and other scholars from the Amsterdam Center for Law and Economics have applied formal economic theory to analyze the relationship between slave and freed agents and their principals. They argue that the Roman system of slavery created a sufficient range of incentives to allow property owners to employ social dependents in a wide variety of sophisticated business arrangements. In one work from this research group, Abatino, Dari-Mattiacci, and Perotti argue that it was possible to use slaves owned in a partnership to create a long-lasting business enterprise that would share many important characteristics of modern enterprises, such as continuity even when the owners changed and protection of assets that belonged to the owners and were distinct from the enterprise.[19] Admittedly, our lack of evidence for real-world business arrangements makes it difficult to verify that Roman property owners used partnerships and the common ownership of slaves to develop the types of enterprises whose existence the authors hypothesize. However, this type of careful and theoretically informed analysis

19. Abatino, Dari-Mattiacci, and Perotti, "Depersonalization of Business in Ancient Rome" (2011).

of Roman legal and social institutions enhances our understanding of the complexities of the ancient economy beyond what can be achieved by an analysis of historical and social factors alone. The focus of the Amsterdam approach on the advantages and disadvantages that would accrue to stakeholders in business enterprises, including the principals who owned the business or supplied funds and the agents carrying out the business, helps us to understand the types of business organizations that were feasible in the Roman world. Indeed, analyzing the economic incentives inherent in business enterprises seems crucial to a full understanding of such institutions.

The contract of mandate, together with unauthorized administration, is an institution that can be appropriately analyzed from both historical and economic perspectives.[20] It could, of course, be hypothesized that mandate remained a basic relationship for defining agency, despite a conservative approach on the part of the legal authorities in interpreting the institution chiefly in terms of aristocratic social values, with little concern to adapt it to the changing needs of Roman commercial life. Yet, as I will argue, the Roman legal authorities recognized situations in which mandate and unauthorized administration could play a crucial role in the financial affairs of Roman property owners. The jurist Ulpian, to cite one important example, emphasizes the usefulness of unauthorized administration as a reason for the praetor's creation of the remedy (*D.* 3.5.1, 3.5.9.1). The jurists and, later, the emperors adapted the rules of mandate and unauthorized administration in such a way as to foster the freedom of parties to enter into contracts of their choosing, by carefully defining the rights and obligations of the parties to a contract, thereby providing certainty about how potential disputes could be resolved. At the same time, the legal authorities were constrained in their capacity or willingness to adapt mandate and unauthorized administration, by their understanding of the obligations arising from good faith that they continued to see as valuable to Roman society. But exploring how concerns for social needs were balanced against their assumptions about Roman society can only tell part of the story of mandate as a social institution. The rules developed from social concerns and tradition also created incentives for particular types of economic behavior that affected the organization of the Roman economy and its capacity to grow.[21]

20. See Bresson, *L'économie de la Grèce des cités* (2007), 1:7–36, convincingly defending the idea that it is appropriate to conceive of an ancient "economy" in the first place. For a very different view, see Bruhns, "Cambridge, Bordeaux ou Heidelberg" (2014).

21. For the degree to which the jurists included economic considerations in the law of tutorship, see Kehoe, "Agency, Tutorship, and the Protection of Pupils in Roman Law" (2017). Certainly, as demonstrated by Schiavone, *The Invention of Law in the West* (2012), the jurists' understanding of justice and fairness in contractual relationships was complex.

Basic Principles of Mandate and Unauthorized Administration

A consistent principle underlying the Roman legal authorities' approach to mandate was that the contract was gratuitous, so that any actions taken by the agent were to benefit the mandator. Thus the late-classical jurist Paul emphasized that no contract of mandate existed unless it was gratuitous, since it drew its origin from reciprocal obligations, *officium*, and friendship, *amicitia*. Agency relationships that involved direct compensation for the agent were to be considered under a separate contractual form, lease and hire (*locatio conductio*, *D.* 17.1.1.4).[22] The social background to "unauthorized administration," *negotia gesta*, is likely to have been similar to that of mandate, with allowance made for a person's different roles, whether acting on the instructions of another or performing business for another without that person's knowledge. In his commentary on the provision in the Praetor's Edict establishing the possibility of recovery under *negotia gesta*, Ulpian emphasizes the necessity of this remedy, since the interests (*utilitas*) of absent persons were often at stake; without the intervention of a third party, they might risk the loss of property, particularly when they were unable to provide a defense in a lawsuit (*D.* 3.5.1).[23] As in mandate, the agent could only act to benefit the absent principal and could not take any action that would make the situation of the absent principal worse. Thus, as Gaius describes, one could free someone from a debt by paying it off, even if that person were unwilling and unaware, but an agent could not enforce a debt on behalf of an absent principal without his or her consent (*D.* 3.5.38).[24] Like mandate, unauthorized administration created a mutual set of rights and obli-

22. Paul. (32 *ad ed.*) *D.* 17.1.1.4: *Mandatum nisi gratuitum nullum est: nam originem ex officio atque amicitia trahit, contrarium ergo est officio merces: interveniente enim pecunia res ad locationem et conductionem potius respicit.* (A mandate does not exist unless it is gratuitous: for it draws its origin from duty and friendship, and payment is incompatible with duty. When money is involved, it rather looks toward lease and hire.) For the social values underpinning the gratuitous nature of mandate, see Finazzi, "Amicitia e doveri giuridici" (2010) 766–73.

23. Ulp. (10 *ad ed.*) *D.* 3.5.1: *Hoc edictum necessarium est, quoniam magna utilitas absentium versatur, ne indefensi rerum possessionem aut venditionem patiantur vel pignoris distractionem vel poenae committendae actionem, vel iniuria rem suam amittant.* (This edict is necessary, since the great utility of absent people is involved, lest without a defense they suffer the taking possession of their property or its sale, the alienation of a pledge, or an action on incurring a penalty, or unlawfully lose their property.)

24. Gaius (3 *de verborum obligationibus*) *D.* 3.5.38: *Solvendo quisque pro alio licet invito et ignorante liberat eum: quod autem alicui debetur, alius sine voluntate eius non potest iure exigere. naturalis enim simul et civilis ratio suasit alienam condicionem meliorem quidem etiam ignorantis et inviti nos facere posse, deteriorem non posse.* (Someone frees another person by paying on his behalf, even if it is against his will and he is unaware, but another person cannot lawfully enforce what is owed to someone without that person's will. For natural and legal reasoning have both persuaded that we can make the situation of a person better even when he is unaware and unwilling, but not worse.)

gations between the agent and the principal. As Gaius describes, when an agent performed a useful service on behalf of an absent principal, even without the latter's knowledge, he simultaneously had the right to compensation for his expenses and had to account to the principal for the actions that he had taken (*D.* 3.5.2).[25] Moreover, as Ulpian states, the actions taken by the agent on behalf of the principal did not have to have a positive outcome, as long as the agent had undertaken them "usefully" (*utiliter*, *D.* 3.5.9.1), although what was considered useful could be a matter of debate.

In cases of mandate, the legal authorities consistently focus on the good-faith obligations that were essential to the contract. These obligations precluded any arrangement by which the agent profited from his service. A case discussed by the jurist Iavolenus illustrates this point (*D.* 17.1.36.1). In this case, an agent received a mandate to purchase, at a specified price, a property of which he was one of several owners. A complication would arise when the other owners were willing—for example, because of financial difficulties—to sell their shares at a price beneath what the mandator had specified. In this case, the agent acting on mandate would not be required to sell his own share at the reduced price, but he would also not be able to profit from this situation—for example, by holding out for a higher price from the principal.[26] The mandator, not the agent, was to gain the savings that accrued as a result of the economic necessity pressing on the co-owners of the property in question.

---

25. Gaius (3 *ad ed. prov.*) *D.* 3.5.2: *Si quis absentis negotia gesserit licet ignorantis, tamen quidquid utiliter in rem eius impenderit vel etiam ipse se in rem absentis alicui obligaverit, habet eo nomine actionem: itaque eo casu ultro citroque nascitur actio, quae appellatur negotiorum gestorum. et sane sicut aequum est ipsum actus sui rationem reddere et eo nomine condemnari, quidquid vel non ut oportuit gessit vel ex his negotiis retinet: ita ex diverso iustum est, si utiliter gessit, praestari ei, quidquid eo nomine vel abest ei vel afuturum est.* (If someone performs the business of an absent person, even though he is unaware, nevertheless he has a cause of action for what he has spent usefully for that person's interest or if he has obligated himself to someone in the interest of another. Thus in this case there arises a reciprocal action, which is called unauthorized administration. And admittedly just as it is fair that he give an accounting of his actions and be condemned on that account if he did something that he should not have or retained some something from the business, so too is it just if he did something useful that he be provided whatever he is missing or will be missing on that account.) Gaius here applies a "synallagmatic" understanding of contract, in which the obligations of the parties arise from a mutual exchange: see Schiavone, *The Invention of Law in the West* (2012) 319–37.

26. Iav. (7 *ex Cassio*) *D.* 17.1.36.1: *Quid enim fiet, si exiguo pretio hi, cum quibus tibi communis fundus erat, rem abicere vel necessitate rei familiaris vel alia causa cogerentur? non etiam tu ad idem dispendium deduceris. sed nec lucrum tibi ex hac causa adquirere debes, cum mandatum gratuitum esse debet: neque enim tibi concedendum est propter hoc venditionem impedire, quod animosiorem eius rei emptorem esse quam tibi mandatum est cognoveris.* (For what will happen if these people, with whom you had a commonly owned farm, should be compelled by financial difficulties or some other cause to throw the property away? For you will not be brought to the same expense. But you should not gain any profit on this account, since a mandate is supposed to be gratuitous; nor are you to be allowed to impede the sale because you know that there is a more enthusiastic buyer for the property than was mandated to you.)

Also fundamental to the Roman contract of mandate was the protection it afforded the mandator against any unauthorized actions taken by the agent on his or her behalf. The stringent standards to which Roman law held the agent carrying out a mandate can be seen in an extended discussion of the issue by Paul (*D.* 17.1.5 pr.–5). In Paul's formulation, the limits of the mandate were to be diligently observed.[27] Thus, for example, if an agent under a mandate issued by a property owner was to sell the mandator's farm for one hundred but sold it for ninety, the mandator would have the right to hold onto the property, unless the agent paid the mandator the difference between the mandated price and the actual sale price and indemnified the mandator against all other claims (*D.* 17.1.5.3).[28] The same principle applied if a slave ordered to sell a piece of his owner's property sold it for a price lower than the owner specified. Again, the mandator could claim back the property (*D.* 17.1.5.4). However, an agent's discretion that worked to the advantage of the mandator—for instance, if the agent were able to purchase a slave for a price lower than what the mandator had instructed—would result in a legally valid transaction (*D.* 17.1.5.5). As Paul says in the same book of his commentary on the Praetor's Edict, the law allowed the situation of the mandator to be more favorable, but never less favorable, than prescribed in the mandate (*D.* 17.1.3 pr.).[29]

The agent's duty to protect the interests of the mandator included preserving any legal claims that the latter might make in connection with the business assigned as part of the mandate. This point becomes clear in an opinion of the republican jurist Q. Mucius Scaevola, as quoted by Celsus (*D.* 17.1.48 pr.). The case concerns a surety (*fideiussor*), a person performing the function, common under mandate, of guaranteeing a loan, in this case, a loan with interest. If the surety, by paying off the loan together with the interest, blocked a potential claim by the mandator that the loan was interest-free, he would not be able to recover what he paid in an action on mandate. However, the duty of the agent to protect the interest of the mandator had limits: in this case, the surety could not be expected to harm his own reputation by claiming, at the original debtor's

27. Paul. (32 *ad ed.*) *D.* 17.1.5 pr.: *Diligenter igitur fines mandati custodiendi sunt.* (Therefore the limits of the mandate are to be maintained diligently.)

28. Paul. (32 *ad ed.*) *D.* 17.1.5.3: *Item si mandavero tibi, ut fundum meum centum venderes tuque eum nonaginta vendideris et petam fundum, non obstabit mihi exceptio, nisi et reliquum mihi, quod deest mandatu meo, praestes et indemnem me per omnia conserves.* (And if I order you to sell my farm for one hundred and you sell it for ninety and I seek it, I will not be blocked by a defense, unless you provide the remainder to me that is missing from my mandate and protected me from any loss through everything.) The text from *nisi* onward may be interpolated.

29. Paul. (32 *ad ed.*) *D.* 17.1.3 pr.: *Praeterea in causa mandati etiam illud vertitur, ut interim nec melior causa mandantis fieri possit, interdum melior, deterior vero numquam.* (Besides, in a case of mandate this is also at issue, that for a while the situation of the mandator might not become better, or on occasion become better, but never become worse.)

behest, that the loan was without interest.[30] Moreover, if someone acting as a surety under a mandate paid off a debtor's obligations to the creditor's procurator, the surety would be able to recover the debt from the principal through an action on mandate (Paul. *D.* 17.1.26.5). The action by the surety would discharge the debt. Of course, if the surety paid the debt to someone other than the creditor's procurator, this action would not discharge the debt, and the surety could only recover his money by proceeding, against the receiver, with a claim for a sum not owed (*condictio indebiti*).[31] This discussion indicates the jurists' concern with the interests of the mandator, but in all likelihood, their privileging of the mandator's interests above all others simplified the actual relationship between a surety and a mandator.

Procurators and Mandate

The likely complexity of the legal terms that practically defined agency relationships in Roman society can be seen in the case of business managers, or procurators. The term *procurator* generally denoted no particular legal status, since it can refer to an agent performing under a variety of legal arrangements. It only carried a precise legal significance when the procurator was performing certain specific functions related to representing another person in court or, in some cases, was managing all of the property belonging to another person.[32] To be

30. Celsus (7 *dig.*) *D.* 17.1.48 pr.: *Quintus Mucius Scaevola ait, si quis sub usuris creditam pecuniam fideiussisset et reus in iudicio conventus cum recusare vellet sub usuris creditam esse pecuniam et fideiussor solvendo usuras potestatem recusandi eas reo sustulisset, eam pecuniam a reo non petiturum. sed si reus fideiussori denuntiasset, ut recusaret sub usuris debitam esse nec is propter suam existimationem recusare voluisset, quod ita solverit, a reo petiturum. hoc bene censuit Scaevola: parum enim fideliter facit fideiussor in superiore casu, quod potestatem eximere reo videtur suo iure uti: ceterum in posteriore casu non oportet esse noxiae fideiussori, si pepercisset pudori suo.* (Quintus Mucius Scaevola says that if someone guaranteed a sum lent with interest and the defendant upon being sued in court, when he wanted to deny that the money had been lent with interest and the guarantor by paying had taken away from him the power to deny that the debt included interest, he [the guarantor] will not seek the money from the defendant. But if the defendant instructed the guarantor that he should deny that the debt included interest and he [the guarantor] was unwilling to deny this on account of his own reputation, he will seek from the defendant what he has paid in this way. Scaevola rightly held this opinion: the guarantor hardly acts faithfully in the first case, since he is deemed to take away from the defendant the power to make use of his own right. But in the second case it must not harm that guarantor that he spared his own reputation.) Lenel considers the references to a guarantor in this text to be interpolated, while the last sentence explaining Scaevola's opinion has also been suspected as interpolated. On the social considerations surrounding this case, see Finazzi, "Amicitia e doveri giuridici" (2010) 801–2.

31. The same principle applied in *negotia gesta*: see Paul. *D.* 3.5.22, where this is the prevailing view. Cf. Paul. *D.* 3.5.24, in which an agent who pays more than he should have can only recover what was actually owed.

32. See Klinck, "Zur Bedeutung des Wortes procurator" (2007); the specific functions included

sure, a procurator serving as a business manager could perform this function on the basis of a mandate, as Ulpian posits when discussing both the procurator taking charge of a specific task and the one managing all of the affairs of a principal (*D.* 46.3.12 pr.).[33] Likewise, Ulpian uses the term *procurator* to denote someone performing a (financial) service on behalf of another on the basis of a mandate (*D.* 3.3.1 pr.).[34] But as the text from Paul discussed earlier concerning the distinction between mandate and lease/hire suggests, it was not uncommon for procurators to be compensated (*D.* 17.1.1.4). Thus Papinian asserted that a procurator could recover an honorarium (*salarium*) through *cognitio extraordinaria*, but only as compensation for services, as opposed to a situation in which the principal had purchased the outcome of a legal case, which was contrary to the law (*D.* 17.1.7).[35] Furthermore, as Papinian ruled, it was not possible to sue for an honorarium (*salarium*) promised for an uncertain purpose, either in the action on mandate or through *cognitio extraordinaria* (*D.* 17.1.56.3). If salaries or honoraria frequently accompanied assignments subsumed under mandate, the Roman legal authorities simplified reality by maintaining a strict distinction between mandate and forms of agency in which the agent was compensated. But the issue of the procurator's precise legal relationship to the principal could arise when he sought compensation for the expenses he bore in managing the property. In Labeo's analysis, as cited by Ulpian, only a procurator acting on a mandate would be entitled to recover such expenses; a procurator receiving a salary would be expected to pay for traveling expenses out of this salary (*D.* 17.1.10.9).

When procurators carried out broad responsibilities in managing property, the restrictions on agents inherent to mandate created complications that potentially carried significant economic costs. In general terms, as formulated by Paul, the procurator was not allowed to cause the situation of the property owner

the *procurator omnium bonorum*, who could represent the principal in court by virtue of managing all of the principal's property, and the *procurator absentis*, formally appointed to represent an absent person in a court case.

33. Ulp. (30 *ad Sab.*) *D.* 46.3.12 pr.: *Vero procuratori recte solvitur. verum autem accipere debemus eum, cui mandatum est vel specialiter vel cui omnium negotiorum administratio mandata est.* (A payment is rightly made to a true procurator. But we should understand that he is a person to whom a specific mandate has been given or to whom the administration of all business has been mandated.)

34. Ulp. (9 *ad ed.*) *D.* 3.3.1 pr.: *Procurator est qui aliena negotia mandatu domini administrat.* (A procurator is a person who administers another person's business on the mandate of the owner.) Cf. *D.* 3.3.1.1, where Ulpian challenges the view of Pomponius and other jurists that a person who is assigned a single task is not appropriately considered a procurator. Cf. *D.* 3.3.1.2: *Usus autem procuratoris perquam necessarius est, ut qui rebus suis ipsi superesse vel nolunt vel non possunt, per alios possint vel agere vel conveniri.* (The use of a procurator is quite necessary, as those who are unwilling or unable to oversee their affairs themselves can pursue actions or be sued through others.)

35. Cf. Finazzi, "Amicitia e doveri giuridici" (2010) 773.

to be made worse without the latter's knowledge: *Ignorantis domini condicio deterior per procuratorem fieri non debet* ([54 *ad ed.*] *D.* 3.3.49). In practical terms, this means that the procurator potentially acted with great risk to himself if he exercised discretion on behalf of the property owner. This was the case even when the procurator had been assigned the general administration of a person's property. As Paul formulates the principle, such a procurator had the capacity to enforce loans, to reassign them (*novare*), to make exchanges on behalf of the principal, and to pay the principal's creditors (*D.* 3.3.58, 3.3.59).[36] Any alienation of property required the ratification by the principal, except for crops or other things that would perish (Modestinus, *D.* 3.3.63). But the procurator had no discretion to negotiate on behalf of the principal to reach settlements with debtors, since the procurator would be diminishing the principal's property by doing so. If the procurator took such measures, they would have no legal validity, and the principal would be able to pursue any claims against debtors, unless he ratified the settlements made by his agent (Paul. *D.* 3.3.60).[37] Another potential risk for the procurator is that he might take on substantial obligations that would benefit the principal alone. Thus, as discussed by Papinian, if a procurator selling properties on behalf of another provided a guarantee against the eviction of the buyer, he would even be responsible for this promise after he had ceased to administer the property of the original owner (*D.* 3.3.67).[38] The promise to which Papinian refers is the *stipulatio duplae*, wherein the seller became liable to the buyer for twice the purchase price paid, in the event of the latter's eviction.[39]

A potential conflict of interest arose when a procurator, acting on a mandate, controlled funds that belonged to the mandator, since this might provide

---

36. Paul. (71 *ad ed.*) *D.* 3.3.58: *Procurator, cui generaliter libera administratio rerum commissa est, potest exigere, novare, aliud pro alio permutare.* (A procurator to whom the free administration of affairs has been entrusted generally can enforce an obligation, assign a loan, or exchange one thing for another.) Paul. (10 *ad Plaut.*) *D.* 3.3.59: *Sed et id quoque ei mandari videtur, ut solvat creditoribus.* (But this is also deemed to be mandated to him, that he pay creditors.)

37. Paul. (4 *resp.*) *D.* 3.3.60: *Mandato generali non contineri etiam transactionem decidendi causa interpositam: et ideo si postea is qui mandavit transactionem ratam non habuit, non posse eum repelli ab actionibus exercendis.* (A general mandate does not include a settlement introduced for resolving a dispute. And for that reason, if afterward the person who gave the mandate has not ratified the settlement, he cannot be repelled from exercising his causes of action.)

38. Papin. (2 *resp.*) *D.* 3.3.67: *Procurator, qui pro evictione praediorum quae vendidit fidem suam adstrinxit, etsi negotia gerere desierit, obligationis tamen onere praetoris auxilio non levabitur: nam procurator, qui pro domino vinculum obligationis suscepit, onus eius frustra recusat.* (A procurator who bound his own faith for (the purchaser's) eviction from properties that he has sold, even if he ceases to manage the business, will not be released from the burden of his obligation by the praetor's aid. For a procurator who has undertaken the bond of an obligation on behalf of an owner refuses his burden in vain.)

39. Kaser, *Das römische Privatrecht* (1971) 555–56.

the agent an opportunity to profit from his service in performing the mandate. Thus Ulpian states that a procurator who delayed in returning money belonging to the mandator was liable to pay interest on the sum. Likewise, if the agent lent out, at interest, funds belonging to the mandator, he would be required to pay the mandator whatever gain the agent realized from this transaction, whether or not the mandator ordered the agent to make the loan. As Ulpian says, that the agent should realize a profit from money belonging to another person is inconsistent with good faith. The procurator would also be liable to pay interest if, contrary to his mandate, he failed to lend money at interest or, as Papinian stated, if he did so but used the interest gained for his own purpose (*D.* 17.1.10.3).[40] The strict rule formulated by Ulpian would seem to hamper arrangements in which the mandator might offer the agent a share of the interest as a financial incentive for the agent to engage in credit arrangements on the mandator's behalf, since a claim on the part of the agent for any profit from the transaction would be unenforceable. Even so, it is not hard to imagine that Roman property owners with funds to invest by lending at interest might assign this task to agents who would derive some share of the profits. But direct financial incentives were incompatible with Roman law's definition of mandate. Arguably, this type of purpose could more easily be arranged by using a slave as an agent, but the concern of the jurists with the legal implications when the procurator lent out the principal's money suggests that procurators acting on a mandate could also make such loans.

The legal authorities simplified reality by insisting that specific instruction by the mandator was necessary to create a claim on the part of the agent for compensation for expenses. In reality, it is likely that procurators or other people tasked with managing a property owner's business could be expected to exercise some discretion, but if they exceeded the specific terms of the mandate, they risked shouldering all the costs. Only if the mandator specifically ratified the actions taken by the agent did those actions assume legal validity. The type of situation that might arise is suggested in a rescript of Diocletian, in which

40. Ulp. (31 *ad ed.*) *D.* 17.1.10.3: *Sed et si pecuniam meam faenori dedit usurasque consecutus est, consequenter dicemus debere eum praestare quantumcumque emolumentum sensit, sive ei mandavi sive non, quia bonae fidei hoc congruit, ne de alieno lucrum sentiat: quod si non exercuit pecuniam, sed ad usus suos convertit, in usuras convenietur, quae legitimo modo in regionibus frequentantur. denique Papinianus ait etiam si usuras exegerit procurator et in usus suos convertit, usuras eum praestare debere.* (But if he has lent out my money and he gained interest, accordingly we will say that he should provide whatever emolument he has experienced, whether or not I gave him a mandate, since it is in keeping with good faith that he not feel a gain from another's property. But if he had not invested the money but had turned it to his own uses, he will be sued for interest that is common in the regions within the legal limit. Finally Papinian also says that if a procurator exacted interest and turns it to his own uses, he must provide the interest.) The phrase *legitimo modo* may be interpolated.

the emperor ruled that a procurator who exceeded the terms of his mandate by selling a farm could not compromise the mandator's rights unless that person specifically ratified the sale (*C.* 4.35.12).[41] In this particular case, without the mandator's ratification, the sale would be null and void, but the procurator would be liable to the buyer, in an *actio ex empto,* for the latter's interest in having the sale go through. The agent's potential liabilities from a failed sale or other transaction certainly must have restricted the agent's scope of action, not to mention the willingness of a third party to do business with him. The underlying legal principle can also be seen in another rescript from Diocletian to a woman named Eutychiana, in which the emperor emphasized that neither a son nor anyone else could prejudice the rights of a property owner without her specific mandate; this case concerns whether the woman's son could compromise her rights by swearing an oath in a formal legal procedure (*C.* 4.1.7, 293).[42] The Roman definition of the mandator's rights and obligations privileged the mandator's interests above all others, even at a potential cost to society, since the uncertainty that a mandator would ratify actions by his agent would have deterred some third parties from entering into otherwise productive contractual arrangements.

The potential pitfalls arising from these restrictions imposed on procurators can be seen in the delicate situation that arose when Pliny's freedman Hermes promised to sell to Corellia, the sister of Pliny's revered mentor Corellius Rufus, property that Pliny had inherited (*Ep.* 7.11, 14). Corellia had previously expressed an interest in acquiring property near Pliny's own at Comum, and when Pliny received an inheritance that included property in the desired location, an opportunity arose for her to acquire it. The freedman brought letters from Pliny to Corellia, with the news that Pliny's portion of the property would be for sale for 700,000 sesterces. At her request, the freedman assigned

41. *C.* 4.35.12: *Cum mandati negotii contractum certam accepisse legem adseveres, eam integram secundum bonam fidem custodiri convenit. unde si contra mandati tenorem procurator tuus ad te pertinentem fundum vendidit nec venditionem postea ratam habuisti, dominium tibi auferre non potuit.* (Since you assert the contract for the mandate of a business involved specific terms, it is accepted that these terms be observed fully in accordance with good faith. Therefore if, contrary to the tenor of the mandate, the procurator sold a farm belonging to you and afterwards you did not ratify the sale, he could not take ownership away from you.)

42. *C.* 4.1.7: *Nec filius nec quisquam alius neque litigando neque paciscendo, sed nec iusiurandum citra voluntatem domini rei deferendo praeiudicium ei facere potest. unde si citra mandatum tuum aliquid erga rem tuam filius tuus gessit nec ratum habuisti, nihil tibi oberit.* (Neither a son nor anyone else can prejudice the interests of a property owner by litigation or pact, or by tendering an oath without his consent. Hence, if your son transacted any business in connection with your property without your mandate, and you have not ratified it, it will not harm you.) For efforts to protect the resources of decurions, see Kehoe, *Law and the Rural Economy* (2007) 169–70; Kehoe, "Urbanization, Land, and Political Control" (forthcoming).

this property to her. The problem was that the property could have been sold at auction for a higher price, 900,000 sesterces, the valuation on which Pliny paid the 5 percent inheritance tax. Corellia proposed to pay the higher price, but Pliny stood by the promise made by his freedman. One question connected with this transaction concerns the capacity in which the freedman Hermes was acting on behalf of Pliny. Hermes may have been merely a messenger, but it seems more likely, in view of the actions he took at Corellia's request, that he was Pliny's procurator, presumably acting on a mandate.[43] In terms of the law, Pliny was under no obligation to ratify what his freedman had done. He did so out of consideration for his friendship with Corellia, but he also supported the actions that Hermes took, since he acted in accordance with Pliny's own character (*meis moribus*, *Ep.* 7.11.6). The delicacy of Pliny's personal situation notwithstanding, this episode illustrates how a procurator might have to take initiative to perform what he considered to be in the interest of his principal, since it would not be possible for the principal to provide him with complete instructions on every possible decision that might arise. That the principal's intent could involve his own financial sacrifice (as occurred in Pliny's case) does not change this point.

Classical Roman law's insistence on protecting the mandator's interests above all others stems from a basic conception of mandate as a gratuitous service that required both the good faith of the agent to perform the service and the good faith of the mandator to compensate the agent for expenses incurred in that performance. This conception of mandate did not consider the interests that some property owners and agents might have in adapting the contract to make it more responsive to changing business conditions. The considerations informing the jurists' conception of mandate are particularly evident in a scenario that attracted the interest of jurists in the Sabinian school, namely, the first-century jurists Sabinus and Cassius, as discussed by Gaius in his *Institutes* (3.161). In this scenario, an agent purchased a farm for a higher price than specified in the mandate (in this case, for 150 rather than 100).[44] The principle

43. For the interpretation that Hermes was a messenger, see Sherwin-White, *The Letters of Pliny* (1985) 416, *ad Ep.* 7.11.6, based on the distinction in Ulp. *D.* 3.3.1.1 between a procurator and a mere messenger. Kirschenbaum, *Sons, Slaves, and Freedmen* (1987) 139–40, considers the precise legal relationship between Pliny and Hermes to be irrelevant.

44. Gaius, *Inst.* 3.161: *Cum autem is, cui recte mandauerim, egressus fuerit mandatum, ego quidem eatenus cum eo habeo mandati actionem, quatenus mea interest inplesse eum mandatum, si modo implere potuerit; at ille mecum agere non potest. itaque si mandauerim tibi, ut uerbi gratia fundum mihi sestertiis C emeres, tu sestertiis CL emeris, non habebis mecum mandati actionem, etiamsi tanti uelis mihi dare fundum, quanti emendum tibi mandassem; idque maxime Sabino et Cassio placuit. quod si minoris emeris, habebis mecum scilicet actionem, quia qui mandat, ut C milibus emeretur, is utique mandare intellegitur, uti minoris, si posset, emeretur.* (However, when the person to whom I have rightly issued a mandate has exceeded it, I will have an action on mandate with

that Gaius addresses in this text is that an agent who exceeded the terms of the mandate would not only lose his own claims under the action on mandate but would also make himself liable to the mandator for the latter's interest in the mandate being performed. In his careful analysis of this text, Dieter Nörr focuses on the significance of the stance of Sabinus and Cassius that the agent had violated the good-faith obligations of his mandate.[45] The agent was expected to abide by the strict terms of the mandate and faced great legal peril if he exceeded them. The position of Sabinus and Cassius is not inevitable: Proculus had held that the agent would be able to claim compensation up to the mandated price, a view that Gaius approves of as "kinder" (*benignior*, *D.* 17.1.4).[46] In Paul's time, the position of Sabinus remained controversial. Paul disagrees with the position of some jurists (presumably including Sabinus) denying the agent an action on mandate to recover expenses, even if the agent were willing to remit that part of the purchase price that exceeded the price specified by the mandator (*D.* 17.1.3.2).[47] At issue in the position that Sabinus takes is not simply the matter of allocating the costs for a contractual arrangement gone awry; rather, in an adverse judgment on mandate, the agent would suffer *infamia*, a quite serious penalty that would affect his ability to plead cases in court, among other things.[48] In the interpretation of Sabinus, in paying more for the

him to the extent of my interest that he fulfilled the mandate, as long as he was able to fulfill it. But he cannot have any cause of action with me. Thus if I have mandated to you that you buy a farm for me, say, for one hundred sesterces, and you buy it for 150, you will not have an action on mandate with me, even if you are willing to give me the farm at the price at which I mandated you to buy it. This was the position especially of Sabinus and Cassius. But if you buy it for less, you will plainly have an action with me, since the person who mandates that it be bought for one hundred is in any case understood to mandate that it be bought for less if it can be.)

45. Nörr, "Mandatum, fides, amicitia" (1993) 15–20.

46. Gaius (2 *de rerum cottid.*) *D.* 17.1.4: *Sed Proculus recte eum usque ad pretium statutum acturum existimat, quae sententia sane benignior est.* (But Proculus rightly judges that he will sue up to the established price, which is certainly a kinder opinion.) The last phrase has been suspected of interpolation.

47. Paul. (32 *ad ed.*) *D.* 17.1.3.2: *Quod si pretium statui tuque pluris emisti, quidam negaverunt te mandati habere actionem, etiamsi paratus esses id quod excedit remittere: namque iniquum est non esse mihi cum illo actionem, si nolit, illi vero, si velit, mecum esse.* (But if I established a price and you bought it for more, some have denied that you have an action on mandate, even if you should be prepared to remit what exceeded (the mandate): for it is unfair that I not have an action with him, if he should be unwilling, but he, if he should be willing, have one with me.)

48. See Kaser, *Das römische Privatrecht* (1971) 274–77; Kirschenbaum, *Sons, Slaves, and Freedmen* (1987) 194; Nörr, "Mandatum, fides, amicitia" (1993) 15 n. 10. As argued by Wolf, "Lo stigma dell'ignominia" (2010), the disabilities imposed on certain classes of individuals dishonored or condemned in laws from the late republic and early principate came to be described, in the later principate, under the term *infamia*. At this time, *infamia* denotes the specific legal status that it would have in Justinianic law. Thus Iul. *D.* 3.2.1 includes a person condemned in an action on mandate among others who were subject to certain disabilities, including appearing in court on behalf of others (with certain exceptions): for the disabilities, see Ulp. *D.* 3.1.1.8; Wolf, "Lo stigma dell'ignominia" (2010), especially 501, emphasizes that the disabilities were a legal consequence of

property than the mandator had instructed, the agent failed to live up to his obligations based on good faith. Sabinus' view takes little account of the likely consequences of this strict position or of the considerations that would lead agents to take such actions, since we can imagine that good faith could require agents to exercise discretion on behalf a principal to achieve some broader goal, such as to complete a purchase that the mandator evidently desired. But unless the mandator ratified the agent's actions, the latter would face both serious financial risk and grave legal liability.

The doctrine of the first-century jurist Sabinus would seem to suggest that the legal institution of mandate can best be analyzed in terms that Boldizzonni would approve, as a product of Roman social values, not as a flexible form of agency. Even the more favorable position taken by Proculus and eventually by Paul, which removed the serious penalty of *infamia* and allowed the agent's claim to expenses up to the price specified in the mandate, can be seen as protecting the interests of the mandator without regard for the economic consequences of doing so, a goal that can be ascribed to the original conception of mandate. But this perspective does not seem adequate for understanding mandate in Roman law. A property owner was not bound by the terms of a sale when his procurator sold land on terms not in accordance with the mandate he had been given (*C.* 4.35.12, 293), and a procurator could not make a settlement on behalf of a mandator (Paul. *D.* 3.3.60). It is not hard to imagine many cases in which wealthy people with property that they had no capacity to supervise themselves would assign this task to procurators precisely because they expected them to be able to exercise some discretion. This is the crucial role that Mouritsen sees freedmen as filling in the financial affairs of upper-class Romans.[49]

It thus seems likely that procurators administering property at some geographical remove were expected to make independent decisions about the welfare of the property owner whom they served. Formally, however, since any settlement that the procurator made required the property owner's ratification, the procurator faced some personal risk in managing another's property. The formal law surrounding mandate emphasized the good-faith obligations of both the mandator and the agent: the agent, upon accepting the mandate, was expected to perform his task in a way that protected the interests of the

condemnation in various actions. Gaius (*Inst.* 4.182) includes mandate among other actions under which condemnation resulted in *ignominia*. See also Finazzi, "*Amicitia* e doveri giuridici" (2010) 761–76: *infamia* may have originally been conceived as a penalty for *dolus*, deliberate misconduct, on the part of the agent.

49. Cf. Kirschenbaum, *Sons, Slaves, and Freedmen* (1987) 171–93, with a focus on Cicero's affairs.

mandator alone; the only consideration given to the agent is that he was to be compensated for the expenditures that he made in working to carry out the specific instructions of the mandator, and when these instructions were not fully specified, the jurists placed limits on the ways in which the agent could obligate the mandator. If the agent exceeded these limits, he took on himself the risk for doing so. In the Roman law of mandate, then, the agent was not a person contracting with a property owner to perform a service and receiving a premium for acceptance of the risk. Rather, the agent was required to protect the principal against any risk or potential loss in connection with the performance of the contract, and he received no compensation for doing so. There is no formal recognition that procurators enjoyed long-term working relationships with property owners, a situation that would almost necessitate that a procurator anticipate a property owner's wishes. Rather, from the perspective of the law, each action that a procurator took was discrete and created its own set of rights and obligations.

To consider the legal situation of procurators from a modern perspective, both Sabinus' and the kinder interpretation of the agent's actions established a rule that property owners and agents might work around, since the property owner, in any case, could ratify what the agent had done and accept the property at the higher price. From the perspective of the Coase theorem, the establishment of a clear rule about each party's rights and obligations would allow them to achieve "efficient" bargains, but it seems that the possibility of a disastrous verdict against the agent in Sabinus' interpretation would create for the agent an uncertainty not present in the interpretation that Paul makes.[50] The formal rules surrounding mandate would leave the procurator, who was expected to exercise some discretion, in a potentially precarious situation. His rights to recover for expenses that he undertook for the principal would be uncertain, and he simultaneously faced potentially crippling liabilities.

The distinction that Paul makes (*D.* 17.1.1.4, discussed above) between mandate and lease and hire suggests that the reality of agency relationships was more complicated than might be assumed from the jurists' treatment of the contract as arising from Roman upper-class reciprocity. Indeed, in the late classical period, an agent could be paid an honorarium for his services, which was interpreted not as direct compensation for services (recompense excluded in the contract of mandate) but as a recognition of services rendered. Thus, in a rescript from Septimius Severus and Caracalla, an agent acting on a mandate

50. For the Coase theorem, see Coase, "The Problem of Social Cost" (1990); Medema and Zerbe, "The Coase Theorem" (2000).

could recover the expenditures that he undertook on behalf of the principal through an action on mandate, but the agent had to pursue the promised salary through a separate action, before the provincial governor, through *cognitio extraordinaria* (*C.* 4.35.1).[51] The possibility of a compensation for serving as a procurator under a mandate suggests that the arrangements between property owners and their agents could be complex, with incentive systems not directly traceable in the juristic sources.

The contract of mandate thus could be used to provide a legal description for agency relationships that had little in common with the original conception of this contract. Property owners chose these forms of agency presumably because they provided a reasonable solution to the problem of obtaining revenues from properties or funds whose management they could not personally supervise. The linking together of the role of procurator and lessee in late antique legislation (see below) suggests that the job of some procurators was similar to the role played by large-scale middlemen, who leased properties from estate owners and took on the task of collecting the rents from the people actually cultivating the land. Such middlemen would have shielded the property owners against risk and would have been paid for this service by the premium they were paid for performing their service as middlemen. The chief means of enforcement available to the property owner was not to renew the middleman's lease. Otherwise, the property owner had little control over how the lessee performed his duties. Other people performing the service of managing property did so under a different contractual relationship, in that they were defined formally as acting under a mandate, but they received a payment of some sort for their services. In this situation, the property owner could enforce the obligations of the agent by withholding ratification from actions that the agent had undertaken, if they were contrary to the property owner's instructions.

As a practical matter, procurators managing property belonging to others had to exercise some discretion in enforcing obligations and buying and selling property. Withholding ratification would represent a drastic step, then, since a property owner's resort to this action would make it far more difficult for the agent to perform business with third parties, while also imposing substantial financial burden on the agent. It seems to be a reasonable hypothesis that withholding ratification from actions taken by an agent would result in the end

51. *C.* 4.35.1: *Adversus eum cuius negotia gesta sunt de pecunia, quam de propriis opibus vel ab aliis mutuo acceptam erogasti, mandati actione pro sorte et usuris potes experiri: de salario quod promisit a praeside provinciae cognitio praebebitur.* (You can sue a person whose affairs have been managed (by you) for the money that you spent out from your own resources or received on loan from others, in an action on mandate both for the principal and interest; a hearing will be provided by the provincial governor concerning the honorarium that he promised.)

of the agent's contractual relationship with the property owner (more on this below).[52] It is useful to consider this use of mandate from the perspective of the "relational contract," a term that legal scholars use to characterize a contract in which both parties have a continued interest in maintaining their relationship and are thus willing to make adjustments to the contract's terms. The parties must do so because it is impossible to foresee at the outset how changing circumstances might affect their interests and their ability to abide by the original terms of the contract.[53] The good faith of the parties played a key role in such arrangements. It not only provided a basis to define the obligations and liabilities of the two parties to the contract, but it also characterized what was essential to maintain an ongoing business relationship. A lawsuit on mandate represented a drastic action, since it involved such high stakes (including, potentially, the penalty of *infamia* for the loser) and since, from an economic perspective, it would serve to allocate resources arising from the contract, that is, to divide up the surplus.[54] The high stakes involved in a suit on mandate would encourage the parties to engage in "private ordering" by coming to a friendly settlement.

The financial risks involved in serving as a procurator for a property owner are likely to have informed the late imperial government's policy of forbidding members of town councils (decurions) from engaging in this activity. In 439, the emperors Theodosius II and Valentinian III ruled that "a decurion [*curialis*] should not be a procurator or a lessee [*conductor*] of someone else's property, or a surety or a mandator of a lessee (i.e., ordering that person to take up a lease). Indeed We ordain that no obligation arise either to a lessor or a lessee from a contract of this type" (*C.* 4.65.30).[55] The motivation for this prohibition lies in the late imperial government's efforts to protect local town councils' integrity and ability to perform fiscal functions, especially those connected with the collection of taxes. Accordingly, decurions were restricted in their right to alienate their property during their lifetimes and to dispose of it after their deaths.[56] Any service as a procurator put the decurion's property at risk.

From another perspective, the legal authorities in other areas of the law as-

52. Kehoe, "Mandate and the Management of Business in the Roman Empire" (forthcoming).

53. For this type of relational contracting, see especially Macneil, "The Many Futures of Contracts" (1974); Macneil, "Contracts: Adjustment of Long-Term Economic Relations" (1978); Goetz and Scott, "Principles of Relational Contracts" (1981); Furubotn and Richter, *Institutions and Economic Theory* (2005) 154–61, 173–90, 292–92; Hviid, "Long-Term Contracts and Relational Contracts" (2000).

54. Cf. Craswell, "Performance, Reliance, and One-Sided Information" (1989) 388.

55. *C.* 4.65.30 (= *Nov. Theod.* 9): *Curialis neque procurator neque conductor alienarum rerum nec fideiussor aut mandator conductoris existat. alioquin nullam obligationem neque locatori neque conductori ex huiusmodi contractu competere sancimus.*

56. See Kehoe, "Urbanization, Land, and Political Control" (forthcoming).

sumed that procurators could act with considerable discretion, since authorities took steps to limit the possibility that procurators might abuse their positions—for instance, by being too aggressive in enforcing debts owed to their employer or even by enriching themselves at the expense of people with whom they did business. The bad reputation that some procurators gained is partly why soldiers were enjoined from serving in this capacity. Diocletian ruled that payments made to a soldier serving as a procurator in contravention of the law had no legal effect and could be reclaimed (*C.* 4.6.5, 290).[57] In the later empire, the use of soldiers as procurators was seen to be an abuse. The emperor Leo (*C.* 4.65.31, 458) forbade soldiers from, among other functions, becoming lessees of other people's property or procurators, "lest, neglecting the use of their weapons, they turn to rural work and become oppressive to their neighbors on the presumption of their military rank."[58] Justinian also established rules against soldiers serving as lessees of other people's property (presumably on a large scale to collect the rents for the owners), decrying how soldiers would "dare to come to such sordid jobs and, abandoning their public pursuits and their victorious standards, to jump into leases of other people's property and not to show the ferocity of their weapons against the enemy, but to turn them against their neighbors and perhaps the very wretched bound tenants [*coloni*] whose management they have undertaken" (*C.* 4.65.35 pr., 530?).[59] In Justinian's conception, procurators were employed on the basis of leases, which suggests that a practice documented in classical law had become more widespread in late antiquity.

The Actions on Mandate and Unauthorized Administration

The discretion that agents in many cases were expected to exercise on behalf of property owners raises the question about the economic significance of the actions on mandate and unauthorized administration.[60] In these actions, the

57. Ulpian specifies that soldiers could not serve as procurators in court cases unless they were pleading a case on behalf of their entire unit (*D.* 3.3.8.2).

58. *C.* 4.65.31: . . . *ne omisso armorum usu ad opus rurestre se conferant et vicinis graves praesumptione cinguli militaris existant.*

59. *C.* 4.65.35 pr.: . . . *ad huiusmodi sordida audeant venire ministeria et relictis studiis publicis signisque victricibus ad conductiones alienarum rerum prosilire et armorum atrocitatem non in hostes ostendere, sed contra vicinos et forsitan adversus ipsos miseros colonos, quos procurandos susceperant, convertere . . .*

60. The Praetor's Edict apparently provided for two causes of action, namely, praetorian *formulae in factum conceptae*, when someone willingly managed the business of an absent or deceased

principal could enforce the agent's obligations, and the agent could claim the expenses that he had undertaken while carrying out business for the principal. Previously, I have discussed how the action on mandate effectively ended a "relational contract," one in which the parties were connected to one another in a long-term economic relationship that they generally wanted to preserve. In many cases, the same observation would apply to an action on unauthorized administration, when we consider the types of arrangements defined under it. Under this circumstance, we should expect that most disputes would be resolved privately by the parties involved, without recourse to the courts. But the Roman jurists and the chancery, the latter when responding to petitions, sought to give the clearest and most precise definitions possible for the rights and duties of the parties involved in a contract of mandate. A lawsuit on mandate, with potentially high stakes involving *infamia*, is likely to have represented a breakdown of this relationship, and the role of the law was to make predictable and equitable judgments when a dispute arose that could not be resolved through negotiation.[61] This effort meant that, although most legal disputes would never come to court, precise legal rules would provide a kind of legal endowment, on the basis of which private negotiations could take place, as Mnookin and Kornhauser argue in their famous 1979 article about the negotiation surrounding divorces in American law.[62] This does not mean that all economic relationships operated within what Mnookin and Kornhauser there call the "shadow of the law," since it is highly unlikely that Roman legal institutions were uniformly socially adequate. But it does seem likely, that, on balance, Roman legal institutions fulfilled this complex function, with broader implications for the economy. The law concerning unauthorized administration gave the parties a similar legal endowment and thus made it more likely that people would intervene, when necessary, to take actions that would benefit individuals and, by implication, society as a whole.

Conclusion

To conclude, the contract of mandate (and also the related quasi contract known as "unauthorized administration," or *negotia gesta*) provided a way to define the

person, and the *bonae fidei iudicia,* more generally for the management of the business of another. See Kaser, *Das Römische Privatrecht* (1971) 589; Finazzi, "Amicitia e doveri giuridici" (2010) 807–8, 812.

61. See Kehoe, *Law and the Rural Economy* (2007) 98, and the above discussion of the relational contract.

62. Mnookin and Kornhauser, "Bargaining in the Shadow of the Law" (1979).

rights and obligations of people engaged in a wide variety of activities essential to Roman commercial life. In credit arrangements and large-scale purchases, one of the principal uses of mandate was to facilitate large-scale transactions by helping to overcome information problems that otherwise would tend to discourage people from investing. At the root of the relationship between mandator and agent was reciprocity, one that certainly drew its origins from the upper-class values of *fides* and *officium*. But in the complex commercial world of the Roman Principate, an essential feature of this reciprocity was an ongoing business relationship that required cooperation and flexibility. When considered by the jurists or the Roman chancery in response to a petition, a mandate either to stand surety for a borrower or to lend money appears to be a one-off, gratuitous transaction, but most such transactions were likely part of more complex relationships in which the mandator and agent might exchange roles or might be involved in other business deals. This reciprocity was an important feature of the economy of the Roman Empire, and the task of the Roman legal authorities in defining rules for mandate was to define clear-cut rules in accordance with which significant financial relationships could be entered. But the law could not always keep up with the changing roles that property owners developed for agents acting under a mandate, particularly procurators with a broad portfolio in managing property.

The concern of the jurists and the imperial chancery was to promote freedom of contracting by making the legal consequences of contracts as clear and predictable as possible, but in regulating mandate, they remained consistent to the original conception of mandate as a gratuitous contract designed to serve the interests of the mandator alone. The continued insistence on protecting the interests of the mandator perhaps limited the uses to which procurators could be put and also imposed costs on third parties who entered into contracts with agents, since there was always the possibility that the principal would not ratify what the agent did. Mandate, then, did not create a form of agency comparable to that of a modern firm. Its success depended on the understanding between the mandator and the agent, or, more specifically, on the agent's confidence that the mandator would stand behind the agent's actions that required discretion. Even if the institutions of mandate and, under the appropriate circumstances, unauthorized administration did not represent "efficient" solutions to the problem of agency in the Roman economy, their endurance, to judge by their treatment in third-century rescripts in the *Code of Justinian*, suggests their continued importance to Roman commercial life. The Roman legal authorities could define rules that made the legal institutions operate more efficiently within Roman society, but the continuing existence of the institutions themselves created a sort of institutional "path dependence," in that institutions such as mandate helped to establish the basic values of society and would thus influence the ways in which economic activity was organized.[63]

Bibliography

Abatino, B., G. Dari-Mattiacci, and E. C. Perotti. "Depersonalization of Business in Ancient Rome." *Oxford Journal of Legal Studies* 31.1 (2011): 365–89.

Aubert, J.-J. *Business Managers in Ancient Rome: A Social and Economic Study of* Institores, *200 B.C.–A.D. 250*. Leiden, 1994.

Bodel, J. "Slave Labour and Roman Society." In Bradley and Cartledge, *The Cambridge World History of Slavery* (2011) 311–36.

Boldizzoni F. *The Poverty of Clio: Resurrecting Economic History*. Princeton, 2011.

Bouckaert, B., and G. De Geest, eds. *Encyclopedia of Law and Economics*. 5 vols. Cheltenham, 2000. Available in an online 1999 edition at http://reference.findlaw.com/lawandeconomics/contents.html.

Bradley, K., and P. Cartledge, eds. *The Cambridge World History of Slavery*. Vol. 1, *The Ancient Mediterranean World*. Cambridge, 2011.

Bresson, A. *L'économie de la Grèce des cités*. 2 vols. Paris, 2007.

Broekaert, W. "Freedmen and Agency in Roman Business." In A. Wilson and M. Flohr, eds., *Urban Craftsmen and Traders in the Roman World*, 222–53. Oxford, 2016.

Bruhns, H. "Cambridge, Bordeaux ou Heidelberg: À quoi servent les 'classiques'?" In C. Apicella, M.-L. Haack, and F. Lerouxel, eds., *Les affaires de Monsieur Andreau: Économie et société du monde romain*, 29–41. Scripta antiqua 61. Bordeaux, 2014.

Bürge, A. "Vertrag und personale Abhängigkeiten im Rom der späten Republik und der frühen Kaiserzeit." *ZRG* 97 (1980): 104–56.

Camodeca, G. *Tabulae Pompeianae Sulpiciorum, edizione critica dell'archivio dei Sulpicii*. 2 vols. Vetera: Ricerche di storia epigrafia e antichità 12. Rome, 1999.

Coase, R. H. "The Problem of Social Cost." *Journal of Law and Economics* 3 (1960): 1–44. Reprinted in R. H. Coase, *The Firm, the Market, and the Law*, 95–156. Chicago, 1990.

Corbino, A., M. Humbert, and G. Negri, eds. *Homo, caput, persona: La costruzione giuridica dell'identita nell'esperienza romana: Dall'epoca di Plauto a Ulpiano*. Pavia, 2010.

Craswell, R. "Performance, Reliance, and One-Sided Information." *Journal of Legal Studies* 18 (1989): 365–401.

de Ligt, L. "Legal History and Economic History: The Case of the *Actiones Adiecticiae Qualitatis*." *Tijdschrift voor Rechtsgeschiedenis* 47 (1999): 205–26.

Finazzi, G. "Amicitia e doveri giuridici." In Corbino, Humbert, and Negri, *Homo, caput, persona* (2010) 633–861.

Finley, M. I. *The Ancient Economy*. Updated edition, with a foreword by I. Morris. Berkeley, 1999.

Frier, B. W., ed. *The "Codex" of Justinian: A New Annotated Translation, with Parallel Latin and Greek Text*. 3 vols. Cambridge, 2016.

63. On institutional path dependence, see Frier and Kehoe, "Law and Economic Institutions" (2007) 137–42.

Frier, B. W., and D. P. Kehoe. "Law and Economic Institutions." In W. Scheidel, I. Morris, and R. Saller, eds., *The Cambridge Economic History of the Greco-Roman World*, 113–43. Cambridge, 2007.

Furubotn, E. G., and R. Richter. *Institutions and Economic Theory: The Contribution of the New Institutional Economics*. 2nd ed. Ann Arbor, 2005.

Goetz, C. J., and R. E. Scott. 1981. "Principles of Relational Contracts." *Virginia Law Review* 67 (6): 1089–1150.

Greif, A. *Institutions and the Path to the Modern Economy: Lessons from Medieval Trade*. Cambridge, 2006.

Hodgson, G. M. *Evolution and Institutions: On Evolutionary Economics and the Evolution of Economics*. Cheltenham, 1999.

Hviid, M. "Long-Term Contracts and Relational Contracts." In Bouckaert and De Geest, *Encyclopedia of Law and Economics* (2000) 3: 46–72.

Kaser, M. *Das römische Privatrecht. Erster Abschnitt, Das altrömische, das vorklassische und klassische Recht*. 2nd ed. HdA 10.3.3.1 Munich, 1971.

Kehoe, D. P. "Agency, Tutorship, and the Protection of Pupils in Roman Law." In D. Mantovani, ed., *Diritto romano e economia: Due modi di pensare e organizzare il mondo (nei primi tre secoli dell'Impero)*, 119–40. Pavia, 2017.

Kehoe, D. P. "Contracts, Agency, and Transaction Costs in the Roman Economy." In Kehoe, Ratzan, and Yiftach, *Law and Transaction Costs* (2015) 231–52.

Kehoe, D. P. "Law, Agency, and Growth in the Roman Economy." In P. J. du Plessis, ed., *New Frontiers: Law and Society in the Roman World*, 177–91. Edinburgh, 2013.

Kehoe, D. P. *Law and the Rural Economy in the Roman Empire*. Ann Arbor, 2007.

Kehoe, D. P. "Mandate and the Management of Business in the Roman Empire." In G. Dari-Mattiacci, ed., *Roman Law and Economics*. Oxford, forthcoming.

Kehoe, D. P. "Urbanization, Land, and Political Control in the Roman Empire." In B. Palme et al., eds. *Land and Power in the Ancient and Post-Ancient World*. Vienna, forthcoming.

Kehoe, D. P., D. Ratzan, and U. Yiftach. "Introduction: Transaction Costs, Ancient History, and the Law." In Kehoe, Ratzan, and Yiftach, *Law and Transaction Costs* (2015), 1–35.

Kehoe, D. P., D. Ratzan, and U. Yiftach, eds. *Law and Transaction Costs in the Ancient Economy*. Ann Arbor, 2015.

Kirschenbaum, A. *Sons, Slaves, and Freedmen in Roman Commerce*. Jerusalem, 1987.

Klinck, F. "Zur Bedeutung des Wortes procurator in den Quellen des klassischen Rechts." *ZRG* 124 (2007): 25–52.

Macneil, I. R. "Contracts: Adjustment of Long-Term Economic Relations under Classical, Neoclassical, and Relational Contract Law." *Northwestern University Law Review* 72.6 (1978): 854–905.

Macneil, I. R. "The Many Futures of Contracts." *Southern California Law Review* 47.3 (1974): 691–816.

Medema, S. G., and R. O. Zerbe Jr. "The Coase Theorem." In Bouckaert and De Geest, *Encyclopedia of Law and Economics* (2000) 1: 836–92.

Mnookin, R. H., and L. Kornhauser. "Bargaining in the Shadow of the Law: The Case of Divorce." *Yale Law Journal* 85 (1979): 950–97.

Morley, N. "Slavery under the Principate." In Bradley and Cartledge, *The Cambridge World History of Slavery* (2011) 265–86.

Mouritsen, H. *The Freedman in the Roman World.* Cambridge, 2011.

Nörr, D. "Mandatum, fides, amicitia." In D. Nörr and S. Nishimura, eds., *Mandatum und Verwandtes: Beiträge zum römsichen und modernen Recht*, 13–37. Berlin, 1993.

Ogilvie, S. "'Whatever Is, Is Right'? Economic Institutions in Pre-industrial Europe." *Economic History Review* 60.4 (2007): 649–84.

Plescia, J. "The Development of Agency in Roman Law." *Labeo* 30 (1984): 171–90.

Randazzo, S. *Mandare: Radici della doverosità e percorsi consensualistici nell'evoluzione del mandato romano*. Milan, 2005.

Schiavone, A. *The Invention of Law in the West*, trans. J. Carden and A. Shugaar. Cambridge, MA, 2012.

Sherwin-White, A. N. *The Letters of Pliny: A Social and Historical Commentary*. Oxford, 1966. 2nd ed., 1985.

Temin, P. *The Roman Market Economy.* Princeton, 2013.

Terpstra, T. T. *Trading Communities in the Roman World: A Microeconomic and Institutional Perspective*. Columbia Studies in the Classical Tradition 37. Leiden, 2013.

Verboven, K. *The Economy of Friends: Economic Aspects of* Amicitia *and Patronage in the Late Republic*. Collection Latomus 269. Brussels, 2002.

Wacke, A. "Die adjektizischen Klagen im Überblick." *ZRG* 111 (1994): 280–362.

Wolf, J. G. "Der neue pompejanische Urkundenfund: Zu Camodecas 'Edizione critica dell'archivio puteolano dei Sulpicii.'" *ZRG* 118 (2001): 73–132.

Wolf, J. G. "Lo stigma dell'ignominia." In Corbino, Humbert, and Negeri, *Homo, caput, persona* (2010) 491–550.

Zimmermann, R. *The Law of Obligations: Roman Foundations of the Civilian Tradition*. Oxford, 1996.

CHAPTER 7

Cui Bono? The True Beneficiaries of Roman Private Law

Thomas A. J. McGinn

It is a truth universally acknowledged that law and legal systems as a rule serve the interests of the wealthy and powerful. The idea can trace a pedigree back as far as Plato's *Republic*, though what Thrasymachus actually says there is that justice is nothing other than the interest of the stronger—if he had said this about law, he might have received less pushback.[1] In any case, we might do better to take a point of departure from the critical legal studies movement of the 1970s and 1980s.[2] Its exponents, often known as the "crits," make a number of claims of direct relevance to our theme, including the argument that law tends to serve the interests of the elite by protecting them against demands for justice on the part of the subelite—identified by these scholars in terms of the poor and the marginalized. In Roman law studies, this argument was anticipated, in a sense, by an important book published by John Kelly in 1966.[3]

One might venture to assert that this point, when stated in very general terms, is unremarkable, uncontested, and unoriginal. All the same, a counterquestion can be put: if it were so obvious that their legal system operated on this principle, just how were the Romans able to manage a system of such drastic socioeconomic inequality so successfully for so long? To address this question in this essay, I begin by introducing work that bears directly on this theme, perhaps not coincidentally produced by a pair of Bruce Frier's students, Dennis Kehoe and Cynthia Bannon. I then examine some further perspectives relevant to the problem, above all, an important study by Edoardo Volterra. Finally, I survey a variety of material drawn from Roman private law to help elucidate what approach or

1. Plato, *Rep.* 1.338C.

2. See the classic statement in Gordon, "Critical Legal Histories" (1984).

3. J. M. Kelly, *Roman Litigation* (1966) esp. 1–84. More recently, North, Wallis, and Weingast (*Violence and Social Orders* [2009] 44–45, 48–49, 159–60, 195) present Rome as a "natural state" (oscillating, in fact, between a "basic" and a "mature" natural state) in which legal institutions largely or wholly advance the interests of the elite. Their analysis lacks the sophistication of Kelly's, however.

approaches seem best.[4] The focus of this essay is on the classical period of Roman law and what immediately precedes, ca. 100 BCE to ca. 235 CE.

Most historians argue or at least assume that Roman private law, like other aspects of their legal system or, indeed, of Roman society in general, was stacked in favor of the elite. In broad terms, this is entirely correct, as I hope to make clear. My particular concern here lies in coming to a better understanding first of how to define the term *elite* for this specific purpose. In other words, I ask whether we should construe the beneficiaries of this system to include only the very top of Roman society—the upper 1.5 percent—or, more flexibly, to embrace the entire range of the upper classes and even some elements definable as "subelite." On a deeper level, I am also curious to know whether it is possible to arrive at a more nuanced appraisal of the meaning of the term *interests* in this context, that is, to inquire whether wealthy and influential Romans conceived of their interests largely or exclusively in a narrow, material, short-term manner or shared a broader perspective. In concrete terms, the latter alternative would mean that the political and legal authorities deemed it worth their while to accommodate the needs of a relatively wider sector of society than one might otherwise assume. This is a very difficult set of questions but worth at least some modest share of our attention. What I hope to show in this essay is that the private law system does seem to have been designed and to have operated, only in appearance paradoxically, along the lines of greater inclusion in both senses, if ultimately in order better to serve those at the very top.

The Kehoe-Bannon Thesis

The Roman system of courts has a certain reputation for dysfunctionality.[5] In antiquity, the outcomes of lawsuits were thought to be heavily influenced by the three factors of money, power, and influence (*pecunia*, *potentia*, and *gratia*), meaning that forensic verdicts were deemed to be largely determined by those possessed of certain economic, social, and political advantages. This perception generated a conspicuous amount of complaints and cynicism.[6] One huge difficulty lay in the fact that, in principle, appeal from or even review of civil

4. More along these lines can be found in the companion piece to this article: McGinn, "Celsus and the *Pauper*" (2016).

5. See, above all, Frier, *The Rise of the Roman Jurists* (1985) esp. 27–41.

6. J. M. Kelly, *Roman Litigation* (1966) 31–68. For a very well-known piece of evidence, see Petron. *Satyricon* 14.2, with Nörr, *Rechtskritik in der römischen Antike* (1974) 150. See also Drexler, "*Potentia*" (1959) 86–89; Garnsey, *Social Status and Legal Privilege* (1970) 207–13; MacMullen, *Corruption and the Decline of Rome* (1988) esp. 87–96.

verdicts was long impossible, meaning that there was, apart from a very few exceptions, no effective means to challenge a decision either by a public official or a finder of fact, even in cases of manifest injustice.[7]

It is true that countervailing influences mitigated some of the effects produced by this situation. These factors include the web of client-patron relationships that offered protection to many of the less-advantaged in Roman society; the prospect of a loss in reputation for misbehaving actual or potential litigants, whether generated by sanctions unofficial in nature (a blow to one's *existimatio*) or official (the infliction of praetorian *infamia* or censorial *nota*); and judicial remedies such as the *missio in bona/possessionem*.[8] Finally, in recent years, scholars have become sensitive to the often subtle ways in which the *iudex* and the private trial itself might be "managed" so as to avoid or soften some of the types of outcomes decried by our sources.[9] The distinction the jurists drew between *bonae* and *malae causae* suggests that they were or believed themselves to be routinely capable of differentiating valid from invalid cases in the abstract, even in situations where a *bona causa* did not prevail in the courts.[10] This arguably helped them not to eliminate dysfunction on this level (a tall order, this side of Plato's *Republic*) but better to manage it.

7. Frier, *The Rise of the Roman Jurists* (1985) esp. 213, 227–30. For the means available to raise such challenges in the republic, see A. H. M. Jones, "Imperial and Senatorial Jurisdiction" (1955) 464–71 (more optimistic than most); Licandro, *In magistratu damnari* (1999) esp. 77–136; Masi Doria, "A proposito di limiti e responsabilità" (2011); Masi Doria, "Giusto processo" (2011) 400–405; Metzger, "Litigation" (2013/2015) 276–78. The right to judge cases on appeal was, on the better view, voted to Octavian in 30 BCE by the Senate (see Dio 51.19.5–7) and was soon to emerge as a cornerstone of the imperial legal system, which, all the same, in important respects developed gradually over time: see, e.g., Jones, op cit., 471–76, 485–87 (holding for 19 BCE, with the grant of *imperium consulare*); Galsterer, "Administration of Justice" (1996) 407–8; Kaser and Hackl, *Das römische Zivilprozessrecht*[2] (1996) 501–10; Fanizza, *L'amministrazione della giustizia* (1999) 11–60; Rainer, "Zum Ursprung" (2003); Randazzo, "Doppio grado" (2003); Spagnuolo Vigorita, "La repubblica restaurata" (2007/2013) 413–19; Wankerl, *Appello ad Principem* (2009) 16; Masuelli, "Il principe come giudice privato" (2012); Metzger, op. cit., 287–88; Venturini, "La responsabilità del giudice" (2013) 472; Peachin, "Augustus' Emergent Judicial Powers" (2015); Tuori, *The Emperor of Law* (2016).

8. On these, see J. M. Kelly, *Roman Litigation* (1966) 20–30; Kelly does not, however, accord them all that much weight. On *missio*, see Metzger, "Litigation" (2013/2015) 279. See also the next note.

9. See, recently, Metzger, "Lawsuits" (2007); Metzger, "Remedy" (2012). On the much-discussed theme of liability for the negligent or corrupt *iudex*, see, in place of a vast literature, Rampazzo, *Sententiam dicere* (2012) 141–64; Metzger, "Litigation" (2013/2015) 277–78; Venturini, "La responsabilità del giudice" (2013); Pergami, "Il ruolo e la funzione del giudice" (2014). Also much discussed is the repression of malicious behavior on the part of litigants, on which see Giomaro, "La scelta del mezzo giudiziale" (2011); Centola, "La disciplina della condotta vessatoria" (2012). See also Metzger, "Litigation" (2013/2015) 287–88, on the sanctions for contempt available under the procedure known as *cognitio*. For a discussion of a variety of challenges and how they were met, see Wacke, "*Res iudicata pro veritate accipitur*?" (2011).

10. See the discussion in Wacke, "*Bonam sive malam causam habere*" (2003). This is not to say, of course, that all or even most cases were crystal clear.

At the same time, there is evidence of a higher-order purpose, namely, that some Romans believed that law, in terms of its own operation, ideally ought to perform the function of a leveler or effacer of the social and economic differences between litigants.[11] This value was shared by many of the political and legal authorities responsible for the development of Roman private law in the early empire. My focus here is on the formation and application of certain legal rules by those same authorities.[12]

In his recent book on law and the rural economy, Dennis Kehoe develops two points of major relevance to the discussion in this essay.[13] Both concern the contract of hire-lease, *locatio conductio*. In his second chapter, he argues that the Roman government generally protected the land-tenure rights of small-scale tenants, *coloni*, on imperial properties, against the interests of the *conductores*, or middlemen. The *conductores* collected the rent from the *coloni* on behalf of the imperial treasury but, in Kehoe's view, did not sublet the land to them. They also farmed certain properties not cultivated by the *coloni*, though these tenants were supposed to provide labor and draft animals to assist in their exploitation. Kehoe shows how the government's concern to maintain the security of the food supply encouraged, albeit at some cost to efficiency, the development of a policy that supported the interests of the indispensable small-scale cultivators, even when these collided with those of a group that was no less important and perhaps better placed to assert itself.

In his third chapter, Kehoe goes on to show how this policy informed the actions of the political and legal authorities in balancing the interests of wealthy private landowners and their tenants. In a sense, the *colonus* (tenant) who leased agricultural property from a landlord to farm was an agent or even a sort of employee of the latter. The challenge for the owner was to lay down appropriate incentives to improve tenant's performance and then to monitor this.[14] Since qualified *coloni* were in short supply, landowners were motivated to make concessions in negotiating and applying the terms of their contracts,

11. See Quint. *IO* 12.7.6: *non enim fortuna causas vel iustas vel improbas facit.* (For the [social] status [of the litigant] does not make a case either right or wrong.).

12. The discussion that follows deals with the matter of equity and the law as it arises in particular contexts. I follow, in principle, the line adopted by Nörr (review of Bürge [1975/2003] 949 with literature), namely, that, broadly speaking, law and equity are not in essential opposition to each other and that equity serves the realization of law as correctly understood. See also the trenchant comments of Honoré, review of Frier (1983) 389–90. The useful reflections of E. P. Thompson on law as "a logic of equity" are noted in the concluding section below.

13. Kehoe, *Law and the Rural Economy in the Roman Empire* (2007). There is insufficient space here to develop a true intellectual genealogy for what follows. Important in addition to the honorand's work discussed below are Frier's "Law, Technology, and Social Change" (1979) and "Law, Economics, and Disasters Down on the Farm" (1989–90).

14. Kehoe, *Law and the Rural Economy in the Roman Empire* (2007) 95.

meaning to show a degree of flexibility and disposition to compromise. Kehoe illuminates these trends with reference to the modern concept of the relational contract.[15] Both the treatment of agricultural hire-lease contracts by emperors and jurists and the conduct of landlords just described belie the great social and economic asymmetry that prevailed between their tenants and themselves.[16] This is not to say that all owners pursued a policy of enlightened self-interest, of course. The difference in status and power was just too tempting for some. The legal authorities generally refrained from favoring the interests of one side over another and encouraged resort to bargaining by the parties, as a way of improving overall productivity, over a reliance on litigation.[17]

At first glance, it might seem that policy makers behaved more aggressively in support of the "little guy" in the first instance, but closer inspection suggests that their aim in both cases was simply to protect the rights of a crucial but low-status group—the farmers who actually raised the crops vital to Rome's economy and the material existence of its population—against the interests of those who were in a position to exploit them in a manner that was not only unjust but possibly dysfunctional to the system. Thus, when I speak of the interests of the latter group, composed of imperial *conductores* and private landlords, I mean these interests as they were often too narrowly construed by some of these exploiters. The authorities were attempting to resolve what might be described as a collective action problem.[18]

Our next example takes us from the law of contracts to that of property. Cynthia Bannon, in her book *Gardens and Neighbors*, discusses a lawsuit, resolved through an imperial rescript, over a servitude concerning a Statilius Taurus, his neighbors, and the water they channeled from a spring on his farm in southern Etruria.[19] Certainty over the identity of this Statilius and, therefore, the emperor in question is strictly impossible, but Bannon offers the plausible

15. Relational contracts are long-running agreements in which the parties display a flexibility and willingness to renegotiate the terms without recourse to the legal system, out of a need and/or a desire to work together and an inability to predict important future contingencies. See, e.g., Hviid, "Long-Term Contracts and Relational Contracts" (2000); Furubotn and Richter, *Institutions and Economic Theory*² (2005) 154–61, 173–90, 291–92.

16. Kehoe, *Law and the Rural Economy in the Roman Empire* (2007) 100.

17. Kehoe, *Law and the Rural Economy in the Roman Empire* (2007) 129.

18. Collective action problems are often invoked by expressive law theorists. There are two main types, both of which draw on game theory. One is the "cooperation problem," where ideals of the common good conflict with individual self-interest, such as with littering or cleaning up after one's dog. The other is the "coordination problem," where government or some other neutral arbiter must lay down a convention, for which the most popular example is perhaps the question of what side of the road we drive on. For discussion and literature, see McGinn, "The Expressive Function of Law and the *Lex Imperfecta*" (2015) 8–9; McGinn, "La funzione espressiva del diritto" (2015) 96–97.

19. Bannon, *Gardens and Neighbors* (2009) 125–37.

view that this Statilius is likely to be the competent, loyal, and trusted Augustan general T. Statilius Taurus (*consul suffectus* in 37 BCE, *consul ordinarius* in 26) or one of his sons, which would make Augustus or Tiberius the emperor issuing the rescript.[20]

As Bannon points out, the conflict lies between a very prominent and well-connected figure and a group that must have been composed of either local worthies or smallholders.[21] In either case, there is an evident asymmetry in status between the parties to the suit—mirroring the asymmetry in the claimed servitude between dominant and servient owners. We find the status differential hinted at in the fact that while the plaintiffs found it necessary to petition the emperor—had they already tried their luck in the praetor's court to no avail?—the emperor writes back not to them but to the defendant.

> *Et Atilicinus ait Caesarem Statilio Tauro rescripsisse in haec verba: "Hi, qui ex fundo Sutrino aquam ducere soliti sunt, adierunt me proposueruntque aquam, qua per aliquot annos usi sunt ex fonte, qui est in fundo Sutrino, ducere <se> non potuisse, quod fons exaruisset, et postea ex eo fonte aquam fluere coepisse: petieruntque a me, ut quod ius non neglegentia aut culpa sua amiserant, sed quia ducere non poterant, his restitueretur. quorum mihi postulatio cum non iniqua visa sit, succurrendum his putavi. itaque quod ius habuerunt tunc, cum primum ea aqua pervenire ad eos non potuit, id eis restitui placet."* (Paul. [15 *ad Plautium*] *D.* 8.3.35)

> [And Atilicinus says that the emperor composed a rescript to Statilius Taurus in the following words: "These men who have been accustomed to channel water from the estate at Sutrium approached me and set forth the following situation of fact. It had become impossible <for them> to channel the water from the source on the estate at Sutrium that they had made use of for a number of years because the source had dried up, and afterward water (again) began to flow from that source. And (so) they requested me to restore to them that right which they had lost not through negligence or their own fault but because they were physically unable to channel the water. Since their request did not seem unjust to me, I thought that they ought to be helped. So I have decided that the

20. Bannon, *Gardens and Neighbors* (2009) 126. Nagl, "Statilius" 34 (1929) 2199, tentatively identifies the Taurus in this text with the Augustan general T. Statilius Taurus.

21. Bannon, *Gardens and Neighbors* (2009) 134. As owners, they might be regarded as of higher status than the tenant farmers studied by Kehoe, but the important point is their situation relative to their adversary, here the wealthy and well-connected Statilius Taurus.

right be restored to them that they held at the point in time when access to this water first became impossible for them." (Paul in the fifteenth book on Plautius)]

The decision can be supported perhaps by doctrinal reasons—the outcome would be that where the interruption in use does not result from the fault of the servitude holder, the rule does not apply—and more certainly by considerations of equity that arise plainly from the text.[22] All the same, the result is a bit surprising, as Bannon points out, because the emperor relaxes a strict application of the use-it-or-lose-it rule—of general validity for servitudes—in favor of the side with less political clout.[23] She argues that there may be an unstated economic rationale as well, in that recognizing the existence of the servitude respected a long-standing custom of sharing water in that locality and, by implication, reduced transaction costs by upholding a known and respected rule.[24]

It is tempting to synthesize the results obtained by these two scholars by examining the outcome from a more strictly political perspective.[25] One of the core sources of legitimacy for the principate was the tribunician power.[26] This put the emperor, assisted by the jurists, in the notional position of defending the weak against the depredations of the strong.[27] The principate witnessed the flourishing of a beneficent ruler ideology that emphasized the virtues of accessibility and fairness in administering law and that itself formed a pillar of imperial rule, even as it could trace a centuries-long pedigree to the ancient Near East.[28]

---

22. See Capogrossi Colognesi, "Le servitù prediali" (2011) 417: "Qui infatti non si ha a che fare con una situazione di fatto esercitata nell'arco di un certo periodo di tempo, ma con un vero e proprio *ius amissum* per *non usus*. La consequenza coerente rispetto alle logiche del *ius civile* appare ovviata in via equitativa dall'intervento imperiale." ("Here indeed we do not have to do with a situation of fact that has operated over a certain period of time, but with a true and proper *ius amissum* for *non usus*. The outcome consistent with the logic of the *ius civile* appears to have been forestalled by an imperial intervention grounded in equity.").

23. Bannon, *Gardens and Neighbors* (2009) 129, 133–34.

24. Bannon, *Gardens and Neighbors* (2009) 133–35.

25. Lack of space does not allow for much more that might be said about the role of law in various contexts—political, ideological, and cultural—not only during the principate, of course, but in the late republic as well. For recent contributions to ongoing debates regarding such matters, see Hölkeskamp, *Reconstructing the Roman Republic* ([2004] 2010); d'Aloja, *L'idea di egalitarismo* (2013).

26. Of course, the political style of emperors differed markedly from one to the next, but this is a fairly consistent theme. See Gilbert, *Die Beziehungen zwischen Princeps und stadtrömischer Plebs* (1976) 139–51, 233–243; Yavetz, *Plebs and Princeps*^{2} (1988) 83–102. Not unrelated is the "ritual of condescension" that some emperors employed to represent themselves as ordinary citizens: see Wallace-Hadrill, "*Civilis Princeps*" (1982).

27. In other words, it had a broad ideological significance and was not directed against any specific target, such as the (contemporary) Senate, with which Augustus often worked closely: cf. Gruen, "Augustus and the Making of the Principate" (2005) 39–42.

28. In place of a vast literature on the beneficent ruler ideology, see Ando, *Imperial Ideology*

At this point, it seems opportune to draw a distinction. The ideology of the just and fair ruler acting as the protector of the weak and vulnerable against the importunities of the strong and predatory is hardly irrelevant to the import of the Kehoe-Bannon thesis, except that, as we have seen, the thesis involves considerations of policy that lie beyond those strictly relevant to this ideology. For the thesis, not only are entire groups or classes concerned, but the decision seems to turn on something more than a desire to uphold the legitimacy of imperial justice.[29] One way of drawing the distinction is to observe that only the thesis can be thought to address genuine collective action problems. Relatively little was at stake in protecting a poor widow from bad treatment in isolated cases involving individual malefactors of no great consequence, especially when compared with the decision to rule against the interest of the wealthy and well-connected, such as Statilius Taurus or a group of wealthy landowners, above all when they might be thought to have the law on their side. At the same time, we should expect manifestations of the application of the Kehoe-Bannon thesis to be packaged as instances of the ruler ideology, which exercised a powerful hold on the attitudes and behaviors of those on both sides of the petition process.[30]

An example of how this worked can be seen in the treatment of the *potentiores* in the law.[31] The *potentiores* were more a social and economic category than a legal one, typically signifying the owners of large landed estates.[32] Against their exploitation of the less powerful (often styled as *tenuiores*), the law provided various defensive measures from the late republic onward.[33] These measures

---

and Provincial Loyalty (2000) esp. 73–130; Tuori, *The Emperor of Law* (2016). On the pedigree, see McGinn, *Widows and Patriarchy* (2008) 37.

29. The two phenomena are so closely linked, however, that one may develop into the other in some circumstances. An example is when one or more judicial decisions cohere into a general policy. This can be argued to occur with imperial legislation on the treatment of slaves by their masters: see Gaius 1.53, with McGinn, "The Expressive Function of Law and the *Lex Imperfecta*" (2015) 9; McGinn, "La funzione espressiva del diritto" (2015) 97–98.

30. So we find in the applications of the Kehoe-Bannon thesis examined above. Instances of the two phenomena can look very similar. For example, a well-known petition of Syrian villagers to Caracalla in 216 might initially seem to belong to either category, though I think one can argue, on the basis of its object (a local priesthood), for classification under the rubric of "beneficent emperor": see Crook, *Legal Advocacy* (1995) 91–95. It is fascinating to observe how the strength of the ruler ideology promoted a style of rhetorical presentation in which petitioners in some cases seem to exaggerate their own weakness and vulnerability as well as the power and influence of their adversaries. For the evidence from Roman Egypt, see Bagnall, "Official and Private Violence" (1989) 211–12; Bryen, *Violence in Roman Egypt* (2013) 99–100, 112, 121–22, 145.

31. On *potentiores* and the law, see Wacke, "The *Potentiores*" (1978); Wacke, "Die *Potentiores*" (1980).

32. Wacke, "The *Potentiores*" (1978) 374; Wacke, "Die *Potentiores*" (1980) 579–80.

33. The word *potentia* and its cognates, while showing a variety of meanings, not infrequently refer to power that is illegitimately held or misused: see Boas, "*Potentatus*" (1934); Trifone, "*Potentiores personae*" (1950–51); Drexler, "*Potentia*" (1959). The evidence from late antiquity illustrates,

represent, to my mind, an important application of the Kehoe-Bannon thesis, as they too exemplify an authoritative intervention on behalf of the weaker against the interests of the stronger, but one that played out over a number of years and was aimed at a persistent threat to public order. The anti-*potentiores* regime also serves as support for the thesis of Edoardo Volterra, which I take up below.[34]

Under the regime developed to shelter the vulnerable against *potentiores,* even landlords might be deemed to require protection.[35] This example offers a suggestion of the limits of the effectiveness of the approach described by the Kehoe-Bannon thesis. Though one might debate how accurate the pessimistic portrait painted by the sources actually is (at least for the classical period),[36] we do well to recognize that the policy cannot, on any estimate, be described as completely effective, as Kehoe well recognizes. The equity-rooted ideals of the jurists could only do so much to counter the effects of a system that was tilted in favor of the wealthy and well-connected.[37]

The rationale for this political and legal positioning had an important economic aspect, if we accept the analysis of Yoram Barzel. He draws a contrast between the type of state that upholds the rule of law, in which the impartial enforcement of clearly delineated property rights promotes greater prosperity, and the criminal, tyrannical, predatory, and dictatorial type of government, where unfair pursuit of private advantage can lead to economic contraction.[38] Without entering into the thorny question of just how successful the Roman government was in its efforts, meaning both those directed against the *potentiores* and those aimed more generally against this kind of challenge, it can be conceded that this idea has its attractions, as does the political explanation overall.

---

among other things, concerns with interference in the administration of the empire, especially in the judicial and fiscal systems, which were compromised, to some extent, by the actions of the *potentiores*: see Gaudemet, "Les abus des *potentes*" (1966/1979); Santucci, "*Potentiores* e abusi processuali" (1996); Elia, "Il principio giusnaturalistico" (2010); the work of Andreas Wacke cited above in the notes.

34. A similar concern arose in an earlier period that was addressed by the *leges Publicia* and *Cincia;* see the discussion in McGinn, "The Expressive Function of Law and the *Lex Imperfecta*" (2015) 32–39; McGinn, "La funzione espressiva del diritto" (2015) 132–40.

35. Iul.-Afric. *D.* 19.2.33 (see also Serv.-Afric. *D.* 19.2.35 pr.) concerns a landlord unable to prevent a *potentior* from interfering with his tenant's exploitation of his farm; the landlord is liable only for remission or return of the rent, not for the tenant's interest. See Wacke, "Dig. 19.2.33" (1976) esp. 489–93; Wacke, "The *Potentiores*" (1978) 383–85; Frier, *Landlords and Tenants* (1980) 81–82; Wacke, "Die *Potentiores*" (1980) 596–98.

36. For pessimism about the situation in the classical period and especially in late antiquity, see Wacke, "The *Potentiores*" (1978) 380, 387–89; Wacke, "Die *Potentiores*" (1980) 589, 604–7.

37. In this matter, the reflections of Frier, *Landlords and Tenants* (1980) 218, are of great importance. See also the comments on equity and law above in the notes.

38. Barzel, *A Theory of the State* (2002) esp. 228–75. For an argument that the Roman state was essentially predatory in nature, see P. F. Bang, *The Roman Bazaar* (2008).

Enough has perhaps already been said to suggest that the Roman experience can be located on a spectrum between Barzel's two extremes, while tending toward the former rather than the latter. The question remains whether the Roman government was an essentially impartial, neutral, or even passive one that occasionally intervened to thwart excesses or something else entirely.

The Volterra Thesis

That the situation was more complicated than this explanation of impartiality suggests emerges first from an important study by Edoardo Volterra (originally published in 1967), in which he surveys the economic value of the cases preserved in Justinian's *Digest* and *Codex*.[39] The question Volterra sets himself is whether the evidence shows that the Roman legal system had as its foundation the large-scale economic interests of the groups that held the lion's share of the substantive wealth as well as controlled the chief means of production.[40] He finds that our sources do not support the conclusion that it did. While the data, given the nature of the compilation, can hardly be regarded as, in any sense, complete, enough survives, in his view, to allow us to arrive at a sense of the economic value of the cases in which the jurists develop the rules of private law. In general, he urges, whether the cases are historical or hypothetical in nature, they concern matters of relatively little financial worth. This holds true, he avers, not only for the hypothetical cases. No real distinction in this regard emerges between cases based on a genuine fact situation and those that are invented, in terms of the monetary values preserved therein.

Volterra argues that the "quasi totalità" ("near entirety") of the legal questions and lawsuits placed before jurists, officials, and emperors do not concern significant economic interests. They do not typically, if at all, examine problems surrounding the availability or use of enormous wealth in the hands of private individuals or of the state on any level. Instead, at their foundation lie matters, both practical and theoretical in nature, that are of very limited economic value, so much so that the juristic literature we possess—which, while far from complete, is not exactly a tiny amount—does not allow even an approximate picture to be drawn of the actual economic conditions of contemporary Roman society.[41] Two questions arise in connection with Volterra's argument. First, can

39. Volterra, "La base economica" (1967/1993). On the evidence of the *Codex*, see the notes below.

40. Volterra, "La base economica" (1967/1993) 124–25.

41. Volterra, "La base economica" (1967/1993) 133 ("quasi totalità"); see also 141 on law vs. life.

we exclude entirely the possibility that the jurists cater to significant economic interests, as he describes them? Second, can we more precisely locate the cutoffs above and below which they take a demonstrable interest, exclusively or not?

Now nearly two decades old, Walter Scheidel's study on references to amounts of money in the literary sources certainly bolsters Volterra's assertion that "le cifre da loro [i.e., the classical jurists] esposte siano spessissimo meramente esemplificative" and do not correspond to those that "concretamente si avevano nella effettiva vita sociale."[42] Scheidel argues that "the literature of Roman times as a whole, and in many cases irrespective of literary genres and individual authors, is permeated by conventional or symbolic monetary valuations to an extent that seriously restricts the range even of tentative calculations and quantifying comparisons."[43] "More specifically," he continues, "at least for certain crucial areas of Roman history, between ninety and one hundred percent of all existing financial numerical data are merely conventional figures which cannot be automatically accepted as rough approximations or rounded variants of actual figures known to the authors."[44] One of the three "patterns of stylization" that Scheidel identifies is composed of figures made up of powers of ten.[45] If we accept as suspect such instances of these as are found in the legal sources, we would disqualify the vast majority of numbers reported by Volterra in his survey.[46] One might add examples that are multiples of five, though they are not nearly as numerous as those that can be divided by ten.[47]

One has the impression that the situation regarding reliable monetary data is shakier for the legal sources than for the literary ones surveyed by Scheidel.[48]

42. Volterra, "La base economica" (1967/1993) 134: "le cifre da loro esposte siano spessissimo meramente esemplificative" ("the numbers provided by them [i.e., the classical jurists] are very often simply intended as illustrations"); "concretamente si avevano nella effettiva vita sociale ("definitely existed in actual social life"); Scheidel, "Finances, Figures, and Fiction" (1996). For data, see the collection of sources in Saivert and Wolters, *Löhne, Preise, Werte* (2005).

43. Scheidel, "Finances, Figures, and Fiction" (1996) 223.

44. Scheidel, "Finances, Figures, and Fiction" (1996) 223.

45. Scheidel, "Finances, Figures, and Fiction" (1996) 224.

46. See, e.g., Volterra, "La base economica" (1967/1993) 144–47. See now the salutary skepticism expressed by Maragno, "I numeri nelle fonti giurisprudenziali" (2017). I am grateful to Dr. Maragno for permitting me to see a copy of her article prior to its publication.

47. This is supported and extended by a pattern described by Maragno ("I numeri nelle fonti giurisprudenziali" [2017]), in which figures of ten and one hundred are relatively numerous in the *Digest*, followed by figures that represent half or double their value (five and twenty, fifty and two hundred, respectively).

48. One might well expect a higher proportion of conventional amounts in the legal sources as opposed to the literary ones, to judge from those that appear in illustrations given by the *Restatements* in modern US law, for example. See *Restatement (Second) of Contracts* § 39 (1981), a discussion of whether a parcel of land is to sell for $5,000 or $4,800. It might be objected that the sums given for transactions preserved in the archive of the Sulpicii are typically divisible by ten: see Camodeca, *Tabulae Pompeianae Sulpiciorum* (1999). In many cases, this could be explained by the nature of the transaction, and one might argue that, for example, the sums stated for a *mutuum*

The problem comes into focus when we reflect on the sheer number of hypothetical cases as opposed to actual ones that we encounter in the *Digest*, a point explicitly recognized by Volterra himself.[49] As a sample, I have surveyed six titles dealing with various delicts and contracts, counting instances of numbers.[50] Five of these titles show eleven or fewer instances of numerical values, while the sixth has more than three dozen.[51] The entire sample shows perhaps half a dozen instances that are possibly but not likely to be real cases, while three more are very likely to be so; the rest appear to be invented by the jurists. Even in those cases that are possibly or likely to be real, however, the numbers themselves are not guaranteed to be anything but invented values.[52] Another potential problem emerges from Volterra's exclusive reliance on the evidence of the *Digest* and the *Codex*. A number of passages from pre-Justinianic juristic literature show amounts in the thousands of *sestertii*.[53] The *Digest* and the *Institutes* display numerous instances of nominative or accusative neuter plurals suggesting that the original value was measured in thousands of *sestertii*; sometimes the presence of the word *milia* indicates this less ambiguously.[54] This raises the possibility that we owe many of the apparently low values in these works not to the classical jurists but to the compilers.[55]

---

or for a *vadimonium* (the latter of which are sometimes far from trivial) lend themselves to such "stylization." But such a conclusion seems far from guaranteed. This evidence merits more discussion than space allows, not least concerning the questions of its representative character and its status as legal evidence. For a document that seems especially relevant, one may consult *TPSulp.* 31, which records details of two court cases, one in the amount of six thousand sesterces, the other in the amount of eighteen thousand. These are consistent with the range of amounts for loans in this evidence. Neither, of course, would pass Scheidel's test. While it is hardly a refutation of his thesis to point out that people—in life, as in literature—often employed round numbers, caution is enjoined all the same. These documents merit further study from this perspective alone.

49. Volterra, "La base economica" (1967/1993) 153. This has long been a subject of discussion, particularly regarding the value of juristic evidence as a historical source: see Wacke, "Die *Potentiores*" (1980) 566–68.

50. *D.* 9.2; 19.1, 2; 45.1; 47.2, 10. By far, most of the numbers represent monetary values. When a passage gives two numbers as alternatives, I count them as one instance. None of these are of interest here.

51. The exception in this sample is *D.* 45.1.

52. For example, the amounts given in the three instances likely to be based on real cases cannot escape Scheidel's criticism (above): eight thousand *modii* (of grain) and three thousand *metretae* (of olive oil) in Scaev. *D.* 19.2.61.1; two hundred of an unspecified denomination in Pap. *D.* 45.1.121.1; one thousand *denarii* in Paul. *D.* 45.1.126.2. Volterra's examination of the *Codex* yields very few numerical values at all: see Volterra, "La base economica" (1967/1993) 147–48. Such a result might be taken to reinforce the thesis that the overwhelming majority of those in the *Digest* are invented by the jurists. This is not to deny the existence of exceptions: for some important examples that mostly involve relatively modest sums, see Frier, "Subsistence Annuities" (1993).

53. Frier, "Subsistence Annuities" (1993) 223 n. 5.

54. Frier, "Subsistence Annuities" (1993) esp. 223.

55. Maragno, "I numeri nelle fonti giurisprudenziali" (2017), shows how, in a number of instances, the compilers altered numerical values in the sources to reflect the Justinianic "exchange rate" of one thousand sesterces for one aureus (see, e.g., *Inst.* 3.7.3).

While Volterra's survey suggests that we have few, if any, quantifiable indicators of great wealth in the evidence he examines, it does not prove that this reflects a social reality in which large-scale economic interests were not routinely consulted by the legal system. A hypothetical number can apply to a legal rule capable of application at various social levels. In this regard, one might well quibble over his dismissal of references to farms, houses, servitudes, and slaves.[56] These items were not necessarily of trivial value, for one thing. In fact, the specimen values in hypothetical cases often display a considerable amount of wealth by ancient standards, though perhaps small by the standards of the upper 1.5 percent.[57] While Volterra is right that they are no sure signs of great wealth, it is impossible to exclude the possibility that wealthy persons had an interest in these rules or that the rules were designed to cater to such an interest.

Volterra concludes that conflicts between wealthy members of the elite were resolved not by the private law system, meaning either through trial in the courts or consultation of the jurists, but outside of it.[58] The matter stands somewhat differently for criminal law, which does serve as a forum for the settling of accounts among the rich and famous. He speculates that the upper classes otherwise had strong motives to seek alternative, informal mechanisms for dispute resolution, grounded in a need for absolute discretion. So the private law system operated for the benefit of "i piccoli interessi della stragrande maggioranza degli individui."[59] The emperor intervened in this system in order to respond to the need to preserve "la pace sociale."[60]

There are some difficulties with this conclusion. Volterra does not appear to discount the possibility that the legal system benefited the socially prominent indirectly. Simply because members of the elite preferred to avoid litigation does not mean that the law was not developed with their interests in mind. But Volterra fails to consider these interests as they are manifested concretely—and, thus, not always indirectly—on the level of the lower orders, through the operation of patronage and even agency.[61] So the efforts of slaves, freedpersons, and (often lower-status) friends not infrequently operated to the benefit of

56. Volterra, "La base economica" (1967/1993) 144, 147–48. One might add such items as *naves* and *insulae*, which are not scarce in the *Digest*.

57. The point applies to some of the evidence from the archive of the Sulpicii discussed above in the notes.

58. Volterra, "La base economica" (1967/1993) 152–55.

59. Volterra, "La base economica" (1967/1993) 153: "i piccoli interessi della stragrande maggioranza degli individul" (the small-scale interests of the overwhelming majority of individuals).

60. Volterra, "La base economica" (1967/1993) 154: "la pace sociale" (social tranquility).

61. See, e.g., the discussions in Andreau, *Banking and Business* (1999); Verboven, *The Economy of Friends* (2002); D. Jones, *The Bankers of Puteoli* (2006).

members of the elite. Some aspects of the private law would have been difficult, if not impossible, for them to escape, even had they wanted to do so. One thinks of various sectors of what might be called "family law," such as guardianship, succession (especially under a will), and divorce, the latter involving, at minimum, the disposition of the dowry.[62] Even in these areas that more exclusively catered to the upper classes, the private law system may have functioned more to provide a structure for extrajudicial settlement than to determine the outcome of litigation. It would be helpful, to be sure, if Volterra were more precise about the social groups he has in mind.

Social Status and Private Law

Matters of guardianship, succession, divorce, and dowry raise a crucial question for us. Were there areas of the private law that were designed by the jurists more or less exclusively to accommodate the needs of the upper classes? A useful case for examination is given by the law of urban lease, where the attention of the legal experts focuses on what can only be upper-class leases.[63] As Bruce Frier suggests, this interest was shaped by matters related to access to litigation, rather than to bias in the law, which is, at least in this case, notably evenhanded. It is not that lower-status persons were, in any way, actively excluded from the courts: there is no sign of this, of course. Instead, a range of factors conspired to deter them from pursuing a claim at law.[64] Above all, it seems that the social

62. There is, to be sure, a difference between knowing (and respecting) the rules and involving oneself with the system. An observation of Pliny the Younger (*Ep.* 2.14.1) on the types of cases he saw in the centumviral court is perhaps not to be dismissed as mere self-deprecation: *Sunt enim pleraeque parvae et exiles; raro incidit vel personarum claritate vel negotii magnitudine insignis.* (For most are small and trivial in nature; rarely does one emerge that is remarkable for the social rank of the persons involved or the value of the matter at stake.) See also Tac. *Dial.* 38.2 (Maternus). This evidence must be read in light of the fact that the minimum level of value set for lawsuits in this court was one hundred thousand sesterces for the *petitio hereditatis* as well as (likely) for the *querella inofficiosi testamenti*: *PS* 5.9.1, with Kaser and Hackl, *Das römische Zivilprozessrecht*^{2} (1996) 53–54; Wacke, "*Bonam sive malam causam habere*" (2003) 222 n. 16; Coriat, "Les Tribunaux" (2012) 168. This evidence suggests both that a particular interest in the law of succession held for the elite, sufficient to sustain a dedicated forum, and that this interest, expressed precisely in terms of actual litigation, tended to cluster toward its lower reaches. The matter deserves more attention than it can be given here.

63. See Frier, *Landlords and Tenants* (1980) 48–55.

64. Frier, *Landlords and Tenants* (1980) 48–51, lists ten factors that discouraged litigation and that, importantly, would have done so increasingly as one moves down the social ladder. Some awareness of this phenomenon emerges in a text of Ulpian, where he advises provincial governors to ensure that the procedure for making judicial requests was not dominated by the socially prominent and the unscrupulous, to the disadvantage of those of middle rank (*mediocres*), who might be discouraged by an inability to find trial counsel or by having to settle for someone insufficiently experienced or respectable: Ulp. (1 *off. procons.*) *D.* 1.16.9.4. For more discussion of the general point, see McGinn, "Celsus and the *Pauper*" (2016).

conditions in which leases operated kept them away: "the poor, the vast majority of all tenants, were mostly housed in squalid tenement houses (*deversoria*) where they paid rent on an essentially short-term basis, perhaps most commonly daily."[65] Such a setup was not likely to generate a great many suits, as Frier points out: so little was at stake, and in case of dissatisfaction, it was easier simply to change tenant or landlord respectively. The relative imbalance in the social status of litigants, prompted by the range of factors that discouraged resort to the courts by persons of very modest means, seems to have been transformed into an almost absolute imbalance in this area of the law.

In framing a set of rules for urban lease, the jurists kept sight of who might be expected to pursue claims under this legal regime. In this way, input, in the form of demands on the law, is channeled through litigation, leading first to the development of the relevant rules and then to output in the form of application of those rules, which, in turn, generates new input. Does this scenario contrast with the legal issues raised in the context of the Kehoe-Bannon thesis under the rubrics of agricultural lease and property law? Evidently not, from both perspectives. The smaller-scale cultivators who benefit from authoritative intervention in these areas of the law are hardly indigent. The subjects of the urban lease regime appear to have encompassed a broad social swath, including not just those elements identifiable as upper-class but also entrepreneurial middlemen and occasionally even lower-class tenants.[66] In fact, legal and archeological evidence for divisions of space within rental units within *domus* (upper-class houses) and *cenacula* (apartments, or perhaps "apartment units") suggests that the notion "upper-class" perhaps ought to be understood as a relatively broad and flexible one in this instance.[67] At some point, however, a *cenaculum* split into several parts probably functioned as a *deversorium*, at least from the perspective of the law on urban lease.

In any case, the center of juristic concern in urban lease appears to remain largely fixed on what we would conventionally describe as the elite, certainly to judge from the absence of explicit interventions on behalf of the less privileged, as we see in the areas of the law studied by Kehoe and Bannon. The result is not, however, to be identified as a crude engine of bias. Instead, we find a body of rules that gives the appearance of being class-neutral, though it is in reality anything but. This is consistent, I believe, with the approach the jurists take

65. Frier, *Landlords and Tenants* (1980) 51.

66. See Frier, *Landlords and Tenants* (1980) 52; for examples of elite tenants and some subelite ones, see esp. 40–42. While our information on the status of middlemen is very thin, it does suggest that some hailed from the subelite: see McGinn, "A Conference on Roman Law" (2012) 10 n. 26.

67. See Wallace-Hadrill, *Houses and Society* (1994) 105–10, 132–34.

to the private law overall, including those areas of contract and property law discussed above. They are simply not prepared to sacrifice the doctrinal values that they implicitly advance through their holdings to a blatant assertion of a social or economic agenda. Frankly, though he might have been clearer about this point too, there is nothing in Volterra's analysis to suggest he believes otherwise. The interventions signaled by Kehoe and Bannon, while crucial to an understanding of how the system worked, are not to be understood, in any sense, as the tail that wagged the dog. In general, Roman private law is surprisingly evenhanded, especially given the mix of interests it accommodated.

Elite interests were in play in other ways as well, a consideration of which will allow us to deepen appreciably the sense of Volterra's trenchant observation about the preservation of the "*pace sociale*." First, let me point out what is perhaps obvious. Volterra is not arguing, as Kehoe and Bannon do, that, at least on occasion, the private law system might favor the interests of lower-status persons over those of higher-status persons when these interests are in conflict. He is arguing that the entire system operated to manage conflicts on that lower level and so served the interests of such persons as a group. It accomplished this without much obvious or any consistent reflection in the substance of the law, which itself gives every appearance, as just observed, of being class-neutral.

Despite the difficulties I have raised, this conclusion is plausible,[68] and I argue that it is actually buttressed by the engagement of higher-status persons with the legal system when they perceived such engagement to suit their interests. In other words, Volterra's thesis, suitably qualified, might well stand. There was, for one thing, an established elite ethic against such participation. In a well-known passage, Livy has young aristocrats advocate the return of the Tarquins on the ground that monarchy is superior to law, claiming "that the laws are a deaf thing, averse to entreaty, better and more advantageous for the poor than for the powerful; that they lack potential for flexibility or pardon if you cross a line; that it is dangerous in the midst of so many human transgressions to live by innocence alone."[69] Some aristocrats seem to have felt that they did not need law and the legal system to achieve their ends.[70] Of course, others did

68. It is assisted, in my view, by the Roman ideal conception of the role of law in managing relations in a society characterized by great political, economic, and social inequality, by treating citizens as equal before it: see Lucret. 5.958–59, 1141–51; Cic. *Rep.* 1.49, 53; *Leg.* 3.44; *Off.* 1.124, 2.41–42, with d'Aloja, *L'idea di egalitarismo* (2013) 49–64.

69. Liv. 2.3.4: *leges rem surdam, inexorabilem esse, salubriorem melioremque inopi quam potenti; nihil laxamenti nec veniae habere, si modum excesseris; periculosum esse in tot humanis erroribus sola innocentia vivere.* See also Liv. 9.1.8. For a different reading of the first passage, postulating a contrast at work between *lex* and *ius*, see Peralta Escuer, "*Leges rem surdam*" (2013).

70. For a striking testimony, see the account at Apul. *Met.* 9.35–38.

not take this view.[71] We have here another instance of what might be described as a "cooperation problem."

No such conflicts are visible for those on the lower level of society whom we can identify, somewhat modifying Volterra's thesis, as among the principal consumers of Roman private law.[72] But who were these people?[73] Volterra himself refers to them in vague terms, such as "i modesti interessi economici dei singoli individui" and "[le] classi economicamente meno abbienti."[74] Can we be more precise? In her book *Lives Behind the Laws*, Serena Connolly argues persuasively that "most individuals likely to petition [Diocletian] belonged to the 'middling sort' . . . , who had enough money and property that they could and would undertake legal transactions, but not enough money that they could easily consult a lawyer and subsequently retain him for a court case."[75] Of those persons whose receipt of rescripts in this period is preserved in the *Codex* of Justinian and other collections, only a small number is obviously identifiable as enjoying elite status. Far more are men and women of this "middling sort," and there are a number of soldiers—perhaps to be regarded as a special category of the "middling"—and slaves.[76] The evidence that survives from the classical pe-

71. See Frier, *The Rise of the Roman Jurists* (1985) 73.

72. In relation to Roman private law, I use the terms *consumers* and *beneficiaries* interchangeably in this essay and its companion piece, to denote those who actively participated in the legal system and were sometimes the recipients of favorable treatment in terms of legal rulings. They can also refer, with the appropriate qualification, to those whose interests were served by Roman private law more indirectly, as discussed below.

73. The factors that discouraged plaintiffs from bringing suit operated on various social levels. Though, as we have seen above, they tended to weigh more heavily as one proceeds down the social scale, some of them operated more forcefully for members of the elite: see below. Certainty is impossible, but one might speculate that they were felt least of all in the middle, as described here. A similar point holds for the social profile of potential defendants.

74. Volterra, "La base economica" (1967/1993) 125, 155: "i modesti interessi economici dei singoli individui" (the modest economic interests of individual persons); "[le] classi economicamente meno abbienti." ([the] less economically advantaged classes).

75. Connolly, *Lives behind the Laws* (2010) 68. Mention should be made of the pioneering work of Liselot Huchthausen, which focuses on petitioners who are soldiers, women, slaves, and provincials, both in the period of Diocletian's reign and prior to it: see Huchthausen, "Soldaten des 3. Jahrhunderts u. Z. als Korrispondenten" (1973), "Herkunft und ökonomische Stellung weiblicher Adressaten" (1974), "Kaiserliche Rechtsauskünfte an Sklaven" (1974), "Zu kaiserlichen Reskripten an weibliche Adressaten" (1976), "Thrakerreskripte" (1979), and *Frauen fragen den Kaiser* (1992).

76. Connolly, *Lives behind the Laws* (2010) 73–79. Soldiers, especially veterans, do seem to have populated the lower levels of the elite: see below. It is true that higher-status persons were more likely to receive an *epistula*, as opposed to a rescript, in response to an inquiry, which might appear to explain some of the disproportion in question: see Liebs, review of Connolly (2012) 718, with Connolly, *Lives behind the Laws* (2010) 141. But such recipients were, it seems, most often public officials or collectives, such as towns or provincial councils: see Arcaria, *Referre ad principem* (2000) 3–16, with Spagnuolo Vigorita, review of Arcaria (2001) 247 with n. 10. Since these officials were acting not on their own behalf but in connection with their official duties, they are not relevant for our purposes. A similar point can be made about the collectives, while not all of the letters addressed to private individuals concerned matters of private law.

riod for recipients of rescripts does not suggest an appreciably different result.[77] Of course, the pool of persons who petitioned is not inevitably the same as the pool of those who received responses, not to mention the pool of those whose responses were collected for publication, and selection for inclusion, particularly in the latter case, would have turned on inherent legal interest rather than on status, as Connolly recognizes for the *Codex Hermogenianus* and the *Codex* of Justinian.[78]

Some might regard terms like *middling* and *middling sort* as not much more precise than Volterra's formulation and want to push further. In recent years, a number of challenges have been raised to the traditional binary conception of Roman society in terms of a tiny elite situated above a vast majority of disadvantaged.[79] These challenges have met with varying degrees of success in clarifying the nature and extent of this "middle."[80] Scheidel and Friesen, for example, argue, for the empire as a whole, "that the top 1.5 percent of all households controlled around one-fifth of total income; that economically 'middling' non-élite groups accounted for a modest share of the population (around 10 per cent) but perhaps another fifth of total income; and that the vast majority of the population lived close to subsistence but cumulatively generated more than half of overall output."[81]

Neither the upper nor the lower reaches of this "middle" are easy to identify with any precision.[82] For the latter, we have scarce information, making it difficult to draw clear distinctions.[83] For the former, we have information that

77. See Coriat, *Le prince législateur* (1997) 317, 338–39; Arcaria, *Referre ad principem* (2000) 9 n. 22 with literature.

78. Connolly, *Lives behind the Laws* (2010) 67–73. On the social level of petitioners in Roman Egypt, see below.

79. The Romans themselves offer little help here, using *ordo* terminology in vague references to a vast range of citizens: see Harris, "On the Applicability of the Concept of Class" (1988/2011) 19; Mayer, *The Ancient Middle Classes* (2012) 9–11.

80. See Harris, "On the Applicability of the Concept of Class" (1988/2011); Veyne, "La 'plèbe moyenne'" (2000); Scheidel and Friesen, "The Size of the Economy" (2009); Mayer, *The Ancient Middle Classes* (2012). See also Scheidel, "Stratification, Deprivation and Quality of Life" (2006). On the municipal level, see the case study by Bandelli, "Ceti Medi" (2010) esp. 16–19.

81. Scheidel and Friesen, "The Size of the Economy" (2009) 62–63; see also 84, 88–91. Scheidel, "Stratification, Deprivation, and Quality of Life" (2006) 54, finds "sufficient evidence in support of the notion of an economic continuum from a narrow elite to a steadily broadening middling group as we move down the resource ladder."

82. Great uncertainty might reign over an individual's status, a phenomenon familiar from far down the social scale, as the legal wrangling over the famous case of Petronia Iusta shows. For more examples, see Gardner, "Lower-Class Families" (1997). More interesting for our purposes is the ambiguity that held for some others over membership in the elite, something suggestive of greater diversity on this level than what one might otherwise assume: see, recently, Bannon, "C. Sergius Orata" (2014).

83. Mayer, *The Ancient Middle Classes* (2012) 10, views it as impossible to distinguish between members of *collegia*, priests in the imperial cult (*Augustales*), and town councillors. The *Augustales*

is difficult to interpret. For example, how do we classify the sort of ex-slaves satirized by Petronius?[84] Imperial freedmen and wealthy businessmen are more persuasively identified as members of the upper classes than regarded as falling below this level.[85] It seems easy to identify town councillors (*decuriones*) as members of the elite on the basis of their belonging to an (elite) *ordo*, except that the property qualification seems to have varied considerably from town to town.[86] Were they all members of the same "aristocracy" if we define this group in socioeconomic terms and not according to legal status? An important juristic text suggests that this was far from the case.

> *Eos, qui utensilia negotiantur et vendunt, licet ab aedilibus caeduntur, non oportet quasi viles personas neglegi. denique non sunt prohibiti huiusmodi homines decurionatum vel aliquem honorem in sua patria petere: nec enim infames sunt. sed ne quidem arcentur honoribus, qui ab aedilibus flagellis caesi sunt, quamquam iure suo ita aediles officio isto fungantur. inhonestum tamen puto esse huiusmodi personas flagellorum ictibus subiectas in ordinem recipi, et maxime in eis civitatibus, quae copiam virorum honestorum habeant: nam paucitas eorum, qui muneribus publicis fungi debeant, necessaria etiam hos ad dignitatem municipalem, si facultates habeant, invitat.* (Call. [6 *cognitionum*] *D.* 50.2.12)

> [Those who trade in and sell merchandise of ordinary use, though they be physically disciplined by the aediles, ought not to be overlooked on the ground that they are persons of little (social) worth. In short, persons of this kind are not forbidden from seeking the decurionate or any public office in their own hometowns. For they are not marked by judicial disgrace (*infames*). But not even are those persons who have been beaten by the aediles with whips kept from public office, even if the aediles were acting correctly in discharging that responsibility. All the same, my own view is that it is dishonorable that such persons who have been inflicted with the blows of whips be received into the *ordo* (of

are especially difficult to pigeonhole. See Scheidel, "Stratification, Deprivation, and Quality of Life" (2006) 42, for the idea that their relationship to decurions was essentially horizontal, insofar as they form "a supplementary quasi-*ordo*" while Scheidel and Friesen, "The Size of the Economy" (2009) 78, hold that the relationship was, at bottom, vertical, so that the *Augustales* rank just below decurions in the Roman social hierarchy.

84. See the discussion in D'Arms, *Commerce and Social Standing* (1981) 97–120.

85. Harris, "On the Applicability of the Concept of Class" (1988/2011) 22; Mayer, *The Ancient Middle Classes* (2012) 9.

86. See Patterson, *Landscapes and Cities* (2006) 202, 222; Scheidel and Friesen, "The Size of the Economy" (2009) 78; Alföldy, *Römische Sozialgeschichte*[4] (2011) 170-172.

decurions), and that this is especially true in those communities that contain a supply of honorable men. For a scarcity of those who ought to take up public responsibilities necessarily summons even such persons as these to positions of municipal rank, provided they possess the requisite wealth. (Callistratus in the sixth book on *Judicial Proceedings*)]

The jurist, Callistratus, first gives the rule. Men who deal in *utensilia*, which can refer to provisions and other items typically found in retail contexts,[87] are not automatically excluded from the decurionate and municipal office, even if they have suffered humiliating physical punishment at the hands of the aediles, the town officials entrusted with oversight of the markets.[88] They are not thereby inflicted with *infamia*, official judicial disgrace. This holds, Callistratus is careful to point out, even if they have been whipped by the aediles and despite the fact that the whipping was for good cause, this last qualification evidently anticipating an objection that the rule might only apply in case of an official abuse of power. The explicit extension of the rule to scourging is an important clarification. While free persons of low status might routinely be vulnerable to beating with cudgels, whipping was a penalty more strictly associated with slaves and, thus, more deeply shaming.[89] Beating decurions (and their sons) with rods was prohibited,[90] meaning that, once admitted to the *ordo*, these businessmen would no longer—legally—be exposed to such treatment or worse.[91]

Having stated and elaborated the rule, the jurist expresses some personal reservations. Such businessmen were subject to severe social prejudice on the part of the elite.[92] Callistratus draws a line of sorts at scourging. Those who have been disgraced by infliction of this slavish penalty ought not to be admitted to the decurionate, if at all possible. He appears to articulate this point not as a matter of law but as a social preference, to be observed particularly if honorable men are available. Or perhaps we should regard this in legal terms

87. See L & S s.v. *utensilis*; *OLD*² s.v. *utensilis*. The two verbs may refer to engaging in wholesale and retail business respectively. For a different view, see Gebhardt, *Prügelstrafe und Züchtigungsrecht* (1994) 116–17, who thinks only the latter is meant.

88. Presumably both beating with cudgels and scourging are meant here. The former might affect one's social reputation but could not, by itself, inflict *infamia*: see Call. *D.* 48.19.28.1 and the other texts collected by Gebhardt, *Prügelstrafe und Züchtigungsrecht* (1994) 118–22. In our principal case, Callistratus goes on to make the same point about the latter—not without difficulty, however.

89. Gebhardt, *Prügelstrafe und Züchtigungsrecht* (1994) 114; Saller, *Patriarchy, Property, and Death* (1994) 133–53, esp. 138.

90. Sev. Ant. *C.* 2.11.5 (a. 198); Call. *D.* 48.19.28.2, 5, citing plural imperial constitutions and generalizing application to all *honestiores*. Cf. Marci. *D.* 49.18.3; Pap.-Ulp. *D.* 50.2.2.

91. Gebhardt, *Prügelstrafe und Züchtigungsrecht* (1994) 115.

92. Sources are in Holleran, *Shopping in Ancient Rome* (2012) 5–6, 202–3.

as a guideline rather than a rule. The jurist is enough of a realist to recognize that this solution will not always be possible, insisting, all the same, that the new members possess the requisite census,[93] which, as noted above, could vary significantly from one town to another. Worth emphasizing in this connection is just how accommodating Callistratus is willing to be, first drawing the line further along than many others might, then making that line a soft one.[94] One might conclude that the real-life distinction between elite and subelite could be elusive at times.

Finally, there is the case of soldiers and veterans, typically regarded by historians as falling toward the bottom range of privileged groups in Roman society.[95] The relatively abundant evidence from Egypt shows them to be avid litigants.[96] As comparatively advantaged Roman citizens, they sat atop the social hierarchy in that province and made their influence felt wherever they had interests, especially economic ones.[97] Of course, Roman Egypt hosted an intersection of (at least) three legal systems, rendering simple comparisons with the operation of the *ius civile* elsewhere somewhat challenging.[98] Nevertheless, it should not be ignored. John Crook's important survey of private law trials in Roman Egypt finds that the social level attested by the papyri "is not that of the 'great and grand' but much more humdrum, the Greco-Egyptian middle class (to use that phrase in a general and perfectly intelligible sense). They have a little property and are concerned about its disposition and the taxes on it and about loans and dykes and local violence."[99] Crook's findings have recently been substantiated and broadened by a pair of recent studies of petitioners and litigants in Roman Egypt, which come to much the same conclusion about their social status.[100] In the end, no matter how we wish to define or describe this "middle," there is, with no reasonable doubt, a "there" there, one with a healthy interest in the system of Roman private law.

To be sure, Volterra's base of evidence offers some compelling support for

---

93. Some towns showed themselves more willing to admit such men as decurions than others. See the evidence given by Gebhardt, *Prügelstrafe und Züchtigungsrecht* (1994) 113–14.

94. See McGinn, "Hire-Lease" (2013) 177–80.

95. See, e.g., Garnsey, *Social Status and Legal Privilege* (1970) 245–51.

96. See the sample of cases in Lewis, "Judiciary Routines in Roman Egypt" (2000).

97. See Lewis, *Life in Egypt under Roman Rule* (1983) esp. 18–64. There was a smattering of equestrians in Roman Egypt: see Rathbone, *Economic Rationalism and Rural Society* (1991) 479; Rowlandson, *Landowners and Tenants in Roman Egypt* (1996) 380.

98. Lewis, *Life in Egypt under Roman Rule* (1983) esp. 185–95; Rowlandson, *Landowners and Tenants in Roman Egypt* (1996) 139–40; Yiftach-Firanko, "Law in Graeco-Roman Egypt" (2009).

99. Crook, *Legal Advocacy* (1995) 62–63; see also 72. As the description makes clear, the Egyptian evidence concerns not just private law but criminal law as well.

100. B. Kelly, *Petitions, Litigation, and Social Control* (2011) 123–67 (see esp. 124 n. 2); Bryen, *Violence in Roman Egypt* (2013) esp. 45–48, 99–100, 115–17, 141–42, 166–70, 200.

his thesis after all. My sample of half a dozen titles from the *Digest* suggests that the jurists had a remarkable interest in the legal woes of shopkeepers, goldsmiths, coachmen, cobblers, jewelers, builders, barbers, copyists, fullers, warehousemen, movers, (tenant) farmers, freedpersons, fishermen, innkeepers, astrologers, and others of the same stripe. Legal problems explicitly and directly affecting members of the upper orders only rarely seem to arise, and when they do, they typically concern only those on the bottom rungs, such as town officials and soldiers.[101] The objection that the vast majority of the cases are hypothetical has no force here, unless we are prepared to reject wholesale the evidence of the *Digest* as a source for social history.[102]

A weightier objection arises from the possibility that these types serve as mere stand-ins for upper-class owners or patrons. There is little or no direct evidence to support this claim, however. Moreover, it risks misunderstanding some important aspects of the structure of the Roman economy. Manufacturing remained largely with independent craftsmen who operated relatively small-scale firms that relied on a combination of subcontracting networks and the hiring of additional workers on a temporary basis in order to accommodate increases (and attendant decreases) in demand, rather than large integrated firms with numerous employees.[103] In the agricultural sector as well, many farmers seem to have operated relatively small farms, one reason that encouraged them to migrate to the city to seek work in the off-season.[104] Though all of these factors have to be set aside the evidence (mentioned above) that the relations of agency and patronage benefited members of the elite, such considerations should hardly be ignored.

Despite a modest level of plausibility, the Volterra thesis meets with serious challenges that suggest it can only be accepted in modified form. The most

101. Exceptions are very few and somewhat qualified at that. They include a case involving the staff of an imperial legate (Pap.-Ulp. *D.* 19.2.19.10), another concerning *advocati* (Paul. *D.* 19.2.38.1), and a rule that, as formulated, applies to all officeholders, not just municipal ones (Ulp. *D.* 47.10.32).

102. See the statement of Matthews, "Roman Law and Roman History" (2006) 483: "Whether real, or imagined in order to illustrate points of law, such situations are part of the thought-world of the writers, and so part of the history of their society." On the many and various challenges in using the work of the jurists as historical evidence, see, e.g., the observations of J. M. Kelly, *Studies in the Civil Judicature* (1976) 71–92; Stolfi, review of Nörr (2007) 558; du Plessis, *Letting and Hiring* (2012) 5–6.

103. See Hawkins, "Manufacturing" (2012); Mayer, *The Ancient Middle Classes* (2012) 17–19; Hawkins, "Labour and Employment" (2013); Hawkins, *Roman Artisans* (2016); Hawkins, "Contracts, Coercion, and the Boundaries of the Roman Artisanal Firm" (2017).

104. See Scheidel and Friesen, "The Size of the Economy" (2009) 91; Hawkins, "Manufacturing" (2012) 185–86; Hawkins, "Labour and Employment" (2013) 339–46.

obvious difficulty is that the evidence on which Volterra relies is not as probative of his conclusions as one might like. On the basis of these sources, it is notionally impossible to exclude a direct interest of the jurists in the problems surrounding the availability or use of enormous wealth in the hands of private individuals. Plenty of evidence survives to suggest that the legal system was tilted, in important ways, in the direction of the wealthy and powerful. The efforts of the legal authorities, as we find them crystallized in the Kehoe-Bannon thesis, could only do so much.

All the same, it is remarkable that most, though not all, of the evidence that the three factors of money, power, and influence (*pecunia*, *potentia*, and *gratia*) affected court verdicts comes from the republic, especially the late republic,[105] while the bulk of that for the heavy hand of the *potentiores* comes from the principate, overwhelmingly from late antiquity.[106] Regarding the latter phenomenon, we have, for the earlier period, some thirteen passages from the high and late classical jurists, beginning with Africanus and Gaius, though a couple of these cite earlier opinions by Labeo and Ateius Capito.[107] This evidence shows that some, though not all, of their interference was extrajudicial in nature. It must be conceded, however, that the possible leveraging of such power in the context of the judicial system was a constant preoccupation in this period and subsequently. Evidence of such anxiety may be sought in the works of the declaimers, where cases involving disputes between a *dives* and a *pauper* are the single most popular theme.[108] In the best of reigns, certain persons enjoying the emperor's favor might be tempted to flout the law.[109] Expressions of anxiety about vast differentials in

105. See J. M. Kelly, *Roman Litigation* (1966) 31–68. On the introduction of the practice of appealing verdicts under Augustus and on other relevant developments, see the notes above.

106. This was recognized long ago by Mitteis, "Ueber den Ausdruck *Potentiores*" (1912). MacMullen, *Corruption and the Decline of Rome* (1988) esp. 168, sees markedly increased corruption, including perception of such by contemporaries, after 250.

107. See the full survey in Wacke, "Die *Potentiores*" (1980) 589–604. Wacke regards two texts attributed to Ulpian's *Opiniones* as postclassical. For yet another passage suggesting the phenomenon without using the terminology, see Wacke, "Gefahrerhöhung als Besitzverschulden" (1984) 688. See also the discussion in MacMullen, *Corruption and the Decline of Rome* (1988) 94–95.

108. Gunderson, *Declamation, Paternity, and Roman Identity* (2006) 232–33. In particular, there is a recurring emphasis on the bad effects of wealth, especially in terms of the impact on political and social stability: Sussman, *Declamations of Calpurnius Flaccus* (1994) 112, 129.

109. See the case of the imperial freedman and procurator Eurythmus, accused of forging a will under Trajan, who compels a group of reluctant plaintiffs to follow through with their charge: Plin. *Ep.* 6.31.7–12. Worth emphasizing is that the emperor acts to remedy the situation. See also the behavior of Tiberius described at Tac. *Ann.* 1.75.1. In the absence of a strong direction provided by an emperor, matters could be very different: see Tac. *Hist.* 2.10.1.

wealth, power, and influence are not hard to find.[110] These factors presented a recurring challenge.[111]

Our sources permit both an optimistic and a pessimistic reading. In chronological terms, the influence of the *potentiores* seems to have been highest in the third through fifth centuries and correspondingly lower for the early principate and the sixth century.[112] For the classical period of Roman law, at least, the literary sources support pessimism, though not in an unqualified way,[113] while the approaches taken by jurists and emperors, consistently with the evidence examined by Kehoe and Bannon, suggest that the problem, while a real one, was being addressed by the legal authorities and to some good effect.[114] We might hesitate to draw the inference that justice was always and inevitably inclined in favor of the wealthy and powerful. This is certainly not the impression one has from the legal sources, where one finds rules applied without obvious regard for the status of their objects.[115] Exceptions run along the lines indicated by Kehoe and Bannon, where impartiality, certainly on the surface, yields to a policy preference in favor of the disadvantaged. These considerations sug-

110. In a number of cases, however, these must be qualified in some way. Lucan (1.175–76) holds, *mensuraque iuris vis erat.* (and the measure of law was force.). But, of course, this declaration looks back to the period of civil war in the late republic. Seneca (*Ep.* 14.3–6) gives plenty of reasons to fear the *vis potentioris*, but none concern losing a lawsuit (I discount the observation at 11 that making speeches in court, like any activity that catches the public eye, produces *adversarii*). Fronto (*Ep.* 157.14H), (mis)quoting Sallust (*Hist.* 1.18M) and perhaps channeling Plato's Thrasymachus, treats the expression, in essence, as a trope, opining, *omne ius in validioribus esse.* (all law is on the side of the stronger.). Despite its character as rhetorical, backward-looking, or simply exaggerated, this evidence is all the same best read as betokening a genuine and diffuse anxiety that should come as no surprise in a society as marked by inequality as was ancient Rome. The same might be said for Philo, *Conf. ling.* 112, on which see Nörr, *Rechtskritik* (1974) 49. Dion. Hal. 1.5.2–3 is also of interest, though it has a broader import: see Gabba, *Dionysius* (1991) 196.

111. See the remarks of Quint. *IO* 9.2.68, 12.7.6.

112. For the latter, see Wacke, "Die *Potentiores*" (1980) 576.

113. See the notes above. Concern over Curiatius Maternus' public recitation of a play having given offense to certain powerful persons (*potentes*) helps set the stage for the discussion in Tacitus' *Dialogus* over the contemporary state of oratory (2.1). On a general level, the discussion revolves around the question of to what extent a differential in power can compromise basic values such as freedom and justice. The impact of monarchy on a legal system can have subtle but important consequences for the administration of private law, as Maternus himself makes plain (39.1–4). As Bruce Frier, "Finding a Place for Law" (2010) 73, points out, however, "the entire 'parade of horribles' that Maternus assembles can only be counted as an unqualified legal good." Aper's boast (7.1) of having defended imperial freedmen and procurators before the emperor can sustain a number of readings in this context. For a sample, see Gallia, "*Potentes* and *Potentia*" (2009) 179.

114. This is to judge from the evident confidence shown by the jurists themselves: see Wacke, "Dig. 19.2.33" (1976) 492 n. 181; Wacke, "The *Potentiores*" (1978) 381–83, 386–87; Wacke, "Die *Potentiores*" (1980) 591–95, 601–4. More broadly, see the literature cited in the notes above. There were, of course, a number of legal remedies in cases where the exercise of force or the instilling of fear might amount to undue influence: for a survey, see Hartkamp, *Zwang* (1971). The question here ultimately turns on their effectiveness, something very difficult for us to measure.

115. Wacke, "Die *Potentiores*" (1980) 567 n. 21.

gest that the imperial court system had—if not entirely, then to some extent—succeeded in shifting outside its bounds the venue of such activity as attributed to the *potentiores*. Seneca shows Augustus taunting the conspirator Cinna with having lost a private lawsuit to a freedperson.[116] It is difficult to imagine such an outcome under the republic, a fact that makes the emperor's sarcasm even more pointed.[117] How many aristocrats were willing to risk such humiliation?[118]

With regard to the evidence of the jurists, while an interest of theirs in the legal affairs of the superelite, meaning the wealthiest and most well-connected Romans, cannot be excluded, there is very little direct evidence for such. Instead, we have abundant indications of a concern on their part with a sector of society below this. Though we cannot define this sector with anything close to precision, our legal sources point, in very broad terms, to a tranche embracing the lower levels of what we can define as the elite in terms of legal status and extending downward to include possibly wide stretches of the upper reaches of the subelite.[119] To be clear, while the system seems to have operated to the benefit of the wealthy and powerful, much evidence points to the relevance of legal rules and remedies for a lower level of the population.

At all events, what can we say about the content of this law? Does this favor or disfavor persons of low status? There is nothing, as far as I can see, as prejudicial to their interests as we find in the criminal law with the division between *honestiores* and *humiliores*.[120] Most of it is, in fact, neutral in terms

116. Sen. *Clem.* 1.9.10, with Braund, *Seneca, "De Clementia"* (2009) 275.

117. In accusing Cinna of aiming to substitute himself as *princeps,* Augustus seems to allude to the political implications of the social leveling imposed by the imperial courts. It remains difficult to believe that even under the new dispensation, truly marginalized groups had equal access to justice, but see the episode recorded at Suet. *Claud.* 15.4, involving reliance on the evidence of prostitutes in the trial of an equestrian. Here is another situation unthinkable for the legal system of the republic, notwithstanding the role attributed to Faecenia Hispala in the context of the Bacchanalian scandal, an exception proving the rule, if ever there was one.

118. See, e.g., Calp. Flaccus 6: *Iam pridem arci nostrae tua fortuna minitatur. supra civilem hanc peraequationem divitiae te elevaverunt.* (For a long time now your wealth has threatened our seat of government. Your riches have lifted you above this status of equality appropriate for a private citizen [trans. Sussman, adapted].) The threats to reputation and social standing posed by the act of bringing a lawsuit and the consequent exposure to the threat of public humiliation doubtless weighed more heavily on higher-status litigants. These are fifth and sixth on the list of Frier's ten factors discouraging resort to litigation, in Frier, *Landlords and Tenants* (1980) 48–50. See, further, J. M. Kelly, *Studies in the Civil Judicature* (1976) 93–111.

119. As a kind of negative proof, one can cite the fact that the *potentiores* did not extend to the lower levels of the elite, such as veterans and at least the poorer decurions, and "therefore formed probably only a fairly small portion of the group of *honestiores*": see Wacke, "The *Potentiores*" (1978) 374.

120. The literature on the subject is vast, but for this particular point, it is enough to consult a couple of key works. See Garnsey, *Social Status and Legal Privilege* (1970) esp. 280: "In the juristic writings, for example, they [the terms *honestiores* and *humiliores* and their more commonly used variants] are used in a limited range of instances which relate almost entirely to the administration of the criminal law in the provinces." Even so, a number of qualifications obtrude: see Rilinger,

of status, in the sense that the rules to be applied are evidently valid across the social spectrum: *la legge è uguale per tutti*. There are some areas, however, where this is not quite the case, as the law engages and benefits certain categories of lower-status Romans.[121]

Conclusion

In what precedes, I have sought to test the validity of two major modern conceptions of the working of the system of Roman private law. One of these is the Kehoe-Bannon thesis, which argues for the occasional intervention of the authorities on behalf of less privileged, though not unimportant, segments of society, against the interests, narrowly conceived, of the wealthier and better connected, with the goal of promoting the ideals of utility and justice. The Volterra thesis relies on the evidence of the *Digest* and the *Codex* of Justinian to advance the idea that the entire system was designed to serve the interests not of the very well-off and powerful members of society but of those persons at a more modest social and economic level.

The evidence we have seen allows a better understanding of some of the limitations of both theses and perhaps encourages an appreciation for how varied and sometimes unexpected the interrelationship between them could be. The political and legal authorities were evidently sensitive to the implications of a pronounced status differential when interests conflicted, particularly in the areas of property and contract law.[122] We can hardly be certain that this was so in every case, of course, and it is very likely that it was not. But if the Volterra thesis, as qualified above, is correct, these situations remain—if more numerous than they might at first appear and certainly of great importance—rather exceptional. To a great extent, the consumers of Roman private law appear to have been members of what we might describe as the lower levels of the elite and the upper reaches of the subelite.

The jurists recognized that the interests of such persons could be safeguarded by asserting the interests of individuals on the lower fringes of or even somewhat below this level of society, thus the figure of the "person of modest

Humiliores—Honestiores (1988) esp. 263–79. For reasons that should be obvious, the criminal law is not our concern.

121. *La legge è uguale per tutti* ("the law is the same for everyone"). For the law engaging and benefiting certain categories of lower-status Romans, see McGinn, "Celsus and the *Pauper*" (2016).

122. I would argue that a somewhat different mix of interests was in play in the promulgation of the *SC Vellaeanum*, ostensibly designed to protect women from the implications of their "gender weakness," but lack of space forbids discussion here. See, recently, Chiusi, "Privatautonomie" (2011) 856.

means."[123] At times, they find it useful to proceed even further,[124] as does Maecian (mid-second century) concerning the rules of the *SC Pegasianum* of ca. 73 CE, which allowed persons entitled to a *fideicommissum* (trust) to approach the *praetor fideicommissarius* in order to compel a reluctant heir to comply with its terms.[125]

> *Sed et qui magna praeditus est dignitate vel auctoritate, harenarii vel eius mulieris, quae corpore quaestum fecerit, hereditatem restituere cogetur.* (Maec. [6 *fideicomm.*] *D.* 36.1.5)
>
> [But even a man of high rank or great influence will be compelled to turn over the inheritance of a gladiator or of a woman who has earned money with her body. (Maecian in the sixth book on *Trusts*)]

The extreme case put here by the jurist, that of a socially prominent or politically influential heir and a socially despised and powerless beneficiary of a trust, is clearly intended to underline the theoretically unfettered force of the compulsory entry on the inheritance.

Does that mean that members of the sectors of society just described, straddling elite and subelite, were the true beneficiaries of this system? In other words, *cui bono*? It would seem that those sectors did benefit, but this does not mean they alone did. The "outlook, values, and interests of the upper classes," including the jurists, were of fundamental importance in giving shape to Roman private law, in terms of both its overall texture and its particular rules.[126] Also, the elite, in principle, would have had easy access to the legal system, even as economic wealth and social privilege rendered them notionally more susceptible to the application of its norms. But for reasons I trust have been made clear, the truest justification for both the Kehoe-Bannon and the Volterra theses lies in the ways the phenomena they describe served the elite, even if, in an important sense, indirectly. This is not a matter of either-or, so that the law

123. See McGinn, "Celsus and the *Pauper*" (2016).

124. Examples, as they say, might easily be multiplied: see the material collected by Honoré, *Ulpian*² (2000). One might hesitate to include among them the policy preference for manumission in doubtful or ambiguous cases known as *favor libertatis* or the several imperial measures protecting slaves from physical abuse (see just Gaius 1.53), on the basis of the stark status differential separating slave from free. All the same, the protection of the lowest-ranking members of a social order is almost bound to inspire confidence in those above them and thus serve a broader purpose than might at first appear to be the case.

125. See McGinn, *Prostitution* (1998) 113–14.

126. For a statement regarding the law of the family, see Frier and McGinn, *A Casebook on Roman Family Law* (2004) 6 (quotation).

catered exclusively or even mainly to the interests of the upper classes and not to a broader section of society, or vice versa. We can thus better understand the position of the legal authorities as pragmatic and broadly self-interested, without resorting to cynicism or to (excessive) idealism: there is simply no call for invoking any of the jurists as a "pioneer of the human rights movement."[127]

From what precedes, it is important to avoid drawing an overly sanguine or pessimistic conclusion concerning the role of the jurists and of law itself. Some years ago, the historian E. P. Thompson (now celebrated but then highly controversial) wrote about a heretofore obscure episode in the law and life of early eighteenth-century England, offering a perspective—on the role of law in the service of class interest—that may help shed light on what was at stake for the Romans: "For 'the law', as a logic of equity, must always seek to transcend the inequalities of class power which, instrumentally, it is harnessed to serve. And 'the law' as ideology, which pretends to reconcile the interests of all degrees of men, must always come into conflict with the ideological partisanship of class."[128] Rather than a foretaste of "the human rights movement," what we find with the Romans is an ethic—broadly shared by members of the elite and the subelite, but perhaps especially characteristic of the more respectable and prosperous elements of the latter—that held it a social good to show sympathy for the *pauper*.[129] The interests of the strong did not always and inevitably stand in contrast to those of the weak—if, indeed, these categories are the only ones available to us in coming to an understanding of the identity and role of the true beneficiaries of Roman law.[130] To invoke our friend Thrasymachus, justice is indeed nothing other than the interest of the stronger.

Bibliography

Alföldy, G. *Römische Sozialgeschichte*. 4th ed. Stuttgart 2011.
Ando, C. *Imperial Ideology and Provincial Loyalty in the Roman Empire*. Berkeley, 2000.
Andreau, J. *Banking and Business in the Roman World*. Trans. J. Lloyd. Cambridge, 1999.
Arcaria, F. *Referre ad principem: Contributo allo studio delle epistulae in età classica*. Milan, 2000.
Bagnall, R. S. "Official and Private Violence in Roman Egypt." *BASP* 26 (1989): 201–216.
Bandelli, G. "'Ceti medi,' aristocrazia decurionale, *ordo equester*, e *ordo senatorius* nella

127. See Honoré, *Ulpian*² (2002) 76–93 (quotation at 76).

128. Thompson, *Whigs and Hunters* ([1977] 2013) 210.

129. See, e.g., *CIL* 6.9545 (= *ILS* 7602); *PS* 4.12.5 (suggesting perhaps that an even lower level of society was not to be excluded). Of course, this is not to be confused with Christian teaching on the subject: see Veyne, "La 'plèbe moyenne'" (2000) 1187–94; MacMullen, "Social Ethic Models" (2015).

130. Cf., e.g., Wacke, "The *Potentiores*" (1978) 379; Wacke, "Die *Potentiores*" (1980) 588.

società ravennate della tarda Repubblica e dell'alto Impero." *Ostraka* 19 (2010): 11–29.

Bang, P. F. *The Roman Bazaar: A Comparative Study of Trade and Markets in a Tributary Empire*. Cambridge, 2008.

Bannon, C. J. "C. Sergius Orata and the Rhetoric of Fishponds." *CQ* 64.1 (2014): 166–82.

Bannon, C. J. *Gardens and Neighbors: Private Water Rights in Roman Italy*. Ann Arbor, 2009.

Barzel, Y. *A Theory of the State: Economic Rights, Legal Rights, and the Scope of the State*. Cambridge, 2002.

Boas, M. "Potentatus." *RhM*, n.s., 83.2 (1934) 181–92.

Braund, S. *Seneca, "De Clementia": Edited with Text, Translation, and Commentary*. Oxford, 2009.

Bryen, A. Z. *Violence in Roman Egypt: A Study in Legal Interpretation*. Philadelphia, 2013.

Camodeca, G. *Tabulae Pompeianae Sulpiciorum*. 2 vols. Rome, 1999.

Capogrossi Colognesi, L. "Le servitù prediali: Interessi contrastanti e cooperazione tra vicini." *BIDR*, 4th ser., 1 (2011): 409–19.

Centola, D. A. "La disciplina della condotta vessatoria delle parti nel processo romano." *Teoria e storia del diritto privato* 5 (2012): 1–78.

Chiusi, T. J. "Privatautonomie oder Schutz des Schwächeren? Zu den Grenzen der Bürgenhaftung." In M. Wittinger et al., eds., *Verfassung-Völkerrecht-Kulturgüterschutz: Festschrift für Wilfried Fiedler zum 70. Geburtstag*, 841–57. Berlin, 2011.

Connolly, S. *Lives behind the Laws: The World of the Codex Hermogenianus*. Bloomington, IN, 2010.

Coriat, J.-P. *Le prince législateur: La technique législative des Sévères et les méthodes de création du droit impérial à la fin du Principat*. Rome, 1997.

Coriat, J.-P. "Les tribunaux de l'empire à l'époque du Principat: État de la question et perspectives." In E. Chevreau et al., eds., *Carmina iuris: Mélanges en l'honneur de M. Humbert*, 167–90. Paris, 2012.

Crook, J. A. *Legal Advocacy in the Roman World*. Ithaca, NY, 1995.

d'Aloja, C. *L'idea di egalitarismo nella tarda Repubblica romana*. Bari, 2013.

D'Arms, J. H. *Commerce and Social Standing in Ancient Rome*. Cambridge, MA, 1981.

Drexler, H. *Potentia*." *RhM n.s.* 102.1 (1959): 50–95.

du Plessis, P. J. *Letting and Hiring in Roman Legal Thought: 27 BCE—284 CE*. Leiden, 2012.

Elia, F. "Il principio giusnaturalistico *omnes homines aequales sunt* nella realtà sociale tardoantica." *Atti dell'Accademia Romanistica Costantiniana* 17.1 (2010): 237–55.

Fanizza, L. *L'amministrazione della giustizia nel principato: Aspetti, problemi*. Rome, 1999.

Frier, B. W. "Finding a Place for Law in the High Empire: Tacitus, *Dialogus* 39.1–4." In F. de Angelis, ed., *Spaces of Justice in the Roman World*, 67–87. Leiden, 2010.

Frier, B. W. *Landlords and Tenants in Imperial Rome*. Princeton, 1980.

Frier, B. W. "Law, Economics, and Disasters Down on the Farm: *Remissio Mercedis* Revisited." *BIDR*, 3rd ser., 31–32 (1989–90) 237–70.

Frier, B. W. "Law, Technology, and Social Change: The Equipping of Italian Farm Tenancies." *ZRG* 96 (1979): 204–28.

Frier, B. W. *The Rise of the Roman Jurists: Studies in Cicero's "Pro Caecina."* Princeton, 1985.
Frier, B. W. "Subsistence Annuities and Per Capita Income in the Early Roman Empire." *CP* 88.3 (1993): 222–30.
Frier, B. W., and T. A. J. McGinn. *A Casebook on Roman Family Law*. New York, 2004.
Furubotn, E. G., and R. Richter. *Institutions and Economic Theory: The Contribution of the New Institutional Economics*. 2nd ed. Ann Arbor, 2005.
Gabba, E. *Dionysius and the History of Archaic Rome*. Berkeley, 1991.
Gallia, A. "*Potentes* and *Potentia* in Tacitus' *Dialogus de Oratoribus*." *TAPA* 139 (2009): 169–206.
Galsterer, H. "The Administration of Justice." In *The Cambridge Ancient History*, 10:397–413. 2nd ed. Cambridge, 1996.
Gardner, J. F. "Legal Stumbling Blocks for Lower-Class Families in Rome." In B. Rawson and P. Weaver, eds., *The Roman Family in Italy: Status, Sentiment, Space*, 35–53. Oxford, 1997.
Garnsey, P. *Social Status and Legal Privilege in the Roman Empire*. Oxford, 1970.
Gaudemet, J. "Les abus des *potentes* au Bas-Empire." In *Études de droit romain*, 3:435–442. Naples, 1979. Originally published in *Irish Jurist n.s.* 1 (1966): 128–35.
Gebhardt, J. *Prügelstrafe und Züchtigungsrecht im antiken Rom und in der Gegenwart*. Cologne, 1994.
Gilbert, R. *Die Beziehungen zwischen Princeps und stadtrömischer Plebs im frühen Principat*. Bochum, 1976.
Giomaro, A. M. "La scelta del mezzo giudiziale in ipotesi di temerarietà della lite *ex parte actoris*." In *Atti del convegno "Processo civile e processo penale nell'esperienza giuridica del mondo antico in memoria di Arnaldo Biscardi,"* 131–52. Milan, 2011.
Gordon, R. W. "Critical Legal Histories." *Stanford Law Review* 36.1–2 (1984): 57–125.
Gruen, E. "Augustus and the Making of the Principate." In K. Galinsky, ed., *The Cambridge Companion to the Age of Augustus*, 33–51. Cambridge, 2005.
Gunderson, E. *Declamation, Paternity, and Roman Identity: Authority and the Rhetorical Self*. Cambridge, 2003.
Harris, W. V. "On the Applicability of the Concept of Class in Roman History." In *Rome's Imperial Economy: Twelve Essays*, 15–26. Oxford, 2011. Originally published in T. Yuge and M. Doi, eds., *Forms of Control and Subordination in Antiquity*, 598–610. Tokyo, 1988.
Hartkamp, A. S. *Der Zwang im römischen Privatrecht*. Amsterdam, 1971.
Hawkins, C. "Contracts, Coercion, and the Boundaries of the Roman Artisanal Firm." In K. Verboven and C. Laes, eds., *Work, Labour, and Professions in the Roman World*, 36–61. Leiden, 2017.
Hawkins, C. "Labour and Employment." In P. Erdkamp, ed., *The Cambridge Companion to Ancient Rome*, 336–51. Cambridge, 2013.
Hawkins, C. "Manufacturing." In W. Scheidel, ed., *The Cambridge Companion to the Roman Economy*, 175–94. Cambridge, 2012.
Hawkins, C. *Roman Artisans and the Urban Economy*. Cambridge, 2016.
Hölkeskamp, K.-J. *Reconstructing the Roman Republic: An Ancient Political Culture and Modern Research*. Princeton, 2010. Originally published as *Rekonstruktionen einer*

Republik: Die politische Kultur des antiken Rom und die Forschung der letzten Jahrzehnte. Historische Zeitschrift Beiheft 38. Munich, 2004.

Holleran, C. *Shopping in Ancient Rome: The Retail Trade in the Late Republic and the Principate*. Oxford, 2012.

Honoré, T. Review of B. W. Frier, *Landlords and Tenants*. *American Journal of Comparative Law* 31 (1983): 388–90.

Honoré, T. *Ulpian: Pioneer of Human Rights*. 2nd ed. Oxford, 2002.

Huchthausen, L. *Frauen fragen den Kaiser: Eine soziologische Studie über das 3. Jh. n. Chr.* Constance, 1992.

Huchthausen, L. "Herkunft und ökonomische Stellung weiblicher Adressaten von Reskripten des *Codex Iustinianus* (2. und 3. Jh. u. Z.)." *Klio* 56.1 (1974): 199–228.

Huchthausen, L. "Kaiserliche Rechtsauskünfte an Sklaven und in ihrer Freiheit angefochtene Personen aus dem *Codex Iustinianus*." *Wissenschaftliche Zeitschrift der Universität Rostock, Gesellschafts- und Sprachwissenschaftliche Reihe* 23.3 (1974): 251–57.

Huchthausen, L. "Soldaten des 3. Jahrhunderts u. Z. als Korrispondenten der kaiserlichen Kanzlei." In *Altertumswissenschaft mit Zukunft: Dem Wirken Werner Hartkes gewidmet*, 19–51. Berlin, 1973.

Huchthausen, L. "'Thrakerreskripte' aus dem *Codex Iustinianus*." *Historia: Acta Universitatis Nicolae Copernici* 13 (1979): 7–20.

Huchthausen, L. "Zu kaiserlichen Reskripten an weibliche Adressaten aus der Zeit Diokletians (284–305 u. Z.)." *Klio* 58.1 (1976): 55–85.

Hviid, M. "Long-Term Contracts and Relational Contracts." In B. Bouckaert and G. De Geest, eds., *Encyclopedia of Law and Economics,* 3:46–72. Cheltenham, 2000.

Jones, A. H. M. "Imperial and Senatorial Jurisdiction in the Early Principate." *Historia* 3.4 (1955): 464–88.

Jones, D. *The Bankers of Puteoli: Finance, Trade, and Industry in the Roman World.* Stroud, 2006.

Kaser, M., and K. Hackl. *Das römische Zivilprozessrecht*. 2nd ed. Handbuch der Altertumswissenschaft 10.3.4. Munich, 1996.

Kehoe, D. P. *Law and the Rural Economy in the Roman Empire*. Ann Arbor, 2007.

Kelly, B. *Petitions, Litigation, and Social Control in Roman Egypt*. Oxford, 2011.

Kelly, J. M. *Roman Litigation*. Oxford, 1966.

Kelly, J. M. *Studies in the Civil Judicature of the Roman Republic*. Oxford, 1976.

Lewis, N. "Judiciary Routines in Roman Egypt." *BASP* 37 (2000): 83–93.

Lewis, N. *Life in Egypt under Roman Rule*. Oxford, 1983.

Licandro, O. *In magistratu damnari: Ricerche sulla responsabilità dei magistrati romani durante l'esercizio delle loro funzioni*. Turin, 1999.

Liebs, D. Review of S. Connolly, *Lives behind the Laws*. *ZRG* 129 (2012): 711–24.

MacMullen, R. *Corruption and the Decline of Rome*. New Haven, 1988.

MacMullen, R. "Social Ethic Models: Roman, Greek, 'Oriental.'" *Historia* 64.4 (2015): 487–510.

Maragno, G. "I numeri nelle fonti giurisprudenziali: Prospettive di analisi." In D. Mantovani ed., *Diritto romano e economia: Due modi di pensare e organizzare il mondo (nei primi tre secoli dell'Impero)*, 613–44. Pavia, 2017.

Masi Doria, C. "A proposito di limiti e responsabilità nell'attività del magistrato giusdicente nella tarda repubblica, tra il cd. editto di ritorsione e l'*abrogatio iurisdictionis*." In K. Muscheler, ed., *Römische Jurisprudenz—Dogmatik, Überlieferung, Rezeption: Festschrift für Detlef Liebs zum 75. Geburtstag*, 419–32. Berlin, 2011.

Masi Doria, C. "'Giusto processo' moderno e garanzie processuali romane: Qualche 'motivo di fondo.'" *Archivio giuridico* 231.4 (2011): 383–409.

Masuelli, S. "Il principe come giudice privato: Modelli di intervento personale del principe nel processo civile ordinario." In L. Garofalo, ed., *Il giudice privato nel processo civile romano: Omaggio ad Alberto Burdese*, 2:84–109. Padua, 2012.

Matthews, J. F. "Roman Law and Roman History." In D. S. Potter, ed., *A Companion to the Roman Empire*, 477–91. Malden, MA, 2006.

Mayer, E. *The Ancient Middle Classes: Urban Life and Aesthetics in the Roman Empire, 100 BCE—250 CE*. Cambridge, MA, 2012.

McGinn, T. A. J. "Celsus and the *Pauper*: Roman Private Law and the Socio-Economic Status of Its Consumers." In I. Piro, ed., *Scritti per Alessandro Corbino,* 4:619–45. Tricase, 2016.

McGinn, T. A. J. "A Conference on Roman Law: The Future of Obligations." In T. A. J. McGinn, ed., *Obligations in Roman Law: Past, Present, and Future,* 1–39. Ann Arbor, 2012.

McGinn, T. A. J. "The Expressive Function of Law and the *Lex Imperfecta*." *Roman Legal Tradition* 11 (2015): 1–41.

McGinn, T. A. J. "Hire-Lease in Roman Law and Beyond." *Ancient History Bulletin* 27 (2013): 168–87.

McGinn, T. A. J. "La funzione espressiva del diritto." *Rivista Giuridica del Molise e del Sannio* 2 (2015): 85–142.

McGinn, T. A. J. *Prostitution, Sexuality, and the Law in Ancient Rome*. New York, 1998.

McGinn, T. A. J. *Widows and Patriarchy: Ancient and Modern*. London, 2008.

Metzger, E. "Lawsuits in Context." In P. J. du Plessis and J. W. Cairns, eds., *Beyond Dogmatics: Law and Society in the Roman World*, 187–205. Edinburgh, 2007.

Metzger, E. "Litigation." In D. Johnston, ed., *The Cambridge Companion to Roman Law*, 272–98. Cambridge, 2015. Originally published as "An Outline of Roman Civil Procedure," *Roman Legal Tradition* 9 (2013): 1–30.

Metzger, E. "Remedy of Prohibition against Roman Judges in Civil Trials." In P. Brand and J. Getzler, eds., *Judges and Judging in the History of the Common Law and Civil Law: From Antiquity to Modern Times*, 177–91. Cambridge, 2012.

Mitteis, L. "Ueber den Ausdruck *Potentiores* in den Digesten." In *Mélanges P. F. Girard*, 2:225–35. Paris, 1912.

Nagl, M. A. "Statilius" 34. *RE* 3A.2 (1929): 2199–2203.

Nörr, D. *Rechtskritik in der römischen Antike*. Munich, 1974.

Nörr, D. Review of A. Bürge, *Die Juristenkomik in Ciceros Rede Pro Murena: Übersetzung und Kommentar*. In D. Nörr, *Historiae Iuris Antiqui*, 2:947–50. Goldbach, 2003. Originally published in *ZRG* 92 (1975): 290–93.

North, D. C., J. J. Wallis, and B. R. Weingast. *Violence and Social Orders: A Conceptual Framework for Interpreting Recorded Human History*. Cambridge, 2009.

Patterson, J. R. *Landscapes and Cities: Rural Settlement and Civic Transformation in Early Imperial Italy*. Oxford, 2006.

Peachin, M. "Augustus' Emergent Judicial Powers, the *Crimen Maiestatis*, and the Second Cyrene Edict." In J.-L. Ferrary and J. Scheid, eds., *Il princeps romano: Autocrate o magistrato? Fattori giuridici e fattori sociali del potere imperiale da Augusto a Commodo*, 497–553, Pavia, 2015.

Peralta Escuer, T. "*Leges rem surdam, inexorabilem esse*: Roma es el pueblo del derecho pero no es el pueblo de la ley." In A. Fernández de Buján and G. Gerez Kraemer, eds., *Hacia un derecho administrativo y fiscal romano,* 2:111–30. Madrid, 2013.

Pergami, F. "Il ruolo e la funzione del giudice nel processo romano di età classica." *SDHI* 80 (2014): 395–409.

Rainer, J. M. "Zum Ursprung der *Extraordinaria Cognitio*." In Sondel et al., *Roman Law* (2003), 69–74.

Rampazzo, N. *Sententiam dicere cogendum esse: Consenso e imperatività nelle funzioni giudicanti in diritto romano classico*. Naples, 2012.

Randazzo, S. "Doppio grado di giurisdizione e potere politico nel primo secolo dell'impero." In Sondel et al., *Roman Law* (2003), 75–94.

Rathbone, D. *Economic Rationalism and Rural Society in Third-Century A.D. Egypt: The Heroninos Archive and the Appianus Estate*. Cambridge, 1991.

Rilinger, R. *Humiliores—Honestiores: Zu einer sozialen Dichotomie im Strafrecht der römischen Kaiserzeit*. Munich, 1988.

Rowlandson, J. *Landowners and Tenants in Roman Egypt: The Social Relations of Agriculture in the Oxyrhynchite Nome*. Oxford, 1996.

Saivert, W., and R. Wolters, *Löhne, Preise, Werte: Quellen zur römischen Geldwirtschaft*. Darmstadt, 2005.

Saller, R. P. *Patriarchy, Property, and Death in the Roman World*. Cambridge, 1994.

Santucci, G. "*Potentiores* e abusi processuali." *Atti dell'Accademia Romanistica Costantiniana* 11 (1996): 325–54.

Scheidel, W. "Finances, Figures, and Fiction." *CQ* 46.1 (1996): 222–38.

Scheidel, W. "Stratification, Deprivation, and Quality of Life." In M. Atkins and R. Osborne, eds., *Poverty in the Roman World*, 40–59. Cambridge, 2006.

Scheidel, W., and S. J. Friesen, "The Size of the Economy and the Distribution of Income in the Roman Empire." *JRS* 99 (2009): 61–91.

Sondel, J., et al., eds. *Roman Law as Formative of Modern Legal Systems: Studies in Honour of Wiesław Litewski*. Kraków, 2003.

Spagnuolo Vigorita, T. "La repubblica restaurata e il prestigio di Augusto: Diversioni sulle origini della *cognitio* imperiale." In *Imperium mixtum: Scritti scelti di diritto romano*, 397–419. Naples, 2013. Originally published in *Studi per Giovanni Nicosia,* 7:521–43. Milan, 2007.

Spagnuolo Vigorita, T. Review of F. Arcaria, *Referre ad principem*. *Iura* 52 (2001): 241–55.

Stolfi, E. Review of D. Nörr, *Römisches Recht*. *SDHI* 73 (2007): 552–65.

Sussman, L. A. *The Declamations of Calpurnius Flaccus: Text, Translation, and Commentary*. Leiden, 1994.

Thompson, E. P. *Whigs and Hunters: The Origins of the Black Act*. London, 2013. Originally published in London, 1975. Reprint, with postscript, 1977.

Trifone, R. "*Potentiores personae*." *Atti dell'Accademia Nazionale di Scienze Morali e Politiche di Napoli* 63 (1950–51): 36–43.

Tuori, K. *The Emperor of Law: The Emergence of Roman Imperial Adjudication*. Oxford, 2016.

Venturini, C. "La responsabilità del giudice nell'età classica, tra negligenza e corruzione." *Index* 41 (2013): 455–72.

Verboven, K. *The Economy of Friends: Economic Aspects of Amicitia and Patronage in the Late Republic*. Collection Latomus 269. Brussels, 2002.

Veyne, P. "La 'plèbe moyenne' sous le Haut-Empire Romain." *Annales: Histoire, Sciences Sociales* 55.6 (2000): 1169–99.

Volterra, E. "La base economica della elaborazione sistematica del diritto romano." In *Scritti giuridici*, 5:123–55. Naples, 1993. Originally published in *Rivista italiana per le scienze giuridiche* 94 (1967): 239–71.

Wacke, A. "*Bonam sive malam causam habere*: Erfolgsaussichten im römischen Zivilprozesses." In Sondel et al., *Roman Law* (2003), 217–40. Later published (in more summary form) as "*Bonam sive malam causam habere*: La prospettiva di successo nel processo civile romano," in *Atti del convegno "Processo civile e processo penale nell'esperienza giuridica del mondo antico in memoria di Arnaldo Biscardi,"* 265–75. Milan, 2011.

Wacke, A. "Die *Potentiores* in den Rechtsquellen: Einfluß und Abwehr gesellschaftslicher Übermacht in der Rechtspflege der Römer." *ANRW* 2.13 (1980): 562–607.

Wacke, A. "Dig. 19.2.33: Afrikans Verhältnis zu Julian und die Haftung für höhere Gewalt." *ANRW* 2.15 (1976): 455–96.

Wacke, A. "Gefahrerhöhung als Besitzerverschulden: Zur Risikoverteilung bei Rückgabepflichten im Spannungsfeld der Zurechnungsprinzipien *casum sentit dominus*, *fur semper in mora* und *versari in re illicita*." In G. Baumgärtel et al., eds., *Festschrift für Heinz Hübner zum 70. Geburtstag am 7. November 1984*, 669–95. Berlin, 1984.

Wacke, A. "The *Potentiores*: Some Relations between Power and Law in the Roman Administration of Justice." *Irish Jurist*, n.s., 13 (1978): 372–89.

Wacke, A. "*Res iudicata pro veritate accipitur*? Die Ziele des römischen Zivilprozesses zwischen Verhandlungsmaxime und Untersuchungsgrundsatz." In F. Harrer et al. eds., *Gedächtnisschrift für Theo Mayer-Maly zum 80. Geburtstag*, 489–524. Vienna, 2011.

Wallace-Hadrill, A. "*Civilis Princeps*: Between Emperor and King." *JRS* 72 (1982): 32–48.

Wallace-Hadrill, A. *Houses and Society in Pompeii and Herculaneum*. Princeton, 1994.

Wankerl, V. *Appello ad Principem: Urteilsstil und Urteilstechnik in kaiserlichen Berufungsentscheidungen (Augustus bis Caracalla)*. Munich, 2009.

Yavetz, Z. *Plebs and Princeps*. 2nd ed. New Brunswick, 1988.

Yiftach-Firanko, U. "Law in Graeco-Roman Egypt: Hellenization, Fusion, Romanization." In R. S. Bagnall, ed., *The Oxford Handbook of Papyrology*, 541–60. New York, 2009.

CHAPTER 8

Libertas and "Mixed Marriages" in Late Antiquity

Law, Labor, and Politics in Justinianic Reform Legislation

Charles Pazdernik

I first made the acquaintance of Bruce Frier in March 2000, when he very graciously agreed to speak at a daylong colloquium I had organized as a Mellon postdoctoral fellow at Emory University, on "teaching ancient law in the modern university." The title of the colloquium, *Cupidae Legum Iuventuti*, or "To Young Enthusiasts for Law," was borrowed from the inscription of Justinian's *Constitutio Imperatoriam*: with these words, Justinian addressed the prospective audience of his *Institutes*, the introductory textbook intended to serve as a "cradle of the law" (*legum cunabula*, § 3) for first-year law students.[1] More recently, I have had the pleasure of collaborating with Bruce and the other editors in revising Justice Blume's translation of Justinian's *Codex*.[2] I hope, then, that the following reflections—on the legal, political, and social contexts in which not only the *Institutes* but also the *Digest* first appeared, even as the revisions that produced the extant, second edition of the *Codex* were getting underway—will make an apt contribution to the present volume. I want to dwell on a particular imperial constitution that, I argue, was calculated to herald and to frame the appearance of the *Institutes* and the *Digest* but now, like so many others, can be reconstructed only on the basis of the fragments collected in the *Codex*.

The constitution in question is represented by five fragments addressed, somewhat surprisingly, to Hermogenes as *magister officiorum*, three of which

1. I welcome this opportunity to acknowledge once again the generous support of Emory's Interdisciplinary Program in Classical Studies, together with the Emory University School of Law; the Law and Religion Program; the Center for Language, Literature, and Culture; and the Center for Teaching and Curriculum. Also speaking on the delightful occasion of the 2000 colloquium were Edward Harris, Olivia Robinson, and Alan Watson.

2. I edited book 12 in Frier, *The "Code of Justinian"* (2016).

are dated to 17 November 533. The five fragments share a concern with policing the morality of women of free status, avowedly to protect them from the consequences of illicit sexual relationships (if not to prevent such relationships altogether), on one hand, and to validate licit but insecurely attested relationships, on the other. Cross-references to this legislation in Justinian's *Institutes* and *Novels* provide support for reconstructing the official rhetoric in which these initiatives were originally clothed, and the geopolitical situation into which they were somewhat incongruously fitted suggests that the emperor's investment in defending feminine virtue had little to do with the fortunes of the humble people affected by his legislation.

With reference to the *Codex*, Boudewijn Sirks reminds us that an imperial constitution had purposes, at the time it was issued, distinguishable from those of the moment at which it was selected and excerpted for inclusion in the collection.[3] While the substantive changes introduced into law by the constitution in question, as these are preserved in the *Codex*, were significant and consequential, I wish to suggest that these were by no means the only—and perhaps not even the primary—motivations behind the promulgation of the original legislation, notwithstanding the relatively brief time that elapsed between its issuance and its subsequent incorporation into the collection.

The closing months of the year 533 crowned a time of extraordinary activity and optimism in the imperial palace at Constantinople. The period witnessed the appearance of Justinian's *Institutes*, promulgated by *C. Imperatoriam* on 21 November, and that of the *Digest* on 16 December by the constitutions *Tanta* and *Δέδωκεν*. There were also suggestions that the geopolitical and theological reintegration of the Roman world was proceeding apace. After Belisarius' convincing, though not yet decisive, defeat of the Vandals in September 533, Justinian, in *C. Imperatoriam*, styled himself *Alanicus Vandalicus Africanus* and heralded the restoration to Roman jurisdiction of Africa and "countless other provinces."[4] On 20 November, as reported in the *Pascal Chronicle*,[5] the emperor made a point of reissuing his Theopaschite edict (*Cod. Just.* 1.1.6, originally

3. Sirks, "The Colonate in Justinian's Reign" (2008) 121, esp. n. 7. See also, with reference to third-century rescripts on personal status in *Cod. Just.*, Evans Grubbs, "Between Slavery and Freedom" (2013) esp. 86–93.

4. *C. Imperatoriam*, intitulatio (trans. Birks and McLeod): *Imperator Caesar Flavius Iustinianus Alamannicus Gothicus Francicus Germanicus Anticus Alanicus Vandalicus Africanus pius felix inclitus victor ac triumphator semper Augustus* . . . (The emperor Caesar Flavius Justinian, conqueror of the Alamanni, Goths, Franks, Germans, Antes, Alani, Vandals, Africans, devout, fortunate, renowned, victorious and triumphant, forever *Augustus* . . .); 1: . . . *tam Africa quam aliae innumerosae provinciae* . . .

5. *CP* a. 533 p. 630 ed. Dindorf 1832. See Whitby and Whitby, *Chronicon Paschale* (1989) 128–29 and n. 374.

issued on 15 March), aimed at reconciling supporters and opponents of the Council of Chalcedon by promoting the doctrine that one of the Trinity had suffered in the flesh, to major metropolitan cities in the East and the West, including Rome, Thessalonica, and Alexandria.

The field of family law—the law of persons, the law of domestic relations—might seem to be an unpromising subject to treat in relation to so much self-congratulatory legislation on the theme of imperial *renovatio*. Nonetheless, as has been suggested above, a consciousness of the immediate context and the scope of Justinian's ambitions at this particular moment, the end of 533, is essential for understanding not only the imperatives that influenced the drafting and dissemination of the constitution in question but also why its provisions proved to be controversial.

In a far-reaching innovation with respect to "mixed marriages" between persons of unequal status, Justinian held that a woman of free status who consorted with a man of unfree status did not thereby endanger her own liberty or that of any children she might produce from such a union. The legislation elicited an unintended, but palpable, response from the lowly persons thus affected, provoking, in turn, a sharp reaction among the entrenched interests thereby threatened.[6] We should not suppose that this initiative was the product of what A. H. M. Jones characterized as "mere legal purism";[7] nor was it a deliberate attempt at reordering socioeconomic relationships, motivated by the Roman jurists' traditional *favor libertatis* (the principle of giving a claim of freedom the benefit of the doubt) and what Mario de Dominicis identified as imperial *benevolentia* and *liberalitas*.[8] Instead, we should follow the lead of Diether Eibach and Mariagrazia Bianchini in discovering an unresolved tension between Justinian's professed investment in *libertas,* a value that he identified not only with free status but also with freedom from illegitimate constraint or subjection, on one hand, and his reluctance either to antagonize propertied interests or to leave the lower classes to their own devices, on the other.[9] The instrumental value Justinian attached to this legislation should be described,

6. For the details, see n. 23 below, with Jones, *The Later Roman Empire* (1964) 795–803 and n. 73.

7. Jones, "The Roman Colonate" (1958) 10; cf. Jones, *The Later Roman Empire* (1964) 359 ("that emperor's obstinate legal purism"), 801 ("Justinian . . . was shocked by this breach of the principle of Roman law which declared that the offspring of a free woman was free").

8. De Dominicis, "I *coloni adscripticii*" (1962) 19, 21; de Dominicis, "A proposito di due leggi byzantine" (1963) 82, 85–86.

9. Eibach, *Untersuchungen zum spätantiken Kolonat* (1980) esp. 162–91; Bianchini, "Sul regime delle unioni fra libere e *adscripticii*" (1984) esp. 62–76. See also Collinet, "La politique de Justinien à l'égard des colons" (1939) 600–11; Koptev, "Rimskoye zakonodatel'stvo o brakakh rabov i kolonov" (1985); Schmitz, "Appendix 1 der justinianischen *Novellen*" (1986) 381–86; Koptev, *Ot prav grazhdanstva k pravu kolonata* (1995) 177–210.

therefore, in terms of the enhanced prestige and legitimacy he hoped to attract to a regime that, it bears emphasizing, was still struggling to establish itself less than two years after the Nika riots of January 532 very nearly brought it down.[10]

The available evidence suggests that Justinian's intervention in the field of family law was packaged as a kind of showpiece legislation, intended to demonstrate unmistakable continuities between that emperor's initiatives in the fields of foreign and domestic policy. As the principium of *C. Imperatoriam* states (trans. Birks and McLeod, modified),

> *imperatoriam maiestatem non solum armis decoratam, sed etiam legibus oportet esse armatam, ut utrumque tempus et bellorum et pacis recte possit gubernari et princeps Romanus victor existat non solum in hostilibus proeliis, sed etiam per legitimos tramites calumniantium iniquitates expellens, et fiat tam iuris religiosissimus quam victis hostibus triumphator.*
>
> [Imperial majesty should not only be graced with arms but also armed with laws, so that proper governance may prevail in time of war and peace alike. The head of the Roman state can then stand victorious not only over enemies in war but also over troublemakers, driving out their wickedness through the paths of the law, and can triumph as much for his devotion to the law as for his conquests in battle.]

There is every reason to believe that Justinian's legislation on "mixed marriages," now scattered as a series of fragments incorporated into the revised edition of the *Codex*, which appeared in late 534,[11] was deliberately timed to foreshadow the introduction of the revitalized *Corpus Iuris Civilis* as represented in the *Institutes* and the *Digest* and, accordingly, to stand as a concrete demonstration of "proper governance" in the civil sphere.

These changes had a considerable, if unintended, impact on rural labor relations, especially as they affected tenant farmers classified for fiscal purposes as *adscripticii. Cod. Just.* 11.48.24 preserves a fragment of an imperial constitution holding that free women who establish domestic relations with males *adscripticiae condicionis constituti*, as well as their children born of such relationships, would remain *in sua libertate*. Likewise, children born of unions between a male of free status and a female *adscripticia* were to follow the status of their

10. On the event itself, see Greatrex, "The Nika Riot" (1997). Lenski, "Constantine and Slavery" (2012), finds strikingly analogous motives in that emperor's legislation on personal status.

11. *Codex repetitae praelectionis*, promulgated by *C. Cordi* (16 November 534).

mother.[12] In his *Novel* 54, dated 537, Justinian acknowledged the former rule to be an innovation, enacted contrary to ancient precedents, "because We are a lover of liberty," and in reaction against the prospect that a child of unfree status might issue from a free mother.[13]

These *adscripticii* are distinguished, in a law of Anastasius (*Cod. Just.* 11.48.19, 491–518 CE), from other tenant farmers who, after thirty years of continuous habitation, become "free," although they remain tied to the soil; in spite of this disability, they were capable of owning property, whereas *adscripticii* had merely a *peculium* belonging to their masters.[14] The assimilation of the status of *adscripticii* to that of slaves occasioned the often-quoted remark that appears in *Cod. Just.* 11.48.21.1 (Justinian, 530 CE): *quae etenim differentia inter servos et adscripticios intellegetur, cum uterque in domini sui*

---

12. *Cod. Just.* 11.48.24 pr.: *si qui adscripticiae condicionis constituti mulieres liberas quacumque mente aut quacumque machinatione sive scientibus dominis sive ignorantibus sibi uxores coniunxerunt vel postea coniunxerint, in sua libertate permanere tam eas quam prolem quae ex eis cognoscitur procreata sancimus: illo procul dubio observando, ut, si ex libero marito et adscripticia uxore partus fuerit editus, is maternae condicionis maculam, non paternam sequatur libertatem.* (If any persons of adscript status, with whatever intention or by whatever fraud, with or without the knowledge of the landlord, have married or shall hereafter marry free women, We decree that these women together with the offspring known to have been procreated from them shall abide in their freedom; let there be no doubt, however, that the offspring born from the union of a free husband and a wife who is an *adscripticia* follows the stigmatized condition of the mother and not the freedom of the father.) On the following clause (11.48.24.1), permitting the landlord to separate the couple, see n. 37 below. In view of the vigorous debates over the legal sources for the colonate in the sixth century (see Sirks, "The Colonate in Justinian's Reign" [2008], cautiously affirmed by Grey, "Colonate" [2013]), I leave *adscripticius* and related expressions untranslated.

13. *Just. Nov.* 54 pr.: ἐλευθερίας γὰρ ὄντες ἐρασταὶ ἔναγχος τεθείκαμεν νόμον, ὥστε μὴ κατὰ τὸ παλαιόν, εἰ ἐξ ἐναπογράφου καὶ ἐλευθέρου προσώπου προέλθοι γονή, πάντως αὐτὴν ἀκολουθεῖν τῇ ἐναπογράφῳ τύχῃ, ἀλλὰ κατὰ τὴν τῆς δουλικῆς τύχης παρατήρησιν οὕτω καὶ ἐπὶ τῶν ἐναπογράφων νομίζεσθαι, καὶ πρὸς τὴν τῆς γαστρὸς κατάστασιν καὶ τὴν τοῦ τεχθέντος κανονίζεσθαι τύχην. ἐξ ἐλευθέρας γὰρ μητρὸς προελθεῖν δοῦλον βρέφος ὁ ἡμέτερος εὖ ποιῶν οὐκ ἠβουλήθη νόμος. (Because We are a lover of liberty, We recently enacted a law providing that the offspring of an adscript and a free person should not invariably have adscript status, as was formerly the case, but that the principle governing servile status should apply also to *adscripticii*, and the status of the child should likewise be referred to the condition of its mother. Our law was unwilling, rightly, that the child of a free mother should be a slave.) See also n. 23 below. Cf. *Cod. Just.* 11.48.16, 11.48.21, 11.68.4. The abrogation of the *SC Claudianum*, here taken for granted, is discussed below; see, further, Sirks, "The Colonate in Justinian's Reign" (2008) 127–28.

14. *Cod. Just.* 11.48.19 (restored from *Bas.* 55.1.18): τῶν γεωργῶν οἱ μὲν ἐναπόγραφοί εἰσι καὶ τὰ τούτων πεκούλια τοῖς δεσπόταις ἀνήκει, οἱ δὲ χρόνῳ τῆς τριακονταετίας μισθωτοὶ γίνονται ἐλεύθεροι μένοντες μετὰ τῶν πραγμάτων αὐτῶν. καὶ οὗτοι δὲ ἀναγκάζονται καὶ τὴν γῆν γεωργεῖν καὶ τὸ τέλος παρέχειν. τοῦτο δὲ καὶ τοῖς δεσπόταις καὶ τοῖς γεωργοῖς λυσιτελεῖ. (Some farmers are *adscripticii* [*enapographoi*], and their *peculia* belong to the landowners. Others become *coloni* [? *misthotoi*] after thirty years, remaining free with their property; these are obliged to work the land and to pay the tax. This is to the advantage of both the landowners and the farmers.) This law is cross-referenced in *Cod. Just.* 11.48.23.1 (Justinian, 531–534 CE), where it is said to apply to persons *colonaria detenti . . . condicione*. See further Sirks, "The Colonate in Justinian's Reign" (2008) 129–30, 138–42.

positus est potestate, et possit servum cum peculio manumittere et adscripticium cum terra suo dominio expellere? (Indeed, what difference can be understood between slaves and *adscripticii*, when both are placed in their master's power and he can manumit a slave with his *peculium* and alienate an *adscripticius* with the land?)

The principle that, in the absence of a valid Roman marriage, a child follows the status of its mother according to the *ius gentium* (in particular, that the child of a free mother and a slave father is freeborn) is familiar from Gaius and was carried over into Justinian's *Institutes* (1.4; cf. Gaius, *Inst.* 1.11). As Gaius went on to observe, of course, the *ius gentium* might be modified by the *ius civile*, as it was in the case of the *Senatus Consultum Claudianum* of 52 CE. In bare outline, the *SC* held that a free woman who persisted in a relationship with a slave belonging to another, despite the master's opposition, thereby jeopardized her own liberty and that of any children born of the union. If, as P. R. C. Weaver has argued,[15] the measure was introduced primarily with a view toward the management of the *familia Caesaris*, authorities gradually lost sight of these purposes; under the Christian emperors, the *SC* was cited primarily as an expedient for policing sexual morality. In the postclassical period, the *SC* was the subject of detailed commentary in the *Sententiae* of Paul and was cited a number of times in the *Codex Theodosianus*.[16]

Justinian abolished the *SC* in a constitution preserved as the sole fragment in *Cod. Just.* 7.24.[17] Like *Cod. Just.* 11.48.24, with which it is partially geminate (cf. § 1 of each fragment), this provision originally formed part of a constitution addressed to Hermogenes as *magister officiorum*. Although the two fragments are undated, they have been associated with three additional fragments addressed to the *magister* Hermogenes: *Cod. Just.* 1.3.53, 5.17.11, and 9.13.1, each of which is dated 17 November 533, four days before the promulgation of the *Institutes*. The apparent relationship among the five texts was noted by Krüger in the stereotype edition of the *Codex* (table 1).[18]

15. Weaver, "The Status of Children in Mixed Marriages" (1986) 162–66. See also Sirks, "Der Zweck des *Senatus Consultum Claudianum*" (2005).

16. See Evans Grubbs, "'Marriage More Shameful than Adultery'" (1993); Evans Grubbs, *Law and Family in Late Antiquity* (1995) 263–73; Arjava, *Women and Law in Late Antiquity* (1996) 220–24; Harper, "The *SC Claudianum* in the *Codex Theodosianus*" (2010); Sirks, "The *Senatus Consultum Claudianum* in 438 and After in the West" (2011).

17. See Sirks, "*Ad senatus consultum Claudianum*" (1994); Melluso, *La schiavitù nell'età giustinianea* (2000) 47–52; Astolfi, *Studi sul matrimonio nel diritto romano* (2012) 58–59, 71–80.

18. See also Bianchini, "Sul regime delle unioni fra libere e *adscripticii*" (1984) 68–69 and n. 22; Bonini, "Giustiniano e i problemi del diritto e del processo penale" (1990) 187 n. 49; Fritz, *Studien zur justinianischen Reformgesetzgebung* (1937) 39.

Table 1. THE CONSTITUTION OF 17 NOVEMBER 533

After Krueger, *Codex Iustinianus, editio stereotypa undecima* (1954)

Cod. Just. 1.3 *De episcopis et clericis* etc.
53. *Hermogeni mag. off., d. xv k. Dec. Cp. dn. Iustiniano pp. A. iii cons.*
(p. 37) = 9.13.1; *iunge* 5.17.11, 7.24.1?, 11.48.24?

Cod. Just. 5.17 *De repudiis et iudicio de moribus sublato*
11. *Hermogeni mag. off., d. xv k. Dec. Cp. dn. Iustiniano pp. A. iii cons.*
(p. 213) *iunge* 1.3.53, 7.24.1?, 9.13.1, 11.48.24?

Cod. Just. 7.24 *De SC Claudiano tollendo*
1. *Hermogeni mag. off.* [*a.* 531–534]
(p. 305) § 1 = 11.48.24; *iungendae videntur* 1.3.53, 5.17.11, 9.13.1

Cod. Just. 9.13 *De raptu virginum seu viduarum nec non sanctimonialium*
1. *Hermogeni mag. off., d. xv k. Dec. Cp. dn. Iustiniano pp. A. iii cons.*
(p. 378) *maiore ex parte redit in* 1.3.53; *iunge* 5.17.11

Cod. Just. 11.48 *De agricolis censitis vel colonis*
24. *Hermogeni mag. off.*
(p. 443) § 1 = 7.24.1; *iungendae videntur* 1.3.53, 5.17.11, 9.13.1

The conclusion that the five fragments originally formed part of a single constitution is supported by their complementary subject matter, as suggested above. In addition to the two fragments dealing with relationships between free women and slaves or *adscripticii* (*Cod. Just.* 7.24.1 and 11.48.24 respectively), *Cod. Just.* 1.3.53 and 9.13.1 are largely geminate and assign penalties against persons who have compromised the chastity of religious and laywomen respectively.[19] *Cod. Just.* 5.17.11 upholds the validity of genuine marriages in instances where the relationship, absent a dowry or comparable manifestation of intent, might appear to be illicit, while enumerating grounds on which a divorce might be obtained due to a wife's unmatronly conduct, such as bathing in the company of other men.[20]

19. See Astolfi, *Studi sul matrimonio nel diritto romano* (2012) 147–51, with McGinn, "The Law of Roman Marriage in Late Antiquity" (2014) 228–35.
20. See Astolfi, *Studi sul matrimonio nel diritto romano* (2012) 29–34.

The fact that they were addressed to the *magister officiorum*, Hermogenes, is a curiosity that militates in favor of the unity of the five texts. For most of his tenure in office, Hermogenes had occupied himself chiefly with the diplomatic negotiations leading up to the so-called Eternal Peace with Persia.[21] Laws dealing with public morality and civil order ordinarily will have fallen within the competence of the praetorian prefects, as is confirmed by an examination of the inscriptions of other constitutions that appear under the relevant titles. The two fragments concerned with ravishers of virgins, matrons, widows, and nuns (*Cod. Just.* 1.3.53, 9.13.1) assign the prosecution of such offenders to the praetorian prefects and to the urban prefect of Constantinople, as one would expect, with the assistance of provincial military and civil authorities.[22] When provincial landowners complained, first in 537 and again in 539, that Justinian's measure with respect to *adscripticii* (11.48.24) was despoiling the countryside of its workforce, the emperor addressed his responses to the authorities from whose tribunals the petitions had originated, those of the praetorian prefect of the East and of Illyricum respectively.[23]

It seems quite clear, therefore, that the *magister* was not expected to enforce the law addressed to him on 17 November. Another responsibility of the official to whom a constitution was addressed was to ensure that the new measure received adequate publicity. While the praetorian prefects were capable of accomplishing this in the ordinary course of business, the *magister* was certainly competent to perform such a task.[24] Justinian is known to have utilized alternative

21. Martindale, *Prosopography of the Later Roman Empire,* vol. 3 (1992) 590–92 s.v. "Hermogenes" 1; Clauss, *Der magister officiorum in der Spätantike* (1980) 159–60. The terms of the Eternal Peace were concluded in September 532.

22. *Cod. Just.* 1.3.53.2 and 9.13.1c respectively.

23. *Just. Nov.* 54 pr., 1 Ἰωάννῃ τῷ ἐνδοξοτάτῳ ἐπάρχῳ πραιτωρίων τὸ β′ (1 Sept. 537; see also n. 26 below) holds that *Cod. Just.* 11.48.24 is not retrospective; children born before its enactment could not claim freedom. *Just. Nov.* 162.2, Δομνίκῳ τῷ ἐνδοξοτάτῳ ἐπάρχῳ *[per Illyricum]* (9 June 539), in response to complaints forwarded by Dominicus (Martindale, *Prosopography of the Later Roman Empire,* vol. 3 [1992] 415 s.v. "Domnicus" [Dominicus] 2) from landlords in Illyricum that their estates were being deserted and that they could not pay their taxes, holds that children of mixed marriages were free but remained *coloni* and were therefore tied to their farms. In *Nov. App.* 1, *Dominico praefecto [per Illyricum]* (7 April 540), the provisions for Illyricum are evidently reversed, but this ruling itself seems to have been overturned: in 570, the landlords of Africa, through the praetorian prefect Theodore (*Prosopography of the Later Roman Empire,* vol. 3 [1992] 1254 s.v. "Theodorus" 30), protested that their estates lay desolate and obtained the concession granted to Illyricum in 539 from Justin II (*Nov.* 6, 1 March 570, in Zepos and Zepos, *Ius Graecoromanum* [1931], vol. 1, Coll. I); after his death, the same notables, headed by the bishop of Carthage, pressed for a confirmation of Justin's ruling, which they obtained from Tiberius and Maurice (*Nov.* 13, 11 August 582, op. cit.), in a constitution addressed to another praetorian prefect also named Theodore (Martindale, *Prosopography of the Later Roman Empire,* vol. 3 [1992] 1257 s.v. "Theodorus" 38).

24. Compare, e.g., *Theod. Nov.* 24.6 (12 September 443), addressed to Nomus (Martindale, *Prosopography of the Later Roman Empire,* vol. 2 [1980] 785–86 s.v. "Nomus" 1) as *mag. off.* (trans. Pharr et al.): "Therefore Your Illustrious Authority . . . shall command this general and most salu-

channels to communicate messages to which he attached special importance and toward which he anticipated resistance from the regular administration.[25] Perhaps John the Cappadocian, the praetorian prefect of the East at the time, who was capable of stymieing initiatives to which he was opposed,[26] could not have been relied on to carry the new measures into effect.

We can be more definite, in any case, about the significance Justinian attached to this measure. In his study of Tribonian, Tony Honoré accepted the original unity of the five fragments addressed to Hermogenes and, most significantly for our purposes, attributed each of them to Tribonianic authorship on stylistic grounds—this in spite the fact that Tribonian no longer held the office of *quaestor sacri palatii* at the time, having been dismissed by Justinian in a fruitless attempt to mollify the Nika rioters.[27] Ordinarily it fell to the quaestor to draft legislation, but Honoré has shown how adroitly Tribonian operated behind the scenes until the moment was ripe to maneuver him back into the position.

The constitution of 17 November 533 happens to be the last attestation of Hermogenes prior to his departure from the office of *magister officiorum*. He was succeeded—apparently on 21 November, as *C. Imperatoriam* seems to suggest, and certainly no later than 16 December—by none other than Tribonian himself,[28] who held the office of *magister* until January 535, when

tary sanction of Our Clemency to be delivered to perpetual enforcement and execution, and by posting edicts everywhere (*edictis ubique propositis*) you shall cause it to come to the knowledge of all." On the powers and functions of the office, see Clauss, *Der magister officiorum in der Spätantike* (1980) esp. 15–98. The *magister* controlled the corps of official couriers, the *agentes in rebus*; see also Corcoran, "State Correspondence in the Roman Empire" (2014). Matthews, *Laying Down the Law* (2000) esp. 168–99, reconstructs procedures for issuing and circulating laws in the later empire. Laws were often copied to multiple officials (op. cit. esp. 158-64, 242-53), but details are only occasionally visible: *Cod. Theod.* 6.28.8 (435 CE), e.g., is addressed to the *mag. off.* with instructions for copies to nine other officials, while *Cod. Just.* 12.21.4 reproduces the same law without those instructions.

25. An example is the dossier of documents preserved as *Just. Nov.* 8 (17 April 535), an anticorruption campaign that mobilized the episcopacy as well as the provincial administration in order to publicize and enforce its measures. See Pazdernik, "'The Trembling of Cain'" (2009) esp. 150–51.

26. Martindale, *Prosopography of the Later Roman Empire*, vol. 3 (1992) 627–35 s.v. "Fl. Ioannes" 11 ("the Cappadocian"). Dismissed during the Nika riots in January 532, he was restored to office by October of that year; *Just. Nov.* 54 was addressed to him during his second prefectureship (see n. 23 above). His vocal opposition to the Vandal expedition caused Justinian to hesitate: see Procopius, *Wars* 3.10.1–18.

27. Honoré, *Tribonian* (1978) 110.

28. He is described by *C. Imperatoriam* as *magister* and ex-quaestor (*Triboniano, viro magnifico, magistro et ex quaestore sacri palatii nostri*, § 3); the office could be titular, *inter agentes*, as Honoré, *Tribonian* (1978) 57, suggests; cf. *C. Haec* (13 February 528, establishing the first law commission that produced the original edition of the *Codex*), where he is styled *virum magnificum magisteria dignitate inter agentes decoratum* (endowed with magisterial dignity *inter agentes*, § 1). By 16 December, in *C. Tanta* pr., he is *magister officiorum et ex quaestore sacri nostri palatii et ex consule.*

he resumed his place as quaestor.[29] Thus it came about that Tribonian and not some less enthusiastic minister would be in place to publicize the domestic relations bill of which he was the architect, no doubt in close consultation with the emperor himself.

Further evidence that the timing of the constitution was not coincidental is supplied by the notice of the abrogation of the *SC Claudianum* given in the *Institutes* (3.12.1), which deplores the fact that a woman "carried away by love for a slave" (*servili amore bacchata*) might, on that account, lose her liberty and property. Judging the provision to be "unworthy of Our times" (*indignum nostris temporibus*), the emperor states that he has ordered its repeal and omission from the *Digest*.[30] If, as Honoré surmised, the draft of the *Digest* was completed no later than March 533,[31] this decision will have been taken well in advance of the publication of the constitution on November 17, and the ensuing delay requires explanation. Possibly the omission was ordered earlier, before the success of the African expedition had brought the theme of liberation to the fore, only to be reissued with greater fanfare in November; in that case, it would parallel Justinian's second promulgation of his Theopaschite edict in that month.[32]

If this chain of inferences holds, therefore, the constitution of 17 November should be regarded as a key component of a package of measures enacted, in November and December of 533, in order to crown Justinian's third consulate[33] and to impress firmly on the minds of contemporaries the idea that the geopolitical, theological, and civil reintegration of the Roman world was proceed-

---

29. Martindale, *Prosopography of the Later Roman Empire*, vol. 3 (1992) 1335–39 s.v. "Tribonianus" 1.

30. *Just. Inst.* 3.12.1 (trans. Birks and McLeod): *erat et ex senatus consulto Claudiano miserabilis per universitatem adquisitio, cum libera mulier servili amore bacchata ipsam libertatem per senatus consultum amittebat et cum libertate substantiam: quod indignum nostris temporibus esse existimantes et a nostra civitate deleri et non inseri nostris digestis concessimus.* (There was another wretched case under the Claudian Resolution. The senate resolved that a free woman led astray by love for a slave should lose her freedom and with it her property. We judged this unworthy of Our reign. We have agreed to its repeal and its omission from the *Digest.*) Cf. 4.18.8, which cross-references *Cod. Just.* 9.13.1.

31. Honoré, *Tribonian* (1978) 173–86.

32. Cf. Luchetti, *La legislazione imperiale* (1996) 395–401.

33. Cf. *C. Tanta* 23 (trans. Monro): *bene autem properavimus in tertium nostrum consulatum et has leges edere, quia maximi dei et domini nostri Ihesu Cristi auxilium felicissimum eum nostrae rei publicae donavit, cum in hunc et bella Parthica abolita sunt et quieti perpetuae tradita, et tertia pars mundi nobis adcrevit (post Europam enim et Asiam et tota Libya nostro imperio adiuncta est) et tanto operi legum caput impositum est, omnia caelestia dona nostro tertio consulatui indulta.* (We have done well to make a point of bringing out this body of law in Our third consulship, as that consulship is the happiest one which the favor of Almighty God and of Our Lord Jesus Christ has given to Our state; in it the Parthian wars were put an end to and consigned to lasting rest; moreover the third division of the world came under Our sway, as, after Europe and Asia, all Libya too was added to Our dominions; and now a final completion is made of the great work on Our law, [so that] all the gifts of Heaven have been poured on Our third consulship.)

ing apace. Arguably the initial impulse behind this legislation had been a desire to defend the sanctity of *iustae nuptiae* by stigmatizing illicit relationships. This would accord with the moralizing rigor of Justinian's early legislation.[34] But with the dawning optimism of the mid-530s, sunnier images predominated. The defense of feminine virtue and the vindication of the civil law principle that the offspring of a free womb is free were feel-good themes, even in an age uncontaminated by focus-group-driven politics. Perhaps Justinian wished to associate himself with the tradition of good emperors like Vespasian and Hadrian, who, according to Gaius (*Inst.* 1.84–85), altered the rules affecting the status of children of mixed marriages in order to correct injustices and restore elegance to the law. Like Justinian's adoption of old-fashioned triumphal titles, the appeal to classical principles was intended to enhance the legitimacy of the regime and render change palatable, even as intervening patterns of legal development were set aside.

It does not follow that the legislation was well considered. Justinian's vindication of *libertas* in the case of free women and their offspring did not compass any improvement in the condition of *adscripticii,* whom he readily consigned to the status of slaves. In the face of pressure from provincial landowners in Illyricum and, later on, in Africa, the emperor and his successors offered, in their *Novels,* concessions that did not renounce the free status of such offspring but nonetheless tied them to their places of origin.[35]

Justinian never meant to endorse or promote relationships between free women and their status inferiors or to effect substantive demographic changes in the composition of the rural labor force. In repealing the *SC Claudianum,* the emperor expresses horror at the prospect that a wayward daughter or niece might disgrace her family and earn for herself a master of inferior standing to her own relations (*Cod. Just.* 7.24.1 pr.). Both the *Institutes* and the *Codex* attribute rascally motives and servile underhandedness to the men involved in such relationships, while casting the women as the hapless victims of their seducers.[36] The possibility that the operation of the law will diminish the ranks of *adscripticii* is deplored by the legislator (*Cod. Just.* 7.24.1.1).[37]

> *sed ne servi vel adscripticii putent sibi impunitum esse tale conamen, quod maxime in adscripticios verendum est, ne liberarum mulierum nuptiis ab*

---

34. See Honoré, *Tribonian* (1978) 14–16.

35. See n. 23 above. Constantine's legislation on personal status created comparable problems: see Lenski, "Constantine and Slavery" (2012) 239, 252–54.

36. Cf., in this respect, *Cod. Just.* 9.13.1.3b.

37. The sentiment is repeated *mutatis mutandis* in *Cod. Just.* 11.48.24.1; see also *Just. Nov.* 22.17 (535).

> *his excogitatis paulatim huiusmodi hominum condicio decrescat, sancimus, si quid tale fuerit vel a servo vel adscripticio perpetratum, liberam habere potestatem dominum eius sive per se sive per praesidem provinciae talem servum vel adscripticium castigatione competenti corrigere et abstrahere a tali muliere. Quod si neglexerit, sciat in suum damnum huiusmodi desidiam reversuram.*
>
> [But lest slaves or *adscripticii* should suppose that such a liaison would go unpunished—something that must be particularly feared in the case of *adscripticii*, lest gradually the ranks of such persons should decrease by marriages with free women devised by these persons—We ordain that, if any such thing shall have been perpetrated either by a slave or by an *adscripticius*, his landlord, whether on his own authority or that of the governor of the province, shall have free rein to correct the slave or *adscripticius* by sufficient castigation and to separate him from such a woman. And if [the landlord] shall have neglected this, he should know that such inactivity will redound to his own hurt.]

The inadequacy of this provision is shown not only in the way in which it dismissively conflates inattention or ignorance on the landlord's part with tacit acquiescence in such relationships but also in the hypocrisy with which it, on the one hand, endorses the principle that free persons are citizens entitled to the protection of law and, on the other hand, concedes to the landlord a vaguely defined right to interfere in the domestic arrangements of persons settled upon his estate. With one gesture, Justinian appears to be reaching out to embrace such women and children within his jurisdiction; with another, he casts that jurisdiction away, leaving them at the mercy of the propertied classes. The emperor and his advisors apparently calculated that by giving landowners ample discretion to act in defense of their own interests, the practical consequences of the measure would be virtually nil.

While concern for the welfare of the humble cannot have been a primary motivation, therefore, the quite genuine (though frequently paternalistic and overbearing) solicitude manifested by Justinian and the empress Theodora toward the plight of unfortunate women[38] does not explain either the careful timing of the measure's introduction or the prominence assigned to the expansion of *libertas* as an animating theme. Nor does it follow that Justinian's measures

38. See Evans, *The Empress Theodora* (2003) 30–34.

with respect to the children of mixed marriages were merely empty gestures guided by a misplaced enthusiasm for legal archaism. To the contrary, Justinian would make the protection of freedom a leitmotif of the reign.

Echoing his language in the *Institutes*,[39] the emperor states in the *Codex* that the *SC Claudianum* must be repealed as inconsistent with the spirit of his age, "in which We have sustained many labors for the sake of the freedom of Our subjects," lest misguided women be deprived of their liberty and lest "the very fate that has been imposed by the ferocity of an enemy against natural *libertas* be likewise inflicted by the lust of the vilest of men" (*Cod. Just.* 7.24.1 pr.):

> *cum in nostris temporibus, in quibus multos labores pro libertate subiectorum sustinuimus, satis esse impium credidimus quasdam mulieres libertate sua fraudari et, quod ab hostium ferocitate contra naturalem libertatem inductum est, hoc a libidine nequissimorum hominum inferri.*

The association between the defense of freedom at home and its recovery abroad is explicit. Even in the face of opposition, as noted above for his *Novel* 54 of 537,[40] Justinian continued to insist that he was a lover of liberty and that his measure was a salutary improvement on ancient precedents. Later *Novels* would reiterate the correlation between the emancipation of slaves at home and the recovery of captive Roman territories and populations abroad as complementary objects of imperial policy.[41]

At the end of 533, moreover, *libertas* and its links to a particularly Roman identity represented not merely a rhetorical or theoretical basis of allegiance to an imperial world order. With the recovery of Africa not yet assured and with the invasion of Italy already in prospect, *libertas* distinguished those for whose sake Justinian was remaking the world from those who stood in his way. In the constitution establishing the new African prefecture, claimed by Honoré to have been penned by Justinian's own hand in the spring of 534, the emperor prays that the inhabitants of Africa might recognize "from what most severe captivity and barbaric yoke they have been freed and what great freedom they have gained under Our happy rule" (*Cod. Just.* 1.27.1.8): *et cognoscant eius habitatores, quam a durissima captivitate et iugo barbarico liberati in quanta libertate sub felicissimo nostro imperio degere meruerunt.*[42] This *libertas* not only defined an exclusive circle of belonging but also entailed a

39. *Just. Inst.* 3.12.1, quoted in n. 30 above.
40. See n. 13 above.
41. *Just. Nov.* 78.4.1 (18 January 539), 89 pr. (1 September 539).
42. On the authorship, see Honoré, "Some Constitutions Composed by Justinian" (1975).

positive duty of loyalty and support for the emperor's causes, a duty extended to both the inhabitants of reconquered provinces and the taxpayers who supported the expeditionary armies.[43]

From one point of view, Justinian's constitution on mixed marriages must be regarded as a failure. It stirred up an exploited class that was meant to remain docile, and it expanded distinctions of status that it meant to collapse, thereby antagonizing the propertied interests on whose cooperation Justinian's plans depended. From another point of view, the constitution illuminated the very real significance that such distinctions played in the lives of ordinary people, while it also presumably succeeded in mobilizing the loyalties of persons to whom the specifically Roman character of their civilization and the providential victories of their emperor sincerely mattered. By straining to demonstrate the complementary interaction of arms and laws in securing proper governance, Justinian overreached himself, not for the last time.

Bibliography

Arjava, A. *Women and Law in Late Antiquity*. Oxford, 1996.

Astolfi, R. *Studi sul matrimonio nel diritto romano postclassico e giustinianeo*. Naples, 2012.

Bianchini, M. "Sul regime delle unioni fra libere e *adscripticii* nella legislazione giustinianea." In *Studi in onore di Cesare Sanfilippo*, 5:59–107. Milan, 1984.

Birks, P., and G. McLeod. *Justinian's "Institutes."* Ithaca, 1987.

Bonini, R. "Giustiniano e i problemi del diritto e del processo penale: appunti sul libro IX del *Codice*." In *Ricerche di diritto giustinianeo*, 55–222. 2nd ed. Milan, 1990.

Clauss, M. *Der magister officiorum in der Spätantike (4.–6. Jahrhundert): Das Amt und sein Einfluß auf die kaiserliche Politik*. Munich, 1980.

Collinet, P. "La politique de Justinien à l'égard des colons." In *Atti del V Congresso internazionale di studi bizantini, vol. 1, Storia filologia diritto*, 600–11. Rome, 1939.

Corcoran, S. "State Correspondence in the Roman Empire: Imperial Communication from Augustus to Justinian." In K. Radner, ed., *State Correspondence in the Ancient World*, 172–255. Oxford, 2014.

de Dominicis, M. "A proposito di due leggi bizantine sul colonato nelle regioni africane." *Iura* 14 (1963): 139–58. Reprinted in de Dominicis, *Scritti romanistici* (1970) 69–88.

de Dominicis, M. "I *coloni adscripticii* nella legislazione di Giustiniano." In *Studi in onore di Emilio Betti*, 3:85–99. Milan, 1962. Reprinted in de Dominicis, *Scritti romanistici* (1970) 11–24.

de Dominicis, M. 1970. *Scritti romanistici*. Padua, 1970.

Dindorf, L., ed. *Chronicon Paschale*. 2 vols. Corpus Scriptorum Historiae Byzantinae. Bonn, 1832.

43. On this theme and its reflection in contemporary historiography, see Pazdernik, "Procopius and Thucydides on the Labors of War" (2000) esp. 153–59.

Eibach, D. *Untersuchungen zum spätantiken Kolonat in der kaiserlichen Gesetzgebung: Unter besonderer Berücksichtigung der Terminologie*. Bonn, 1980.
Evans, J. A. S. *The Empress Theodora: Partner of Justinian*. Austin, 2003.
Evans Grubbs, J. "Between Slavery and Freedom: Disputes over Status and the *Codex Justinianus*." *Roman Legal Tradition* 9 (2013): 31–93.
Evans Grubbs, J. *Law and Family in Late Antiquity: The Emperor Constantine's Marriage Legislation*. Oxford, 1995.
Evans Grubbs, J. "'Marriage More Shameful than Adultery': Slave-Mistress Relationships, 'Mixed Marriages,' and Late Roman Law." *Phoenix* 47 (1993): 125–54.
Frier, B. W., ed. *The "Codex of Justinian": A New Annotated Translation, with Parallel Latin and Greek Text*. 3 vols. Cambridge, 2016.
Fritz, K.-H. *Studien zur justinianischen Reformgesetzgebung*. Quakenbrück, 1937.
Greatrex, G. "The Nika Riot: A Reappraisal." *JHS* 117 (1997): 60–86.
Grey, C. "Colonate." In R. S. Bagnall et al., eds., *The Encyclopedia of Ancient History*, 1652–54. Malden MA, 2013.
Harper, K. "The *SC Claudianum* in the *Codex Theodosianus*: Social History and Legal Texts." *CQ* 60 (2010): 610–38.
Honoré, A. M. "Some Constitutions Composed by Justinian." *JRS* 65 (1975): 107–23.
Honoré, T. *Tribonian*. London, 1978.
Jones, A. H. M. *The Later Roman Empire, 284–602: A Social, Economic, and Administrative Survey*. Baltimore, 1964.
Jones, A. H. M. "The Roman Colonate." *Past and Present* 13 (1958): 1–13.
Koptev, A. V. *Ot prav grazhdanstva k pravu kolonata* [From the rights of citizenship to the law of the colonate]. Vologda, 1995.
Koptev, A. V. "Rimskoye zakonodatel'stvo o brakakh rabov i kolonov" [Roman legislation on marriages of slaves and *coloni*]. *Vestnik drevnej istorii* 4 (1985): 62–83.
Krueger, P., ed. *Codex Iustinianus*. Vol. 2 of *Corpus Iuris Civilis*. 11th ed. Berlin, 1954. Reprint, Hildesheim, 1997.
Lenski, N. "Constantine and Slavery: *Libertas* and the Fusion of Roman and Christian Values." In S. Giglio, ed., *Atti dell'Accademia Romanistica Costantiniana XVIII*, 235–60. Rome, 2012.
Luchetti, G. *La legislazione imperiale nelle Istituzioni di Giustiniano*. Milan, 1996.
Martindale, J. R., ed. *The Prosopography of the Later Roman Empire. Vol. 2, AD 395–527*. Cambridge, 1980.
Martindale, J. R., ed. *The Prosopography of the Later Roman Empire. Vol. 3, AD 527–640*. Cambridge, 1992.
Matthews, J. F. *Laying Down the Law: A Study of the Theodosian Code*. New Haven, 2000.
McGinn, T. A. J. "The Law of Roman Marriage in Late Antiquity." *Iura* 62 (2014): 208–50.
Melluso, M. *La schiavitù nell'età giustinianea: Disciplina giuridica e rilevanza sociale*. Paris, 2000.
Monro, C. H. *The "Digest" of Justinian*. Cambridge, 1904.
Pazdernik, C. "Procopius and Thucydides on the Labors of War: Belisarius and Brasidas in the Field." *TAPA* 130 (2000): 149–87.
Pazdernik, C. "'The Trembling of Cain': Religious Power and Institutional Culture in

Justinianic Oath-Making." In A. Cain and N. Lenski, eds., *The Power of Religion in Late Antiquity*, 143–54. Farnham, 2009.
Pharr, Clyde, Theresa Sherrer Davidson, and Mary Brown Pharr. *The Theodosian Code and Novels and the Sirmondian Constitutions*. Princeton, 1952. Reprint, Union NJ, 2001.
Schmitz, W. "Appendix 1 der justinianischen *Novellen*: Eine Wende der Politik Justinians gegenüber *adscripticii* und *coloni*?" *Historia* 35 (1986): 381–86.
Sirks, A. J. B. "*Ad senatus consultum Claudianum*." *ZRG* 74 (1994): 436–37.
Sirks, A. J. B. "The Colonate in Justinian's Reign." *JRS* 98 (2008): 120–43.
Sirks, A. J. B. "The *Senatus Consultum Claudianum* in 438 and After in the West." In K. Muscheler, ed., *Römische Jurisprudenz: Dogmatik, Überlieferung, Rezeption*, 623–35. Berlin, 2011.
Sirks, A. J. B. "Der Zweck des *Senatus Consultum Claudianum* von 52 n. Chr." *ZRG* 122 (2005): 138–49.
Weaver, P. R. C. "The Status of Children in Mixed Marriages." In B. Rawson, ed., *The Family in Ancient Rome: New Perspectives*, 145–69. Ithaca, 1986.
Whitby, Michael, and Mary Whitby. *Chronicon Paschale, 284–628 AD*. Liverpool, 1989.
Zepos, J., and P. Zepos. *Ius Graecoromanum*. 8 vols. Athens, 1931. Reprint, Aalen, 1962.

Afterword

Clifford Ando

It is a pleasure and an honor to contribute to this volume in honor of Bruce Frier. Although I enrolled in Bruce's class on Roman law, I did not write on private law matters in my dissertation, nor was that project advised by Bruce. Nonetheless, a conversation with Bruce over lunch was decisive in the design of its argument: as we parted, Bruce suggested that I read Kronman on Weber. I eventually did turn to legal history, albeit my interlocutors in those days had very different theoretical commitments than those on exhibit in Bruce's recent work or, indeed, the essays gathered here, varied though they are. The invitation to think about Bruce's own work and reflect upon that which he has inspired is therefore welcome to me both intellectually and as a matter of piety. In what follows, I offer a personal reading of Bruce's first monographs on law and seek to relate the essays in this volume to the program that he charted for American Roman legal scholarship.

To my mind, *Landlords and Tenants in Imperial Rome* and *The Rise of the Roman Jurists* are truly great works of legal history—daring, elegant, capacious, and knowing. More narrowly, they are phenomenal works of Roman legal history. Let me first explain the latter claim. Together with Bruce's famous essay "Bees and Lawyers," those works share a concern to assess specific features of Roman law—the interests that shaped urban lease law; the precarious autonomy achieved by Roman jurisprudence in private law matters—in light of the broadest possible consideration of the political economic, social, and institutional contexts in which they developed. They also share a profound recognition that the surface rhetorical and formal qualities of Roman jurisprudential literature militate profoundly against success in just this endeavor.[1] As Bruce wrote in *Landlords and Tenants*,

1. Frier, "Bees" (1982–83) 113.

> The texture of Roman juristic writings differs from most modern jurisprudence. One primary difference is the absence of surface urgency in the Roman sources: the absence of any clearly expressed sense that "law-jobs" cannot be put off until tomorrow, and that society stands in pressing need of new rules and new legal institutions. Instead, page after page of juristic writings is filled with a dry, rather unrhetorical prose that for the most part simply declares the law, offering no intellectually sufficient explanation or justification; arguments are not common, and when they do appear, they seem to conceal more than they disclose about the foundation of juristic decisions.[2]

After a fashion, this feature of Roman jurisprudential literature may be explained by the form of autonomy sustained by the jurists in the classical period, whose origins are charted in *Rise of the Roman Jurists*. The independence of the jurists—the autonomy of their social authority; its dependence solely on mastery; the claim that judgment on that mastery should be made solely by others in the guild—is enacted and inscribed in their literary production via its forms (responses to and commentary on each other's works) and content (forms of argumentation that insist on apparent disinterest and radical decontextualization).[3]

As Bruce observes, there is thus a logic underlying the forms of legal scholarship long conducted on Roman sources, namely, analytic jurisprudence and narrowly doctrinal forms of historical study: these were well suited to read, along rather than across the grain, the types of information that ideological pressures in the classical period encouraged the jurists to push to the fore, while others were perforce suppressed.[4] Of course, we can now see that reading Roman law as a "single system," united by a "logical web tying together its diverse propositions," was a mode of analysis deeply suited to the varying contexts in which both Roman law as a prestige body of norms, and legal science as autonomous from politics, were themselves mobilized as ideals, the better to serve profoundly political and ideological needs.[5] In *Landlords and Tenants* and also in "Bees," Bruce dismissed out of hand the pretensions to abstraction

2. Frier, *Landlords* (1980) 196–97.

3. On this feature of Roman legal writing, see Bryen, "When Law Goes Off the Rails" (2016).

4. Frier, *Landlords* (1980) 200–201.

5. See, e.g., Whitman, *Legacy* (1990); Capogrossi Colognesi, *Dalla storia di Roma alle origini della società civile* (2007); Tuori, *Ancient Roman Lawyers* (2007); Tuori, *Lawyers and Savages* (2015). These sources concentrate on early modern legal science, but the same is emphatically true of the radical dehistoricization performed by late medieval modes of legal scholarship, when what was at stake was a superficially different but largely homologous desire to enable the translation of rules across contexts.

advanced by both the jurists and partisans of dogmatic history. As a concrete example, Bruce considered the categories "wild" and "domesticated" as applied to animals. A biologist or gourmet cook might find them crude or unhelpful, he allowed,

> but in law they have proved remarkably useful and durable because they provide a relatively obvious framework for dealing with the major questions of property law that animals raise. There is nothing God-given or inevitable about these categories; their persuasiveness stems solely from pragmatic considerations.[6]

Likewise, in *Landlord and Tenants*, having admitted the difficulty of discerning the extra-doctrinal considerations taken on board in any given piece of jurisprudential reasoning, Bruce insists upon the operation of two factors in Roman academic jurisprudence on urban leases: first, that the jurists accepted "the structure and preexisting social institutions or practices of the rental market . . . as the basis and framework for the *legal* institutions of urban leasehold"; second, "that the development of particular rules in lease law was influenced by the development of legal doctrines or analogous rules in areas outside of urban leasehold."[7] Bruce thus sets before us two methodological challenges or, perhaps, a single one that recurs at each further stage of inquiry. First, should we take it as axiomatic that, in reasoning the law, the jurists *consistently* wrestled with pragmatic considerations regarding the social reality that the law sought to regulate—in order words, that they had a view of "law and society"? If so, by what hermeneutic means shall we determine, in any given case or as a general matter, what interests the jurists took on board or how they understood the ontology—the givenness—of social institutions, and, therefore, the relationship of law to reform or critique? Second, if Roman juristic reasoning had frequent recourse to analogy (as clearly it did), we must *also* seek to account for the nature and influence of social and institutional context on the thinking of the jurists at each remove from the starting point of our investigation.

Viewed in this light, a distinct thread running through Bruce's work has been the search for appropriate theoretical tools by which to bridge the closed world of juristic reasoning and self-regard, on the one hand, and the messy

6. Frier, "Bees" (1982–83) 113.

7. Frier, *Landlords* (1980) 198–99 (emphasis in original). See also Frier, *Rise* (1985) 187: "The importance of the passage [*Caec.* 65–78] lies in two fundamental propositions: 1) private law's central function is to preserve the long-term material security of the existing social order, and for this reason its rules must be insulated from transient social and political influences . . ."

world of private lives and social institutions in which the jurists intervened, on the other. A distinct feature of his grappling with this problem has been his highly sophisticated engagement over time with different toolkits for resolving it, from Roscoe Pound's and Julius Stone's legal sociology on interests to his more recent engagement with new institutional economics and law and economic modes of analysis.[8] Consideration of the theoretical diversity on display in Bruce's own work in this regard provides one means to assess the richness and diversity on display in this volume.

For example, Adriaan Lanni and David Phillips both parse statutory language and, to a point, the history of its application, as problems of institutional design. In Lanni's case, this involves an explicit weighing of anthropological and social scientific approaches. Both Lanni and Phillips seek to excavate the logic imminent in a system—Lanni that of collective punishments, Phillips that of the nonprosecution of certain types of killing under Draco's homicide law. Both scholars adduce modern comparanda of notable anachronism to shed significant light on their endeavors.

Michael Leese, Tom McGinn, and Dennis Kehoe, by contrast, insist, in very different ways and regarding very different contexts, that lenses provided by economics can reveal important facets of the operation of legal institutions. By adducing the notion of social capital, Leese applies a uniform mode of analysis to the purely economic considerations involved in marital decisions—the value of cash exchanged may have made marriage transactions the largest ones any individual was likely to undertake—as well as the affective and social aspirations individuals brought to those decisions. For his part, Kehoe identifies the *explanandum* in the study of mandate by means of a functionalist supposition: Roman society needed a variety of agency relationships; the disutility of mandate and its failure to adapt—its odd allocation of risk and labor—therefore demand study. Along the way, Kehoe cites the unusual status of mandate in that it seems to have been exploited between social equals. McGinn's concern is with the enduring question of the availability, exploitation and fairness of legal institutions for nonelites, particularly in their contractual relations with elite actors, to wit, with their nonequals. Touching on notable work by Cynthia Bannon and Dennis Kehoe, as well as Bruce Frier, McGinn broadly affirms the notion that Romans considered the legitimacy of the civil law to rest on its treating persons equally. Subsidiary to his analysis is the revelation that for the Romans, too, wealth served as a useful proxy for measuring social power: he cites in a note the condemnation addressed by a prosecutor to a would-be ty-

8. Frier, *Landlords* (1980) 203–5; Frier and Kehoe, "Law and Economic Institutions" (2007).

rant in a text by Calpurnius Flaccus: "Your riches have elevated you above the standard of citizenly equality."[9]

Lauren Caldwell stands apart from the aforementioned contributors in advocating a distinctively law-and-literature approach to her material. She studies the analysis of justice advanced by Aelian in a series of anecdotes of Artaxerxes and Xerxes. She proposes that, read in sequence, the anecdotes offer a sustained reflection on justice in natural law and on law as a human institution: justice is both natural and a good offered by nature to us; and justice is realized in human relations when they derive from and sustain natural orders. In closing, Caldwell applies the insights gleaned from this reading to the concerns visible in the Severan jurists about the nature and source of limits upon paternal power. An invitation is thereby issued to read Roman legal sources in light of a wider variety of modes of intellectual and literary study.

The difficulty in doing law-and-society forms of scholarship in Roman legal history arises in the fashion to which Bruce has given such cogent description in large measure because of the distinctive qualities of Roman jurisprudential sources. Roman legislation, including, under the empire, imperial edicts and responses, are an altogether different matter. Not only did they avowedly intervene in policy matters on political grounds, but it was more or less essential that the positive law content of any given enactment be clearly and overtly justified by reference to legal and cultural propriety or substantive justice. Bruce's work on the Blume translation of the *Codex* of Justinian has brought him into direct contact with this material, and Charles Pazdernik's contribution to this volume is an exemplar of one type of reading given to the codes, both in respect of the reconstruction of the original enactment from its multiple citations and in its focus on the context in which that enactment was produced and intervened.

Another means to investigate the contexts of legal reasoning involves a turn to the evidence from practice, which often enough derives from contexts at some remove from Rome, whether geographically, culturally, ecologically, or as a matter of public law. (By this I mean that much evidence from practice derives from contexts in which litigants were aliens in respect of Rome or in which the soil was legally non-Roman, notionally precluding the use of certain Roman legal forms and so forth.) Cynthia Bannon and Dennis Kehoe both engage in this sort of work, in this volume and in their many other contributions to the field. Future scholarship will need to consider anew whether extra-Roman practice, for which the evidence often predates classical jurisprudence, can be shown to

9. Calpurnius Flaccus 6, *Decreto reditu exul occisus: supra civilem hanc peraequationem divitiae te elevaverunt.*

have influenced legal thinking at Rome and, if so, by which routes such influence occurred.

In closing, I'd like to say a word about *The Rise of the Roman Jurists*. This is one of those great books that many cite but few take on board. To a point, this is only to be expected: much citation, and much reading, are instrumental in nature, performed in pursuit of one's own ends and not by way of taking on board the totality of another's argument. What is more, the citations of *Rise* have not been wholly unfair: the book can to a point be legitimately described as pursuing a very traditional story, namely, the history of the first generations of Roman jurists and the earliest chapters in the history of Roman legal reasoning.[10] Bruce gave the framework of this thoroughly conventional topic a hugely significant and modern twist by adducing the notion of autonomy, not least in contradistinction to the adversarial or agonistic understanding of the legal process held by advocates.[11] A window is thereby opened, and light is shed, by which complex issues such as the social position of the jurists, the rhetoric and narrowness of legal argument and the forms of legal writing, and the independence of legal scholarship from politics, are established in historical relation to one another.

But what makes the book great is the remarkable depth of the causal and contextual claims Bruce advances in telling this tale, and the economy of argument and precision of language by which he achieves this end. One strand of his argument concerns the institutional structures of the late republican legal system, with its differentiation of roles between magistrates, lay judges, and informal advisors serving as disinterested experts and repositories of institutional memory.[12] Another concerns the pressure placed on the functioning of the system by the massive increase in case load and the changing demographics and interests of litigants consequent upon the increase in the citizen population after the Social War. In Bruce's view, these new users of the Roman legal system "were certain to have been more rule-oriented in their understanding of law than were the old citizens for whom it was familiar."[13] The supposition is that they will have responded to the incipient rationalization of the system by demanding its furtherance.

> It is probably not amiss, therefore, to describe the mass enfranchisement of the Italians, and the subsequent increase in the judicial caseload, as

10. Schulz, *History* (1946) 38–98; Schiavone, *Invention* (2012) 175–306.
11. Frier, *Rise* (1985) 184–96.
12. This argument is summarized at Frier, *Rise* (1985) 272.
13. Frier, *Rise* (1985) 278.

> the direct "precipitant" for the rise of the Roman jurists within the Roman judicial system.[14]

The flagging of the term *precipitant*, a concept drawn from Robert MacIver's *Social Causation*, is typical of Bruce's generosity toward the scholarship of others and the immense range of his reading.

These various strands of argumentation reach their climax in a passage of great brilliance and thrilling compression, which I quote in full.

> Broadly speaking, the rise of the Roman jurists may thus be attributed to three external factors: the enfranchisement of the Italians (perhaps the most important factor); the increase in commerce and personal wealth during the late Republic; and the political instability of the era. These external factors produced demands upon the internal structure of the Roman judicial system, which in practice could satisfy the demands only through a gradual upgrading of the weight accorded to jurists' pronouncements on law. Most of the change probably occurred on the micro-scale, as new patterns of judicial conduct emerged and were reinforced through social acceptance; hence the evidence for the change is mainly indirect and circumstantial, though rather conclusive. In general, so I would argue, the increasing scale and complexity of late Republican society made it desirable (though not necessarily inevitable) that law become differentiated at a higher and more deliberate level than in earlier Mediterranean societies; and the presence of the jurists at the margins of the Roman judicial system made it possible for this to occur. The factors that caused the rise of the Roman jurists are thus broadly similar to those that created and shaped the Principate.[15]

Let me focus on three strands only of this remarkable paragraph. First, the claim with which it closes is notable not simply for what it asserts about the politics of Roman legal scholarship. Bruce has also torn a veil from before our eyes. The richness of the historical contextualization that has led to this point is now revealed as having been crafted with the full weight of half century's scholarship on the Roman revolution in mind; and the power and cogency of the argument about law is dramatically enhanced by its assimilation to a hard-

14. Frier, *Rise* (1985) 279.
15. Frier, *Rise* (1985) 282.

won consensus in another field. The autonomy of Roman law from politics is thereby revealed as the product of extraordinary political ferment.

Second, I would like to draw attention to the care with which the various strands of argument are both justified and woven together. Each is in its way complex. What is more, each is a distinctly modern argument, ultimately unprovable by recourse to an ancient evidentiary regime. It is not simply that the evidence is partial. Bruce is posing urgent, modern questions, to which *their* language and concerns will provide only limited response. There is also a sense in which the overall argument derives power from precisely this status of its constituent strands. As in statistics, where one can diminish uncertainty by aggregating estimates, so long as the subsidiary systems of estimation do not share independent variables, so Bruce's argument derives some measure of its force precisely from its ambition and from the sense he conveys of controlling the terms of all aspects of his chosen field.

As a final matter, the paragraph gestures both backwards, to Bruce's earlier work, and forward in historical time, to the structures of Roman law in the classical period. As regards Bruce's earlier work, the concluding pages of *Landlords and Tenants* offer a stunning analysis of the relationship between the form of jurisprudential reasoning and its precarious political position in a time of gradually increasing absolutism.[16] Despite considerable discrepancy in their substantive concerns and evidentiary bases, at this high level the two books converge and present a historical portrait of very great sweep. As regards the future history of classical law, Bruce's remarkable explanation for the use made by the Caesars, as he terms them,[17] of private law, should now be read alongside J. G. A. Pocock's analysis of citizenly relations as they emerge from Roman sources of the imperial period. On Pocock's reading, an individual of that age became a citizen

> through the possession of things and the practice of jurisprudence. His actions were in the first instance directed at things and at other persons through the medium of things; in the second instance, they were actions he took, or others took in respect of him, at law—acts of authorization, appropriation, conveyance, acts of litigation, prosecution, justification. His relation to things was regulated by law, and his actions were performed in respect either of things or of the law regulating actions.[18]

---

16. Frier, *Landlords* (1980) 215–16.
17. Frier, *Rise* (1985) 286.
18. Pocock, "Ideal of Citizenship" (1992) 40.

This further convergence, between Bruce's work and an essential but neglected strand of modern political theory, may stand as an illustration of the richness and generative nature of Bruce's scholarship and as a call to action along the lines that he has so usefully and carefully charted.

Bibliography

Bryen, A. "When Law Goes Off the Rails; or, *Aggadah* among the *iurisprudentes*." In C. Ando, ed., "The New Ancient Legal History," special issue, *Critical Analysis of Law* 3.1 (2016): 9–29.

Capogrossi Colognesi, L. *Dalla storia di Roma alle origini della società civile: Un dibattito ottocentesco*. Bologna, 2008.

Frier, B. W. "Bees and Lawyers." *CJ* 78 (1982–83): 105–14.

Frier, B. W. *Landlords and Tenants in Imperial Rome*. Princeton, 1980.

Frier, B. W. *The Rise of the Roman Jurists: Studies in Cicero's "Pro Caecina."* Princeton, 1985.

Frier, B. W., and D. P. Kehoe. "Law and Economic Institutions." In W. Scheidel, I. Morris, and R. Saller, eds., *The Cambridge Economic History of the Greco-Roman World*, 113–43. Cambridge, 2007.

Pocock, J. G. A. "The Ideal of Citizenship since Classical Times." *Queen's Quarterly* 99 (1992): 33–55.

Schiavone, A. *The Invention of Law in the West*. Trans. J. Carden and A. Shugaar. Cambridge, 2012.

Schulz, F. *History of Roman Legal Science*. Oxford, 1946.

Tuori, K. *Ancient Roman Lawyers and Modern Legal Ideals: Studies on the Impact of Contemporary Concerns in the Interpretation of Ancient Roman Legal History*. Frankfurt, 2007.

Tuori, K. *Lawyers and Savages: Ancient History and Legal Realism in the Making of Legal Anthropology*. New York, 2015.

Whitman, J. Q. *The Legacy of Roman Law in the German Romantic Era: Historical Vision and Legal Change*. Princeton, 1990.

Contributors

Clifford Ando is David B. and Clara E. Stern Professor and Professor of Classics, History, and Law at the University of Chicago and Research Fellow in the Department of Biblical and Ancient Studies at the University of South Africa.

Cynthia J. Bannon teaches ancient history at Trinity College in Hartford, Connecticut.

Lauren Caldwell is Visiting Assistant Professor of History at Trinity College, Hartford, Connecticut.

Dennis P. Kehoe is Professor of Classical Studies and associate faculty member of the School of Law at Tulane University.

Adriaan Lanni is Professor of Law at Harvard Law School.

Michael Leese is Assistant Professor of History at the University of New Hampshire.

Susan D. Martin is Distinguished Professor of Classics and Provost and Senior Vice-Chancellor Emerita at the University of Tennessee, Knoxville.

Thomas A. J. McGinn is Professor of History at Vanderbilt University.

Charles Pazdernik is Professor of Classics at Grand Valley State University, Allendale, Michigan.

David D. Phillips is Professor of History at the University of California, Los Angeles.

Indices

Literary Sources

Epigraphical and Papyrological Sources

Legal Sources

Index of Persons

Index of Subjects